"ORDER UNDER LAW"

Readings in criminal justice

"ORDER UNDER LAW"

Readings in criminal justice

Robert G. Culbertson
Mark R. Tezak

Illinois State University

Waveland Press, Inc.
Prospect Heights, Illinois

For information about this book, write or call:

Waveland Press, Inc.
P.O. Box 400
Prospect Heights, Illinois 60070
(312) 634-0081

364
C9670

Cover Design: Mark Tezak and John Stanicek

9/86

Contents

Preface

There are several reasons for the current widespread interest in criminal justice. Part of the appeal of criminal justice as a field of study stems from the fact that the criminal justice system plays an important role in our lives. Rare is the individual who has never had contact with or has never witnessed the operation of the police. A smaller number of us have had occasion to view the courts and the corrections components of the criminal justice system. Criminal justice also generates widespread and intense interest due to the significance of the issues involved. When one studies criminal justice, he or she must come to grips with some of the most emotional and complex questions confronting our society. Do we have two standards of justice, one standard for the wealthy and another for the poor? Does our criminal justice system discriminate against minorities? What is the proper goal of punishment? Have moral and ethical issues been ignored in the "people changing" techniques used in rehabilitation? Is it proper for the state to take a life? One could continue to cite questions such as these—questions which reflect individual and collective value conflict.

A third explanation for our interest in criminal justice can be linked to the fact that much remains to be done in the field. Police organizations need reform and, many would claim, professionalization. Enormous caseloads demand that attention be devoted to the court process in order to improve both its efficiency and fairness. Corrections continues to function in an environment of confusion because of years of neglect and a lack of consensus regarding goals for this component of the criminal justice system.

The issues and controversies in the field of criminal justice have been closely scrutinized over the past ten years and the result is a massive body of literature. In this publication we have attempted to focus on some of the major issues which have emerged from this body of literature. We have assembled a group of articles which we believe will facilitate understanding of the complexities of criminal justice for the general reader. Our primary interest, however, has been to provide a set of readings for the student commencing his or her study in criminal justice.

It is hoped that the reader will find this work to be both enjoyable and illuminating. In order to profit fully from the following selections, the reader should keep in mind the phrase which serves as our title—"order under law." This phrase, coined by Jerome Skolnick in his landmark publication, *Justice Without Trial*, does much to explain the conflicts and controversies found in the criminal justice system. We demand that our police apprehend suspects, that our courts convict the accused, and that our correctional system, in some way, punish the convicted. We demand order. The tasks involved in insuring order would be relatively straightforward were it not for our simultaneous demand that the police, courts and correctional agencies operate within the constraints placed upon them by the law.

Robert G. Culbertson

Mark R. Tezak

Section I

Crime:
An American Institution

During the late 1960s crime was one of the most sensitive and emotional issues in our society. Increasing crime rates, generated in part by demographic factors, led many to conclude that our society was facing serious moral decay. Riots paralyzed a number of our major cities during a series of "long hot summers." Political and social movements were also influenced by assassins' bullets as we witnessed the deaths of President John F. Kennedy, Senator Robert Kennedy, and civil rights leader Rev. Martin Luther King. Politicians exploited the deep philosophical divisions in our society. Some politicians called for responses which placed additional demands on an already overburdened criminal justice system.

Richard Nixon's campaign for the Presidency in 1968 was based on the assumption that complex social problems could be solved with greater levels of crime control. As a part of the "war on crime," various groups pressured the courts to "stop handcuffing the police." At the same time a number of Presidential Commissions described increased racial discrimination in our society and the special problems of the inner city resident — problems which could not be solved with crime control strategies. The 1960s also witnessed new rights for suspects, defendants and inmates in prisons as the U.S. Supreme Court delivered a number of landmark decisions which altered the operations of criminal justice agencies. Official abuses of power were condemned. For example, the Chicago Police Department was accused of "rioting" at the 1968 Democratic Convention. The study of criminal justice emerged from this climate of conflict and confrontation because traditional

1

disciplines had ignored, for the most part, these overwhelming issues.

While politicians focused their attention on crime rates, they tended to ignore two basic problems. First, crime statistics, upon which crime rates are based, have never been very accurate. Published crime rates may or may not reflect the actual amount of crime at any particular time. Rather, these published rates reflect police activity and tend to rise and fall with changes in enforcement policies. Second, many politicians ignored the fact that American society has always been plagued by criminal activity of one kind or another. Youth gangs roamed the streets of our major cities in the early 1800s and by mid-century New York's Central Park was dominated by young thugs during hours of darkness. Lynchings were a common feature in our society during the late 1800s and continued into the 1900s as racial strife permeated America. During the 1920s and 1930s criminals became heroes as John Dillinger and others pursued the American dream of wealth and affluence at a time when our economic system had failed. The 1960s were, therefore, not a departure from a pattern of lawfulness, but rather reflected the historical pattern of lawlessness.

Public concerns in the area of crime have lessened somewhat over the past ten years as we face complex issues and problems related to inflation and energy shortages. At the same time, crime issues are always close to the surface. Occasionally they dominate our attention as did the recent series of violent riots in Miami and other cities. As resources become increasingly scarce, as adequate housing becomes increasingly difficult to find, and as unemployment rates continue to rise, we can anticipate continued high levels of violence. Finally, our society has never come to grips with the tremendous impact of organized and white collar crime. Some writers contend that the tolerance for organized and white collar crime simply reflect the pervasive nature of crime throughout American society. The articles in this section focus on the crime problem and on our society's reaction to that problem.

In "Fear," Charles Silberman discusses one of the most damaging effects of crime. Crime statistics attach numbers to specific criminal acts and attempt to give us a dollar cost of crime in our society. For the individual citizen, reality is not reflected in crime statistics or cost figures. Rather, reality is the emotional and psychological process of fear. We cannot place a dollar cost on fear. We cannot quantify the impact of crime on the quality of life in a society when individuals are afraid to leave their homes at night because they believe that they may be assaulted. Crime statistics lose their importance when a large number of persons live in fear and believe that the police, courts and correctional institutions are not doing an adequate job of protecting society.

Jonathan Casper's "The Nature of Law and the Causes of Crime," examines the criminal justice system from the perspective of the offender.

Casper's research, conducted in Connecticut prisons, demonstrates the severe problems our criminal justice system faces in its attempt to gain the respect of the criminal defendant. Such respect, Casper contends, is essential if we are to hold any hope for the rehabilitation and reintegration of the offender.

In the final article in this section, Richter Moore casts doubt on the notion of a "criminal justice system." Moore's title, "The Criminal Justice Non-System," is indicative of problems in this area. The three selections point to the enormity of the task facing criminal justice practitioners, researchers, and American society.

1

Fear

Charles Silberman

Men come together in cities in order to live; they remain together in order to live the good life.
— Aristotle

One of the bargains men make with one another in order to maintain their sanity is to share an illusion that they are safe even when the physical evidence in the world around them does not seem to warrant that conclusion.
— Kai T. Erikson, *Everything in Its Path*

"Every time I'm mugged, I feel like I'm that much less of a person."
— Statement of a Mugging Victim

I

All over the United States, people worry about criminal violence. According to public opinion polls, two Americans in five — in large cities, one in two — are afraid to go out alone at night. Fear is more intense among black Americans than among whites, and among women than among men.

From *Criminal Violence, Criminal Justice* by Charles E. Silberman. © 1978 by Charles E. Silberman. Reprinted by permission of Random House, Inc.

The elderly are the most fearful of all; barricaded behind multiple locks, they often go hungry rather than risk the perils of a walk to the market and back.

These fears are grounded in a harsh reality: since the early 1960s, the United States has been in the grip of a crime wave of epic proportions. According to the Federal Bureau of Investigation's *Uniform Crime Reports,* the chance of being the victim of a major violent crime such as murder, rape, robbery, or aggravated assault nearly tripled between 1960 and 1976; so did the probability of being the victim of a serious property crime, such as burglary, purse-snatching, or auto theft. The wave may have crested—crime rates have been relatively stable since the mid-1970s—but criminal violence remains extraordinarily high. If recent rates continue, at least three Americans in every hundred will be the victim of a violent crime this year, and one household in ten will be burglarized.

In some ways, the crime statistics understate the magnitude of the change that has occurred, for they say nothing about the nature of the crimes themselves. Murder, for example, used to be thought of mainly as a crime of passion—an outgrowth of quarrels between husbands and wives, lovers, neighbors, or other relatives and friends. In fact, most murders still involve victims and offenders who know one another, but since the early 1960s murder at the hand of a stranger has increased nearly twice as fast as murder by relatives, friends, and acquaintances. (Much of the latter increase involves killings growing out of rivalries between drug dealers and youth gangs.) In Chicago, for which detailed figures are available, the number of murders of the classic crime-of-passion variety rose 31 percent between 1965 and 1973; in that same period, murders by strangers—"stranger homicides," as criminologists call them—more than tripled.[1]

Rape has been changing in a similar direction. In 1967, people known to the victim—estranged husbands and lovers, other relatives and friends, and casual acquaintances—were responsible for nearly half the rapes that occurred. (Some studies put the proportion even higher.) In 1975, two-thirds of all rape victims were attacked by strangers, with such attacks accounting for virtually the entire 140 percent increase in the number of reported rapes since the mid-1960s.

On the other hand, robbery—taking money or property from another person by force or the threat of force—has always been a crime committed predominantly by strangers. The chances of being robbed have more than tripled since the early 1960s, a larger increase than that registered for any other major crime. Robbers are more violent than they used to be: nowadays, one robbery victim in three is injured, compared to the 1967 ratio of one in five. Although firm figures are hard to come by, it would appear that robbery killings have increased four- or fivefold since the early 1960s, accounting for perhaps half the growth in stranger homicides.[2]

The most disturbing aspect of the growth in "street crime" is the turn toward viciousness, as well as violence, on the part of many young criminals. A lawyer who was a public defender noted for her devotion to her clients' interests, as well as for her legal ability, speaks of "a terrifying generation of kids" that emerged during the late 1960s and early '70s. When she began practicing, she told me, adolescents and young men charged with robbery had, at worst, pushed or shoved a pedestrian or storekeeper to steal money or merchandise; members of the new generation kill, maim, and injure without reason or remorse.

It would be an exaggeration to call viciousness the rule, but it is far from exceptional. The day I began revising this chapter for publication, the mother of a good friend—a frail (and frail-looking) woman in her seventies—was thrown to the sidewalk in the course of a mugging; she sustained a fractured hip and collarbone and will have to use a cane or "walker" for the rest of her days. During an earlier stage of my research, an acquaintance who was moonlighting as a cabdriver was held up by two passengers. After they had taken all his money—my acquaintance put up no resistance—one of the robbers shot him through the right hand, shattering a bone, severing a nerve, and leaving him with life-long pain; several operations later, he still has difficulty using his hand with the agility needed in the craft on which his livelihood depends. (Fortunately, my own family has escaped violent crime until now; but my home was burglarized, as was my son and daughter-in-law's, while I was writing this book.)

For a long time, criminologists, among others, tried to pooh-pooh talk about a rise in street crime, pointing out that the *Uniform Crime Reports* provide only a crude measure of the number of crimes committed each year.* But the increase has been too large, and conforms too closely to people's day-to-day experience, to be dismissed as a statistical illusion. The fact is that criminal violence has become a universal, not just an American phenomenon. Once crime-free nations, such as England, Sweden, West Germany, the Netherlands, and France, as well as more turbulent countries, such as Italy, are now plagued with an epidemic of murder, kidnapping, robbery, and other forms of crime and violence—some of it politically inspired, all of it criminal in intent and consequence. (Within the United States, crime has increased more rapidly in suburbs and small cities than in large cities.) Wherever one turns—in virtually every free nation except Japan—people are worried about "crime in the streets." As Sir Leon Radzinowicz, director of Oxford University's Institute of Criminology, has written, "No national characteristic, no political regime, no system of law, police, justice, punishment, treatment, or even terror has rendered a country exempt from crime."[3]

*For an analysis of the problems involved in measuring crime, see Appendix.

Nor does any national characteristic render a country immune to the corrosive effects of crime. Criminal violence is debasing the quality of life in American cities and suburbs. Quite apart from the physical injuries and financial losses incurred, fear of crime is destroying the network of relationships on which urban and suburban life depends. Anger over crime is debasing the quality of American politics as well: witness the fact that the preeminent issue in the 1977 mayoral election in New York City was the death penalty, something over which the mayor has no control whatsoever. The issue was injected by the winning candidate as a way of shedding his previous image as a liberal. (The friend whose mother was robbed and injured told me, only half jokingly, "A liberal is someone who has not yet been mugged.") What is at stake is not liberalism or conservatism as such, but the ability to think clearly about what can (and what cannot) be done to reduce criminal violence, and at what cost. In any society beset by violence, there is a danger that people's desire for safety and order may override every other consideration; the United States has avoided that mistake so far.

II

Why are people as afraid as they are? The answer cannot lie in the number of violent crimes alone; from an actuarial standpoint, street crime is a lot less dangerous than riding in an automobile, working around the house, going swimming, or any number of other activities in which Americans engage without apparent concern. The chances of being killed in an automobile accident are ten times greater than those of being murdered by a stranger, and the risk of death from a fall — slipping in the shower, say, or tumbling from a ladder — are three times as great.

Accidents also cause far more nonfatal injuries than do violent crimes. More than 5 million people were injured as a result of automobile accidents in 1973 and some 24 million people were hurt in accidents at home — about 4 million of them seriously enough to suffer a temporary or permanent disability. By contrast, fewer than 400,000 robbery victims were injured, and about 550,000 people were hurt in incidents of aggravated assault. Yet radio and television newscasts are not filled with accident reports, as they are with crime news; people do not sit around their living rooms trading stories about the latest home or auto accident, as they do about the latest crime; nor has any candidate for high office promised to wage war on accidents or restore safety to our highways and homes.

In fact, it is perfectly rational for Americans to be more concerned about street crime than about accidents, or, for that matter, about white-collar crime. Violence at the hand of a stranger is far more frightening than a comparable injury incurred in an automobile accident or fall; burglary evokes a sense of loss that transcends the dollar amount involved. The reasons have a great deal to do with the nature of fear and the factors that produce it. From a physiological standpoint, what we call fear is a series of complex changes in the endocrine system that alerts us to danger and makes it possible for us to respond effectively, whether we choose to attack or to flee. The first stage—the one we associate most closely with fear or tension—prepares the entire body for fight or flight: the heart rate and systolic blood pressure go up; blood flow through the brain and the skeletal muscles increases by as much as 100 percent; digestion is impaired; and so on. The second stage provides the capacity for rapid aggression or retreat; the third for a slower, more sustained response.

Thus fear serves as a kind of early warning system. The hormonal changes involved also make it possible for us to respond to danger at a higher level of efficiency, as anyone who has been in combat or has faced other emergencies knows from experience. When life or reputation or honor are at stake, we achieve feats of speed, strength, and endurance—not to mention imagination and intellectual clarity—that we never thought possible, and that in fact we cannot attain under ordinary circumstances.

But as most of us also know from experience, fear can be counterproductive as well. The same hormonal changes that alert us to danger and make it possible to perform herculean feats get in the way of normal behavior. If stress continues too long without being resolved, it leads to illness or pathological behavior. If the danger is so great that it overwhelms us, or so sudden that the early warning system, i.e., the first stage of hormonal change, is by-passed, we may become literally paralyzed with fear. The vulgar metaphors of extreme fear accurately describe the physiological processes; loss of control over the bladder and sphincter are common phenomena.

What this means, as the sociologist Erving Goffman writes, is that people exhibit two basic modes of activity: "They go about their business grazing, gazing, mothering, digesting, building, resting, playing, placidly attending to easily managed matters at hand. Or, fully mobilized, a fury of intent, alarmed, they get ready to attack or to stalk or to flee."[4] We can do one or the other; we cannot do both at the same time—at any rate, not for very long.

How, then, do we guard against danger while going about our normal activities? "By a wonder of adaptation," as Goffman puts it, people have "a very pretty capacity for dissociated vigilance" which enables us to monitor the environment out of the corner of the eye while concentrating on the task at hand. Sights, sounds, smells, and a host of other subtle cues give us a continuous reading of the environment. When that reading conveys a hint of danger, we take an unconscious closer look and may return to our task with just a microsecond's confirmation that things are in order; if that second look suggests that something is awry, our full attention is mobilized immediately.*

For this process to work, we have to know what to fear; we have to learn to distinguish cues that signal real danger from those that can be ignored, at least temporarily, without incurring too much risk. If a warning system is too sensitive—if it produces full mobilization at the merest hint of a danger—people so "protected" would live in a constant state of frenzy and thus would be unable to do all the other things, besides defending themselves, that are essential for survival. Too little sensitivity would be equally fatal.

Human beings tend to equate strange with dangerous; the most common early warning signal of approaching danger is the sight of a stranger. Hence armies post sentries; frightened people use watchdogs. In tightly knit urban communities, as Jane Jacobs has described in sensitive detail, people are always watching the street, and an extraordinary network of communication announces the presence of strangers as soon as they appear.[5] (In some German and Polish neighborhoods in Milwaukee, a stranger driving through the streets is enough to trigger several calls to the police.)

Life in metropolitan areas thus involves a startling paradox: we fear strangers more than anything else, and yet we live our lives among strangers. Every time we take a walk, ride a subway or bus, shop in a supermarket or department store, enter an office building lobby or elevator, work in a factory or large office, or attend a ball game or the movies, we are surrounded by strangers. The potential for fear is as immense as it is unavoidable.

We cope with this paradox in a number of ways. The equation whereby strange means dangerous has an obverse, in which familiar means safe. The longer something is present in the environment without causing harm, the more favorably we regard it and the warmer our feelings are likely to be. People who live near a glue factory become oblivious to the smell; city dwellers come to love the noise, often finding it hard to sleep in the country-side because of the unaccustomed quiet. In psychological experiments, people who were shown nonsense syllables and Chinese ideograms for a second time judged them "good" as opposed to "bad" in comparison with other nonsense syllables and ideograms they were shown, later on, for the first time. The more often people were shown photographs of strangers, the warmer their feelings became toward them.

*Police develop this capacity to an unusual degree. Experienced officers can operate a patrol car, listen to the police radio, and carry on a conversation with a partner while they simultaneously monitor the streets, sidewalks, and alleys, picking up cues that are invisible to the civilian.

In cities, familiarity breeds a sense of security. People who know that they have to be on guard in a strange neighborhood, especially at night, feel more secure in their own neighborhood and come to believe that they have a moral right to count on its being safe. This tendency helps explain a phenomenon that has puzzled social scientists: the fact that people's assessment of the safety of the neighborhood in which they live seems to bear little relationship to the actual level of crime there. In one survey, 60 percent of those queried considered their own neighborhoods to be safer than the rest of the community in which they lived; only 14 percent thought their neighborhood was more dangerous. What was striking was that people felt this way no matter how much crime there was in their neighborhood: in Washington D.C., precincts with crime rates well above the average for the city, only 20 percent of respondents thought the risks of being assaulted were greater in their neighborhood than in other parts of the city.[6]

This same phenomenon makes crime a terribly bewildering, as well as fear-evoking, event when it is experienced on one's own turf. "Casual conversations with urban citizens or regular reading of the newspapers in recent years would indicate that many, if not most, inner-city residents live with the fatalistic expectation that sooner or later they will be mugged," Robert LeJeune and Nicholas Alex write in their richly informative study of the experiences of mugging victims. "But closer examination reveals that most of these fear-laden accounts are not associated with a corresponding mental frame necessary to develop the appropriate precautionary behavior."[7]

To the contary, the mugging victims studied by LeJenue and Alex had all assumed before they were mugged that however dangerous *other* neighborhoods might be, they were reasonably safe from attack in their own. "I never felt afraid," said one victim, a widowed secretary. "Well, I'm not willing to say that I wasn't afraid at all," she added. "Everybody has a little bit of a feeling of fear." What she meant, it turned out, was that she had always been afraid of the neighborhood in which her daughter lived. "Because I heard things of that neighborhood—and it wasn't safe. I heard of people being mugged. And there I didn't feel secure." Her own neighborhood was something else again. As she explained, "Here I wasn't afraid. . . . In my neighborhood there are police cars, there are people walking. How can anybody be afraid? . . . And on *my* block—I'm not going to be afraid on Post Avenue."

But city dwellers rarely stay cooped up in their own neighborhood; most adults have to venture elsewhere to go to work, to shop, to visit relatives and friends, or to use the cultural and entertainment facilities that make cities cities. When we enter any environment, whether familiar or strange, we automatically take a quick "reading" or "sounding" in order to decide whether to be on guard or not. If things are as they should be, if appearances are normal, we can be off guard; we can concentrate on the task at hand, confident of our ability to predict what will happen from the cues we pick up out of the corner of the eye. The result is the sense of safety that comes from feeling in control of one's own fate. For if we can predict danger in advance, we can avoid it—if only by retreating in time to some safer haven.

The process is extraordinarily fragile. We can predict danger only if the subtle cues on which we depend—for example, people's dress or attitude or demeanor—are accurate, which is to say, only if things are as they appear. Ultimately, the whole fabric of urban life is based on trust: trust that others will act predictably, in accordance with generally accepted rules of behavior, and that they will not take advantage of that trust. For life to go on in public places—in city streets, building lobbies, elevators, and hallways—people must put themselves in other people's hands.

Consider the elaborate etiquette pedestrians employ to avoid bumping into one another. The American pedestrian maintains a scanning or check-out range of about three or four sidewalk squares, assuming that people beyond this range—whether in front or behind—can be ignored. As other people enter the scanning range, they are glanced at briefly and then ignored if their distance, speed, and direction imply that neither party has to change course to avoid a collision. When people have been checked out in this manner, Goffman writes, they can be allowed to come quite close without evoking concern. Moreover, pedestrians ignore oncomers who are separated from them by other people; thus someone may walk in dense traffic and be completely unconcerned about people just a few feet away.[8]

While one person is checking out those who come into his range in this manner, others are checking him out in the same way; none of them is aware, except in the vaguest sense, that this is what they are doing. And the process can become much more complicated. If an initial body check indicates that the pedestrian and a stranger are on a collision course, or if the stranger's course is not clear, an individual may follow one of a number of procedures. "He can ostentatiously take or hold a course, waiting to do this until he can be sure that the other is checking him out," Goffman writes. "If he wants to be still more careful, he can engage in a 'checked-body-check'; after he has given a course indication, he can make sure the signal has been picked up by the other, either by meeting the other's eye (although not for engagement) or by noting the other's direction or vision, in either case establishing that his own course gesture has not likely been overlooked. In brief, he can check up on the other's eye check on him, the assumption being that the other can be relied on to act safely providing only that he has perceived the situation."

This process of unconscious mutual accommodation is even more complex when traffic is heavy. If pedestrian A is walking behind pedestrian

B, A not only accommodates to the movements B makes to avoid colliding with pedestrian C; he frequently will adjust his movement to what he *assumes* B is about to do to avoid C. And when these adjustments are not possible—for example, if a narrow path has been cut through heavy snow or around a construction site or other obstacle—one of several other adjustments comes into play automatically. As Goffman observes, "City streets, even in times that defame them, provide a setting where mutual trust is routinely displayed between strangers."

This kind of voluntary coordination usually works because, under ordinary circumstances, no one has much to gain from violating the rules. At the same time, the fact that coordination is required provides a standing invitation to gamesmanship, and adolescents often pick up the challenge. When gaining face is important, the psychological payoff from violating the rules—staring someone down, for example, or maintaining a course that requires the other person to step aside—may be large. Under the system of racial etiquette that prevailed in the South until fairly recently, blacks were required to step aside—into a muddy street, if need be—in order to let whites (*any* whites) go past with full possession of the sidewalk. Equally important, eye contact with whites was prohibited as another means of symbolizing white superiority and black inferiority; for a black man to eye a white woman was to invite a lynching.[9]

It is not surprising that some members of the present generation of black adolescents find delight in reversing the old conventions—for example, walking four or five abreast so that white pedestirans have to stand aside, or conversing in the street in a group so that a white driver backing his car out of his driveway has to wait until the youngsters choose to move. As accompaniments to these triumphs of reverse gamesmanship, there may be eye contact as well, in the form of a long, hate-filled glare.

Encounters of this sort are discomforting, for they show how fragile the social order really is—how dependent it is (and always has been) on acceptance of the rules by people who never have had much reason to accept them. "It has always been the case that the orderly life of a group contained many more points of weakness than its opponents ever exploited," Goffman writes, and a breakdown in what we consider civility or decorum exposes those weaknesses.

III

Crime does more than expose the weakness in social relationships; it undermines the social order itself, by destroying the assumptions on which it is based. The need to assume that familiar environments are safe is so great that until they have become victims themselves, many people rationalize that newspaper and television accounts of crime are greatly exaggerated. "This kind of thing happens on television, but not in real life," a college student exclaimed after she and a friend had been held up on the Ellipse, an area adjacent to the White House. (Although the two students were not injured, a migrant worker sitting on a nearby bench was shot in the face and blinded when he told the robbers—correctly—that he had no money.) "You just don't shoot someone in the back like in a Western movie," a young woman who had been shot and seriously injured in a D.C. robbery attempt told a Washington *Post* reporter.

Even when they admit that crime does occur, people comfort themselves with the assumption that it won't happen to them—in much the same way that we assume our own immortality, or our invulnerability to earthquake or flood.* It is only in retrospect, as LeJeune and Alex explain, that victims realize they should have been more aware of their own vulnerability. "Of course the conditions have been getting worse and worse," one of their respondents observed. "Uh, someone thinks that accidents happen to other people but they don't happen to me. Then when it did happen I was very upset because I didn't think it could happen to me."[11]

The need to feel safe is so powerful that people routinely misread cues that should signal danger. They may simply delay responding to a stranger, to give him a chance to explain or apologize; intuitive knowledge of this tendency on the part of pickpockets, assassins, and saboteurs make it possible for them to carry out their mission.[12] People also may redefine a danger signal as a normal event—for example, by assuming that a mugger is merely panhandling or playing a practical joke. Consider these explanations by three of LeJeune and Alex's respondents:

> I was walking down the street. Four young men approached me. I say, "Oh, cut this fooling out." And then they put their hands in my pocket.

> When I got into the elevator I felt a hand, you know, and I thought the fellow was joking. But then I started feeling the pain. He was very strong. It was no joke.

Similarly, a victim may perceive a threatening stranger as a friendly neighbor who forgot his keys:

> I thought: it's one of my neighbors waving to me not to close the door. He must have forgotten his key. Just then somebody grabbed me in the back of the neck and held my head in both his arms.

Or the victim may interpret a robber's demand for money as a request for a loan:

---

*"In this respect, as in many others, the man of prehistoric age survives unchanged in our unconscious," Sigmund Freud wrote. "Thus, our unconscious does not believe in its own death; it behaves as if immortal...." We really believe that "'Nothing can happen to me.' On the other hand, for strangers and for enemies, we do acknowledge death...."[10]

When we started getting off the elevator he turned around and he said: "Give me ten dollars." I thought he wanted to borrow ten dollars. He said, "I don't want any trouble. Give me ten dollars." And I looked him up and down, and I see he has a knife in his hand. So I didn't let myself get knifed. I gave him the ten dollars and he got off.[13]

People *need* to be able to make sense out of their environment; otherwise, life would be intolerable. To "live with fear," as victims call it—to be suspicious of every sound and every person—converts the most elementary and routine aspects of life into an exercise in terror. It is to avoid such terror that people who have not been victimized (and some who have) interpret threatening gestures and events in terms that are more understandable and comfortable.

Thus the emotional impact of being attacked by a stranger transcends the incident itself; it reaches a primordial layer of fear unlike anything evoked by an equally damaging encounter with an automobile or other inanimate object, or even by a crime that does not involve a direct encounter with another person. A criminal attack is disorienting as well, evoking traumatic reactions similar to those the sociologist Kai T. Erikson found among the survivors of the Buffalo Creek Flood.* Victims of criminal violence, like victims of earthquake or flood, develop what Erikson describes as "a sense of vulnerability, a feeling that one has lost a certain natural immunity to misfortune, a growing conviction, even, that the world is no longer a safe place to be." Because they previously had underestimated the peril in which they lived, the survivors of a disaster lose confidence in their ability to monitor their environment; as a result, they live in constant fear that something terrible will happen again.[14]

Crime victims are affected in much the same way; the inability to tell friend from foe—the sense that they no longer know how to monitor their environment—can turn the most ordinary encounter into a nightmare. Until the attack in which he was blinded, James Martin, a nineteen-year-old former handyman, never worried about crime. In the Washington, D.C., ghetto where he lived, talk about crime was a constant, but Martin recalls, "I never paid any attention...I felt safe. I thought people would look at me and say, 'the dude ain't got nothing.'" He was wrong. The men who held him up at a bus stop were enraged when Martin told them he had only $6 on his person; they knocked him down, beat his head against the sidewalk, then smashed a soda bottle on the curb and rammed the jagged edge into his right eye, completely destroying his vision. Although the robbers were convicted and imprisoned, Martin found that there was no way he could continue to live in Washington. Afraid to go out alone and equally afraid to

*On February 26, 1976, 132 million gallons of mud and debris broke through a faulty mining company dam in Buffalo Creek, West Virginia, killing 125 and leaving 4,000 of the hollow's 5,000 residents homeless.

stay home, he could not sleep, either, for fear his assailants would break out of prison and return to attack him again. He and his family moved back home to a small town in North Carolina, to live in a trailer on his mother-in-law's farm.[15]

This sense of vulnerability and fear seems to be a universal feeling, regardless of whether the person attacked is injured or not. Instead of familiar environments being automatically defined as safe, they now are perceived as uniformly dangerous because of the victim's inability to rely on the old cues. Asked whether being mugged had changed their outlook on life in any way, respondents in LeJeune and Alex's survey replied as follows:

> I am just so much more frightened wherever I turn, and it seems as though the entire city has turned into an incredible jungle.... It's incredible that I think that way, that I feel that way; it's so unlike me."

> Yes. It's made the city more of a jungle to me. Yes it has. And I haven't got too long to retire. And where I had really thought I would stay in the city, you believe it, I'll get out.

> Well it has. I mean I don't feel free, like to do things. You feel you like to go to the movies or something. You don't feel you could do it. You always fear that there's somebody, uh, even if you go to the movies and you're safe— you're inside—coming out you'll always have that fear, oh my God, somebody's passing or something.

The worst fear is felt in the area in which the person was attacked, particularly if it is his own neighborhood. "I've been living here for three and a half years, and I've never had any real fear of it," a mugging victim who decided to move out of her neighborhood told LeJeune and Alex. "It's like it's my home. I know the block. I recognize people. It's all very familiar to me. Now it's become very unfamiliar to me, very threatening, very, very much like a jungle. I trust nobody. You know, I'm constantly looking around me.... I will never walk on *that* block again."

The most disorienting aspect of all is the senselessness of the whole experience, which shatters victims' belief that cause and effect have some relationship. They no longer can view the world as a rational, hence predictable, place over which they have some control. "The thing that bothers me, and always will, is why they shot me," says Sally Ann Morris, a twenty-six-year-old woman badly injured in a holdup attempt. "I didn't pose any threat to them; I was running away...."[16] Tommy Lee Harris, a sixty-two-year-old man who was badly beaten by two young muggers after he had given them all his money, says in obvious bewilderment, "I don't know why it happened; I didn't know the men." After beating Harris to the ground, breaking four ribs, the muggers put him in the trunk of his own car, which they proceeded to drive away. Harris' life was saved when a policeman saw the muggers run through a red light and pursued them in his patrol car.[17]

The victim's bewilderment is compounded by the realization of how large a role coincidence and chance had played. For the first week after the shooting, Ms. Morris blamed the friend who had been with her at the time:

> I thought why couldn't it have been him, he could have taken it better. Why me?'' she recalls. "Isn't that just terrible to think like that? ...And then I spent a long time thinking: if it had just taken longer to park, or if we had gone down another street...."

The discovery that life is irrational and unpredictable makes victims feel completely impotent. This, in turn, exacerbates their fear: whether or not we feel in control of a situation directly affects the way we respond to it. Indeed, psychological experiments indicate that fear is substantially reduced if people merely *believe* they have some control over a stimulus, even if their response has no effect. One such experiment, described to the forty students who participated as a study of "reaction time," was conducted at the State University of New York at Stony Brook. The students were given a series of electric shocks lasting six seconds each, after which they were divided into two groups. One group was told that if they pulled a switch rapidly enough, they could reduce the shock they received from six to three seconds; the other group was told that they would receive three-second shocks no matter what they did. In fact, both groups received shocks of the same duration—three seconds.. But the members of the first group, who believed that their actions could reduce the shock, showed far less stress as measured by galvanic skin reactions than did the members of the second group.[18]

Thus accidents are far less terrifying than crime because they do not create the sense of impotence evoked by crime. "You can't slip in the shower unless you're *in* the shower," the psychologist Martin E.P. Seligman points out., and "You can't get into an automobile smash-up unless you're riding in an automobile." One can take precautions, moreover, that extend the sense of control over one's environment and fate—using a skidproof rubber mat in the shower, checking a ladder to make sure it is steady, swimming in the ocean only if a lifeguard is on duty and the surf and undertow are not too strong, and keeping a careful eye out for other drivers and pedestrians.

In some of these situations, such as driving a car, people know in advance that they must be vigilant. And the automobile itself acts as a kind of armor or shield, protecting both driver and passenger from the invasion of self that interpersonal crime involves. Indeed, when riding in an automobile, people usually behave as if they were invisible to other drivers and passengers—which in a psychic sense they are—and as if the other drivers and passengers were invisible to them. It is only young children, who have not yet been socialized into highway etiquette, who make eye contact with people in other cars. The rest of us display what Goffman calls "civil inattention" to others when we drive or walk in public.

In violent crime, there is a direct intrusion on the self that produces anger and shame, in addition to fear. "My whole life has been invaded, violated—and not just by the act itself," says a forty-seven-year-old woman who was raped in her apartment. "It didn't happen just to me but to my husband and children." The rape totally shattered her sense of self, leaving her with a feeling of having been defiled, of being "stained and different," that, ten months later, her husband's love and understanding had not been able to overcome. "She says, 'You don't want anything to do with me because I am so dirty,'" the husband reports, and the wife wonders if she can ever put her life together again. "There have been times when I wish (the rapist) had killed me—it would have been kinder.... It was as though there were something lacking in dignity in still being alive." At times, to be sure, she feels a glimmer of hope: "I know that somehow we will work it out...."But she adds: "I have changed and the world has changed. I don't see things the way I used to." In the best of moods, in fact, she is besieged by fear, afraid to go out alone and afraid to stay home, obsessed, as so many victims are, that the attacker will come back to seek revenge on her or on her two younger children.[19]

Although the sense of shame and defilement is most evident (and most understandable) in instances of rape, robbery and assault victims have similar, if less intense reactions. Our sense of self is bound up with our ability to control the personal space in which we live. As administrators of prisons and concentration camps well know, stripping people of their clothes serves to strip them of the normal defenses of their egos, leaving them far more compliant and docile. Victims of muggings, robberies, and assaults also experience a diminishment in their ego defenses. Male victims feel stripped of some portion of their masculinity as well; hence they often display a compulsive need to explain why it was impossible for them to resist or prevail. This need is strongest of all in men who have been the victims of homosexual rape.

Crimes such as homicide and rape deprive both victims and their relatives of the protective mantle of privacy, converting their intensely private agony and pain into public experiences. "It's impossible for somebody who hasn't been through it to understand the difference between a father dying of natural causes and being murdered," the married daughter of a murdered Bronx pharmacist told a New York *Post* reporter a year after the event. "If I had to name one thing that I hate (the murderer) for the most, it is that he made my father's death—which you should have to cope with privately— a very public thing."[20]

Burglary, too, evokes considerable fear, even though there is no confrontation with a stranger. For one thing, burglary victims are highly conscious of the fact that there might have been a confrontation had they come home earlier, hence they often are afraid to be home alone. Children whose homes have been burglarized sometimes need psychiatric help to cope with the fear.

More important, forced entry into one's home is an invasion of the self, for our homes are part of the personal space in which we live. We express our individuality in the way we furnish and decorate, and in the artifacts we collect; we may view some of our possessions in a casual manner, but others are invested with layers of meaning that bear no relationship to their monetary value. I can still feel the rage that overcame me when I discovered that the person who had burglarized my home had taken a set of cuff-links and studs worn by my father on his wedding day. The fact that they were covered by insurance was irrelevant; their value lay in their power to evoke my father's physical presence seventeen years after his death. I remember, too, the enormous relief my wife and I felt when we discovered that the burglar had been interrupted before he had a chance to take the candlesticks my mother had used to usher in the Sabbath every week of her life.

Because our homes are psychological extensions of our selves, burglary victims often describe their pain in terms strikingly similar to those used by victims of rape—and in a symbolic sense burglary victims *have* been violated. The saying that one's home is a sanctuary is no mere epigram; it expresses a profound psychological truth. One of the oldest and most sacred principles of Anglo-Saxon law held that no matter how humble a person's cottage might be, not even the King could enter without his consent. The principle is recognized, after a fashion, by totalitarian regimes. The dramatic symbol of totalitarianism is the harsh knock on the door in the middle of the night; as Goffman points out, the fact that even storm troopers knock implies their acknowledgment of the territorial rights of the residents. It is not too much to conclude that crime threatens the social order in much the same way as does totalitarianism.

In the United States, because of the abnormally low base from which the crime wave of the 1960s and early '70s began, the upsurge in criminal violence has been even more traumatic than otherwise might have been the case. Americans who came of age during the 1930s, '40s, and '50s had their general outlook and expectations shaped by an atypical, perhaps unique, period of American history. During their formative years, crime rates were stable or declining, and the level of domestic violence was unusually low. Never having experienced the crime and violence that had characterized American life for a century or more, this generation of Americans—the generation from which most governmental and other opinion leaders are drawn—came to take a low level of crime for granted.

For people over the age of thirty-five, therefore, the upsurge in crime that began in the early 1960s appeared to be a radical departure from the norm, a departure that shattered their expectations of what urban and suburban life was like. The trauma was exacerbated by the growing sense that the whole world was getting out of joint, for the explosive increase in crime was accompanied by a number of other disorienting social changes—for example, a general decline in civility, in deference to authority, and in religious and patriotic observance. But this is getting ahead of the story.

Notes

[1] For Chicago, see Richard Block, "Homicide in Chicago: A Nine-Year Study (1965-1973)," *Journal of Crime and Criminology,* Vol. 66, No. 4 (December, 1976), pp. 496-510; Block and Franklin E. Zimring, "Homicide in Chicago, 1965-1970," *Journal of Research in Crime and Delinquency,* Vol. 10, No. 1 (January, 1973), pp. 1-112. On homicide trends generally, see Lynn A. Curtis, *Criminal Violence* (Lexington, Mass.: D.C. Heath & Co., 1974), esp. Ch. 3; A. Joan Klebba, *Mortality Trends for Homicide, by Age, Color, and Sex: United States, 1960-1972* (Rockville, Md.: National Center for Health Statistics, undated, mimeo). I have updated Curtis' analysis of trends in stranger homicide through use of the FBI's *Uniform Crime Reports.*

[2] The discussion of crime trends is based on my own analysis of data contained in the following sources: Donald J. Mulvihill and Melvin M. Tumin, with Curtis, *Crimes of Violence,* A Staff Report to the National Commission on the Causes and Prevention of Violence, Vol. 11, Ch. 5 (Washington, D.C.: U.S. Government Printing Office, 1969); J. Edgar Hoover, *Crime in the United States: Uniform Crime Reports, 1967* (Washington, D.C.: U.S. Government Printing Office, 1968); Clarence M. Kelley, *Crime in the United States, 1975 (Uniform Crime Reports),* and Kelley, *Crime in the United States, 1976 (Uniform Crime Reports)* (Washington, D.C.: U.S. Government Printing Office, 1976 and 1977); *Criminal Victimization in the United States, 1973,* A National Crime Panel Survey Report (U.S. Government Printing Office, 1976); *Criminal Victimization in the United States: A Comparison of 1973 and 1974 Findings,* A National Crime Panel Survey Report (U.S. Government Printing Office, 1976); *Criminal Victimization in the United States: A Comparison of 1974 and 1975 Findings,* A National Crime Panel Survey Report (U.S. Government Printing Office, 1977). See also Curtis, *Criminal Violence,* Ch. 3.

[3] Leon Radzinowicz and Joan King, *The Growth of Crime* (New York: Basic Books, Inc., 1977), p. 3. On the growth of crime throughout the world, see also Ted Robert Gurr, "Contemporary Crime in Historical Perspective: A Comparative Study of London, Stockholm, and Sydney," *Annals of the American Academy of Political and Social Science,* Vol. 434 (November, 1977), pp. 114-36; Gurr, *Rogues, Rebels and Reformers: A Political History of Urban Crime and Conflict* (Beverly Hills, Calif.: Sage Publications, 1976); Marshall B. Clinard and Daniel J. Abbott, *Crime in Developing Countries* (New York: John Wiley & Sons, 1973).

[4] Erving Goffman, *Relations in Public* (New York: Harper Colophon Books, 1971), p. 238. [4]

[5] Jane Jacobs, *The Death and Life of Great American Cities* (New York: Random House, Inc., 1961).

[6]Jennie McIntyre, "Public Attitudes Toward Crime and Law Enforcement," *Annals of the American Academy of Political and Social Science,* Vol. 374 (November, 1967), pp. 38-39. See also *Crimes and Victims: A Report on the Dayton-San Jose Pilot Survey of Victimization* (Washington, D.C.: U.S. Department of Justice, Law Enforcement Assistance Administration, 1974), Table 13.

[7]Robert Lejeune and Nicholas Alex, "On Being Mugged: The Event and Its Aftermath," *Urban Life and Culture,* Vol. 2, No. 3 (October, 1973), reprinted in *The Aldine Crime and Justice Annual, 1973* (Chicago, Ill.: Aldine Publishing Co., 1974), pp. 161-89.

[8]Goffman, *Relations in Public,* pp. 11-12.

[9]For a discussion of the complex rules governing eye contact in human society, see Michael Argyle, "The Laws of Looking," *Human Nature,* Vol. 1, No. 1 (January, 1978), pp. 32-40.

[10]Sigmund Freud, "Thoughts on War and Death," in Freud, *On War, Sex, and Neurosis,* reprinted in Richard D. Donnelly et al., *Criminal Law* (New York: The Free Press, 1962), p. 347.

[11]Lejeune and Alex, "On Being Mugged," p. 171.

[12]Goffman, *Relations in Public,* pp. 265ff. On pickpockets, see David W. Maurer, *Whiz Mob* (Gainesville, Fla.: American Dialect Society, November, 1955), esp. Ch. 5.

[13]Lejeune and Alex, "On Being Mugged," pp. 167-69.

[14]Kai T. Erikson, *Everything in Its Path* (New York: Simon & Schuster, 1976), p. 234.

[15]John Saar, "Attack at Bus Stop Wrecks Man's Life, Denies Ambition," Washington *Post* (March 9, 1975).

[16]Ron Shaffer, "Tormented Gun Victim Asks Why," Washington *Post* (November 29, 1975).

[17]Shaffer and Alfred E. Lewis, "You Go Out . . . and Might Not Get Back," Washington *Post* (August 23, 1975).

[18]Maggie Scarf, "The Anatomy of Fear," *New York Times Magazine* (June 16, 1974), pp. 18-20.

[19]John Saar, "Rape Victim's Memories Haunt Her," Washington *Post* (April 20, 1975).

[20]Barry Cunningham, "Murder Victim's Family: One Year Later," New York *Post* (September 12, 1974), p. 54.

2

The Nature of Law and the Causes of Crime

Jonathan Casper

The law is, among other things, a series of commands about how people in a society ought to behave. The criminal law consists of a series of negative propositions—for example, Thou shall not steal or rob or rape or murder or shoot drugs. These norms tell us what we ought not to do and at the same time—if they are obeyed—define the quality of life in our society. Some of the norms are directly tied to the economic system—for example, those protecting private property—and others are derived from basic moral notions about how people ought to treat one another. These norms not only provide a framework for social and economic life in a society but also provide a regularity and predictability to one's relations with others.

The norms that comprise the criminal law are in part the product of morality and convention among members of the society. That is, the formal doctrine is produced by notions of what is right and wrong. Norms that no longer comport with moral standards begin to fall into disuse and may become "dead-letter" laws—still on the books but not obeyed or enforced—or may be formally expunged from the criminal code. Thus, conduct conforming to the law is not only the product of a socialization process that teaches the value of obedience to law. It is also the product of unthinking moral imperatives that have no direct reference to the content of

Jonathan D. Casper, *American Criminal Justice: The Defendant's Perspective,* ©1972, pp. 145-167. Reprinted by permission of Prentice-Hall, Inc. Englewood Cliffs, N.J.

the law itself. Most people in the society refrain from breaking into their neighbor's houses for reasons more complex than simply because they know this conduct is illegal and may produce sanctions by officers of the law; neither do most fail to steal simply because they realize that it is in their own interest for people to respect the property of others. Most also do not steal because they believe that it is *wrong* to do so.

The relationship between law, morality, and convention is two edged. In part the norms are the product of convention and morality; in part obedience to the law is itself a matter not only of the dictates of the law but also of one's own moral code.

In this chapter we shall explore the defendants' views of the law and of violation of the law. The question of why some people engage in "criminal" behavior is one that has long plagued societies and students of behavior. Many explanations and theories have been developed, none of which seem particularly fulfilling. Is it too much to expect that criminals themselves — when asked, "Why did you do it?" — will provide us with ready answers to the question. They, too, are quite confused about why they behave as they do and would welcome an answer. This chapter will analyze their notions about the law and violation of it and offer an interpretation of what they had to say. The discussion is speculative. Since our system is so willing to permit defendants to "participate" in deciding how their criminal behavior ought to be punished, it seems reasonable to listen to some of their notions of why they broke the law.

What do the defendants think about the laws they violated? With the exception of a few arrested on drug charges, all the defendants believed that they had done something "wrong," that the law they violated represented a norm that was worthy of respect and that ought to be followed:

> I knew everything I did out there, it was wrong. I knew. You know, like, I was breaking the law; I knew what I was doing. I knew I wasn't sup-posed to do that. There was nothing they need to tell me I had to do. It's just like I think that when you have a country, the thing is, it is true, if you have a country, you got to have laws to keep people from — this man work all year for his money, and you go and take it from him. Got to keep you from doing that, you know. If you didn't, you couldn't have a country. It couldn't be run.

Like the man quoted above, about half the men interviewed (thirty-five of seventy-one) were charged with property crimes. Without exception all felt that laws against taking property from others were "good" laws and that such behavior should not be tolerated but merited punishment. They felt that the people they stole from "deserved" the property they had and that it was wrong to take it from them:

> *How did you feel about the people who owned the stuff you were taking?*

Well, nine times out of ten I didn't know the people, you know? I didn't know the people. But I know when they came home and found their TV set was missing, well, I knew they felt bad. They're out there working all day, man, and come home and they see that their things are missin. I knew they felt pretty bad. But that didn't bother me, because I felt as though I got what I wanted. I'm satisfied. I'm only lookin out for myself, you know. Wasn't thinkin about the others.

Some guys tell me that, you know, they do B and E's or robberies, or other property crimes — that they in some sense feel like the people they are robbing don't deserve to have the stuff; so it's OK to take it. I gather you didn't feel that way?

No, I didn't feel that way. They deserved it because they worked for it. They probably worked forty, forty-eight hours a week, and most of the stuff probably wasn't even paid for. They deserved it. It wasn't that why I took it. I took it for the simple reason that I had a habit of drugs, and I knew that called for TV or the tape recorder. I knew I could sell it; so this is why I took it. But the people deserved it, oh yeah, they deserved it.

*   *   *

I don't hold any animosity whatsoever for somebody who has money. Matter of fact, I respect them for it. That they're intelligent enough to have it. And you know, if I ever do get it, I'll be happy to be in that same position, see what I mean? As I say, I respect them for it. And that's why I wouldn't want to change too much myself — because if I ever do get some money, which I intend to sometime, I would want to be in a position where I can, you know, control my destiny or whatever it is.

*   *   *

I don't feel too much of anything. Just as I say, like certain class of people, the way the system is set up, certain class of people have an — the system is set up and geared to their success and prosperity more so than others and another class — where it's geared that they should stay oppressed and it's hard to get out of it. Now, I felt it was in suburbia, these people *in a sense had the advantages of society more so than I did. But this still don't make what I did right.* You understand what I mean? I'm not trying to justify. I can't. (Emphasis added.)

These men, like almost all, admit to an envy of the property of others and to a desire to get the things that they don't have. But at the same time they are not really radicals bent upon destroying the system of private property, feeling that the rich have no "right" to possess what the poor do not. Rather, they feel that the law against stealing is justified, primarily because when they get the things they desire, they don't want someone (like themselves) to come along and take it from them. They understand the idea of reciprocity upon which the law is based.

The men interviewed have by and large "accepted" the norms implicit in the criminal law. But they have not "internalized" them. This is a somewhat subtle distinction, but I think it is crucial to understanding their relationship to the law and the reasons that they broke it. "Internalizing" a norm can be conceptualized as involving four steps: (1) acknowledging that the norm exists and understanding what behavior is prescribed or proscribed; (2) acknowledging the authoritativeness of the norm: accepting that it "ought" to be followed (such acceptance may be the product of a variety of factors: of a sense that the behavior prescribed enjoys a moral status; of an instrumental calculation that following a norm will provide benefits to the person by maintaining his property or protecting himself; of knowledge that failure to obey the norm will produce punishment that makes disobedience not worthwhile); (3) developing feelings of virtue (or self-worth) when one engages in conduct in conformity with the norm and guilt (negative feelings about oneself) when one violates the norm. (4) As a consequence of the first three steps, a norm is internalized when a person has a basic predisposition to behave in ways that are congruent with the norm. Only in extraordinary circumstances will the person consider violating the norm. In a man's day-to-day life the notion of disobeying the norm usually does not occur. Thus, internalization is a product both of a socialization process which teaches that the behavior prescribed by the norm is inherently desirable and satisfying in and of itself and of instrumental calculations that following norms will produce more personal benefit than disobedience.

Most norms violated by the men I have interviewed have been internalized by most citizens in our society — at least by those who have a modicum of money and status. Most citizens, even when they are in some financial difficulty, do not consider the possibility of actually breaking into a house or robbing a liquor store; when they become angry at someone, they do not typically think seriously about beating him up or perhaps killing him; when they are anxious or despairing, they do not cop heroin and shoot up. The fact that most citizens do not think about committing these "crimes" is not simply the product of their being "crimes," nor of a fear of going to jail. They do not think of them, for they have learned that such behavior is not within the range of alternatives that they can actually consider. In part, it is also the product of a Kantian imperative, a view that if everyone engaged in these acts, each man would be worse off than if no one did them. Thus, because of both socialization and calculation, most norms in the criminal law have been internalized by most people in our society.

The men I have interviewed have not, by and large, internalized these norms. They have achieved the first two steps, but not the third or fourth.

Difficulties encountered in their lives quickly bring to mind course of action that involve law violation. Although they are aware of the norms and acknowledge their authoritative status, they are typically aware of and consider the possibility of violating them, and in fact do violate them with great frequency.

Some evidence of this emerged in their replies to the question, "What do you think would happen if there were no law against (the crime that you were charged with or convicted of committing)?" Without exception they responded, in effect, that everyone would begin doing it. Although a few introduced some subtlety into their response—for example, those who were richer would be less likely to steal; some people were less prone to violence than others—most were quite convinced that in the absence of a law, behavior now proscribed would become rampant. This view imputes to the law powers that, of course, it does not possess, but indicates a great faith in the efficacy of the law.

More important, it suggests that most of the men believe that law-abiding behavior is the product not of convention, morality, or internalization of the norm itself, but rather of external force imposing constraints upon a person. They seem to be suggesting that man's natural inclination is to steal and fight and kill and shoot dope. It is clear that there is in fact something to this argument, for if there were not such inclinations, there would be no need for laws against such behavior. But they are saying something more than this; they are indicating the extent to which they have not internalized the norms of the law. They impute a morality to the law but think that people will not behave in a lawful manner in the absence of force.

In a very real sense these men are living in a Hobbesian state of nature, a war of all against all. Each man is subject to his own passions and greed, and in the absence of a Leviathan, each will wreak violence on another's person and property. They long for this Leviathan but do not find it. In fact, they do know it exists, for they see it around them every day; but it is not theirs.

The see a "civil" society in the middle-class and rich society in which their lives are embedded but of which they are not members. This distance from "civil" society accounts in part for their failure to internalize the norms of the criminal law and for their propensity for law-violating behavior. The norms of the law are the product of a "they"—the middle class and rich—whose general style of life and whose norms the defendants accept and in fact covet deeply.

We can view the defendants as spectators at a game. They see the players; they see the rules they live by; and they envy them the opportunity to play and the rules by which the game proceeds. At the same time, they are *not* players. The rules, therefore, are not theirs. They are involved in another game, and the rules of civil society do not serve their interests—they serve the interests of the members of that society. Thus, they have not internalized the rules—the thought and the practice of violating them occur to them frequently—even though they recognize them and accept them as desireable guides to life. Let us look now at the defendants' views of the causes of crime. It is useful to distinguish between those who were drug addicts at the time of their last arrest and those who were not.

The Junkie

About half the men interviewed reported that they had been using heroin at the time of their last arrest.* It is difficult to tell whether this is an accurate reflection of the proportion of those who commit crimes in Connecticut. The men in prison were selected randomly, and the estimate of prison officials suggests that 50 percent is probably reasonably accurate.

The drug addicts—who were in prison for drug offenses or property crimes, most frequently breaking and entering—reported that they had committed their crimes for the purpose of obtaining money to support their drug habits, which ranged from about eighteen to one hundred dollars a day. Thus, for these men the real question seems to be not why they committed crimes, but rather why they became drug addicts. It may not be that simple, for I have the impression that many of them might well have been involved in criminal activities even if they had not been addicted. Many had criminal records that preceded their experience with drugs. Moreover, a number of men interviewed had been drug addicts in the past but apparently had not been addicts at the time of their last arrest.

Why does a man become a drug addict? Most of the men who were addicts had theories, though none really thought they completely understood their behavior or the general phenomenon. Most suggested that their initial experience had to do with watching people around them apparently quite happy on drugs and being curious about what it was like. This led to experimentation, to enjoyment, to habitual use, and to addiction. Others spoke of the notion of "escape," of being in a position in which nothing could bother them, in which life became tolerable. Others talked of the status attached to use of drugs; others of psychological weakness and the need for a crutch. All agreed that heroin was enjoyable, though supporting a habit was not:

> What kind of person would be an addict, and what kind of person wouldn't?
>
> What kind of person? Anybody can get hooked—anybody can get hooked. you can be around the wrong crowd; you could have your best

*Thirty-seven of seventy-one reported that they were heroin users at the time of their last arrest. Thirty-one reported that they were addicted to heroin.

friends, they'll get you hooked. Anybody—your wife, your girlfriend; maybe your mother and your father, your uncle and your aunt. Anybody can get you hooked. You bein around it so much, that's what it is now. There's so much in the street—all your friends are doin it—you can't help from getting around it. It's in the ghettos, it's in the suburbs. You can't help from gettin around it. In the ghetto there is nothin to do, really, nothin to do but shoot pool. Maybe go to a party or a dance, that's it. We don't bowl, we don't swim; so you get tired of liquor. You know, when you're young, you get a lot of wine—muscatel, Thunderbird, Gypsy Rose—all that fade away. You graduate gradually. Now you about thirteen, fifteen, sixteen, you in the pool room shootin pool—BAM! Dude is here sellin dope. Got a big bankroll in his pocket. So he say, "Try a snuff, man." So, man, this is out of sight—BAM! It relaxes your nerves. you don't care about nobody—and don't nobody pay any attention to you. When you got it, you real friendly and everything. It just calms you down automatically.

*   *   *

Curiosity. There's a lot of things—curiosity, problems—a lot of things, you know, that lead a person falling into the cooker. More people are trying to solve—no, not trying to solve, but they're trying to escape the reality of their problems by getting into their cooker. And where they used to fall into the liquor bottle, well, they're not fallin into the liquor bottle anymore. They're falling into the heroin cooker.

Why?

Well, like this—I don't know; I can't say. I used drugs because, you know, like problems—well, I can face (them), but there's just something that I like to do, you know?

You just enjoy it?

Right. But, now, some of my friends—well they use drugs because they have problems, and they're trying to hide from them. But as long as they hide, they can forget their problems. But as soon as they come down, the problem's still there. So actually they didn't solve anything. They've got a bigger problem then, when they get a habit.

*   *   *

Why do you suppose most people start using heroin?

Out of curiosity—you know? Just bein curious. Like I started just wantin to know what it was like, and then once you find out what it's like, really, you invovled. You can't just pull away from it.

A lot of people say it's fun.

From the beginning it's fun. Once you get a habit, it's not fun no more, you know. Now, a lot of people come to jail and kick their habit, go back on the street again. They kicked the habit physically, but mentally they still have the shootin the drugs in their mind, you know.

Why do they go back? Because they like it?

Well, not because they like it. Well, that could be a part of it too—because they like it—that could be a great part of it too. But nine out of ten of 'em go back to it because they need the feeling; they dig the feeling of the high. And most likely live in an environment where most people use it. Maybe half of their associates use it, you understand? So they have no choice: either run away from the problem or stay there and try to fight it. If you stay and try to fight it, you're not gonna win, because you don't have very much will power, I don't think. A person that never experienced that, can't, you know, say nothin about it—what it do to you or what it don't do to you. Because when you sick, then junk is best, really, the very best. But we start out usin it from curiosity, want to see what it's like. We see this fellow noddin, meditatin, you know. Say, "Man, you look pretty nice"; man, he's high. So you try it. It feel nice. You don't get no habit the first time you try it, you know; so you try it again, and then you start doin it every day, like high every day. Then after two weeks, three weeks, your back starts hurtin when you get up in the mornin. Then you go get you some stuff—you feel pretty nice now. After two months, man, you strung out. You got to have it, got to have it. Before, you had to have it, but now you got to have it or you suffer.

*   *   *

If you're in a good frame of mind, heroin is not that enjoyable. But if you're depressed—when I started using it, I was coming out of a really bad crisis in my life, and so, you know, it enabled me to forget about it. It gave me something to do more than anything (else). I'd get up in the morning and I'd say, "Well, I got something to do today. I got to get the money together. I got to cop without getting caught. I got to make sure it's good stuff, and I got to get off." And then I would worry about what I'm going to do for pleasure after that. And it was that as much as (it was) the sensation of being high—it was a lifestyle.

Thus, a man gradually was drawn into addiction. With his addiction went a good deal of criminal activity since habits can cost a lot of money. Some sold drugs to support their habits; others concentrated on "boosting" (shoplifting) or breaking and entering. Their lives had a Sisypehan quality, for success in copping dope and getting off was simply a prelude to further search for money to get more drugs. Most seemed to hate their lives as addicts, for they were on a treadmill. But their attitudes toward heroin were more than a little equivocal. Most felt that it was a "bad" drug; it destroyed lives. But many—as the third man quoted above—seemed in their discussion of their experience as junkies to be arguing with themselves as much as they were describing their past experience. They didn't want to go back to drugs, but then again they did.

What would you like to be doing (ten years from today)?

Have my family. Have a nice home. Shoot all the drugs I want to. Just make me happy; all I want to do is be happy. I want to be just like anybody else. I want to bowl, I want to fish. But I don't have time for it, because I'm chasin that bag, tryin to get that cash to get that bag.

What do you think you'll be doing in ten years?

Wish I could predict the future, but — the way things are now, sometimes — like now — I got the urge for some drugs. Somebody drop a bag of it, I probably would shoot it. That's the way it is. No use to beatin around the bush. I'm tellin you how I feel inside. I'm a for real person, and I'm tellin you for real how I feel. And most drug addicts feel the same way. Anytime I get in a conversation with 'em, they talk about it.

This man, and many like him, will probably return to drugs when released from prison. He will then continue to commit a variety of crimes to support his habit. Much of his crime will go undetected, but eventually he will be caught and will return to prison.

Why does he do it? The roots of his behavior lie both within himself and within the social system in which he lives. Clearly, drugs serve some basic need for this man and for most addicts. He desires gratification of his desire to "be happy" or to forget "his problems," and he wants it fast. This man, and most of the other addicts, seem to share a lack of self-control, a tendency to see the world as something beyond their control. In a very real social and economic sense, this is a correct view, for the world offers them few opportunities to get jobs or live lives that have meaning or a future. Moreover, they see themselves as somewhat out of their own control. A common theme expressed by drug addicts was a fear of man's impulses, a notion that he is subject to passions that he cannot control. The addictive quality of heroin produces a kind of physiological equivalent of this psychological feeling of being at the mercy of others' and of one's own impulses. In this sense heroin addiction, for many, may be functional, for it produces external structure to lives that comports with the individual's own image of himself and place in society.

Criminal without Habits

The remainder of the men interviewed were not acting out of the compulsion to obtain drugs that motivated the dope addict. Their crimes, which included breaking and entering, robbery, weapons charges, and assaults, were committed for other reasons: they wanted goods or money; they were angry with someone and punished them or sometimes killed them. Some of their crimes were calculated; some were done in the heat of anger. Many expressed a desire for gratification quickly rather than in the future:

> There was things I wanted and — it's not because I'm too lazy to work for 'em. The things I wanted just seems too far off and pretty hard to — just like a new car and nice clothes, and maybe some day I wanted maybe a nice house and stuff. I was lookin ahead of the future. I know just working take twenty years, ten years to get these things, and I got caught up with my own thoughts, got all messed up, got myself all involved, and that's it. As I was fifteen to sixteen years (old), seemed like everybody else had cars. I didn't, you know. I wanted a car and things like this. I felt, boy, how am I gonna work and save a thousand dollars and another five hundred dollars for insurance. Boy, by the time I do this, then I'll be an old man. Really you're not, but this is the way you think.

This is a common theme offered by the men who committed property crimes: they wanted things, and they didn't see how they could get them soon enough by working at jobs; so they "had" to turn to crime.[1] Thus, crime is a method of obtaining material things for these men, and for many a method that seems simpler than a job:

> Well, like now as far as the employment thing goes, like you have to be a mastermind to get the type of job you want. Like you gotta not only be a high school grad, but you have to specialize in a certain field to get what you want. And people are getting tired of that. Everybody don't have the ability to go to school, or they don't have the patience to go to school and take the time to get these degrees and what not; so they learn somethin in the meantime. They learn how to steal, or they learn how to play card games. There's a thousand and one things that you do. Like I learned to play all these games. You learn how to do 'em because they're easier — aw, no, now I wouldn't — hell, no, they're not easier, not by a long shot. Everything that I can do wrong, it's not easier than being on a job, you know? I'd rather have that eight hours, but it's just that that eight hours would — like the $200 I may get for working that week, you know, I may have $1,600 for that same forty hours; so why should I throw $1,400 away for $200? It's not easier, but it's more profit. No, it's not easier, but it's more profitable. Wrong is more profitable.

> *Do you think that's why more and more people are violating the law?*

> Oh, yes and no. Yes, they violate the laws to get the money, yes. No, they violate the laws because they have to, you know? Some dudes, they

---

[1]For a discussion of the concept of time perspective as a factor in criminal behavior, see Edward Banfield, *The Unheavenly City* (Boston: Little, Brown and Company, 1970), Chapter 8.

try, try, try everything. They're not suited for any of these; so they get disgusted. They're not making no money; so they try something different. He may have a rusty old pistol thrown up in the drawer somewhere, you know, and he see that his shoe is getting sort of low, and the seat of his pants gettin sort of thin, and his shirt don't look too fine no more. So he decides, well, now you see that old pistol over there in that drawer. He goes and gets that pistol and looks at it and says, "Roscoe, we going out and get us some squares tonight." You know? And he goes out and sticks up some joint. He never did it before, no, but he's gotten away with the money; so he got away with it the one time. That may be three hundred dollars, yeah. It may last him a couple of days cause fast money goes fast. The faster it comes, the faster it leaves. Yeah, yeah, you can't save it too tough. Naw, you can't save it too tough. It's hard, it's very hard to save. But, anyway, he start with a three-hundred-dollar stick-up, maybe a liquor store. Right? And he keeps climbin the scale. He's not gonna keep on robbin these liquor stores for three hundred dollars. Then he go to a loan company and get three thousand. Not going to go to the loan company no more if he can go to a bank and get $3 million, you know? He keeps progressin. With a little thought you can do anything and get away with it.

* * *

All the prices on everything is all gettin higher, and stuff like that.
People are stealing just to support themselves?

A lot, yeah. I did for a long time.

Why do people do that instead of getting a job?

It's hard to find jobs now. Hell, it's damn hard to find jobs. Cause I was out there for four months. I couldn't find a job. One job last me a week, and I got fired for not goin in. That was my fault, but I had real bad hours, was only gettin $1.80 an hour.

* * *

Why do you suppose most people break the law against B and E?

To get money, furniture — mostly just money.

Why do you suppose some people get money that way and some people have jobs? What do you think differentiates the people who break and enter from the people who don't?

It's easier work to break into a place than working eight hours and forty hours a week. Break into a place — there half an hour, and you make almost as much pay.

* * *

Probably everything in general. There's more people than ever. Cities are bigger. Narcotics are widespread. Keeping up with the Joneses.

> Everything is more or less geared to material things, personal material things—cars, clothes, etc. And everything is higher now. In the past maybe a man was content to have a mule and forty acres. Now it's a car and maybe a couple of suits.

These men express two common themes: the material gain that criminal behavior can produce and an unwillingness or inability to make similar gains by noncriminal behavior. The notion that crime pays was expressed by many of the men; but very few believe, as the first man quoted suggests, that one can indefinitely get away with the crimes. In the long run the "small-time" criminal will always be caught. But he can get away with a lot before the day of reckoning:

> When you do a B and E, nobody sees you. And although they have a good idea who did it, it's very hard unless the person you're with testifies against you in order for you to get convicted, or they catch you red-handed first. As I say, I've been arrested and actually sent to jail three times on breaking and entering. And when they arrested me, I might give them another five or six that they knew I did. But how many—maybe I've done fifty or seventy-five that, you know, they couldn't ever convict me on. See, the time is very minimal as far as the crime goes, and you can still get a lot of breaking and entering, and it's very hard to catch you on one.

This man suggests the calculation that many go in for: comparing the rewards of working with the gains that may accrue from illegal behavior. Several characteristics of the calculation stand out. First, most assume that for any given job they will not be caught, though in the long run they will. Second, the payoff is seen as typically greater than could be obtained by other, noncriminal activity. This is both a result of distaste for the types of jobs that are available and for the deferment of gratification that working for a living typically entails. Finally, the price that must be paid for failure—for getting caught—is not perceived as too high to warrant the risk involved. This last feeling results from both a self-deception—the denial that they *will* get caught—and from the fact—that prison simply isn't so *bad*. For the younger men who have not been there before, it even holds some mystery and excitement. For the older men who have already done time, it is something they feel that they can "handle." For both, though, the crucial factor is that life on the street is not so good. None of the men wanted to be in prison, for they enjoy freedom and the ability to attempt to meet their needs—for which freedom is essential. But neither is life on the street such a lark either, for it too involves a good deal of frustration in attempting to fulfill their wants. Thus, for the junkie and the nonjunkie, prison is not—relative to life on the street—sufficiently undesirable. At the same time, it does strike me that making prison conditions harsher or lengthening sentences would solve this difficulty.

First, the defendants typically — as suggested before — tend to convince themselves that they will not get caught for any one crime. The "rational" man would probably conclude that the odds of being caught for the typical B & E are quite slight; the defendants imagine the odds as even more in their favor. Moreover, even an extended stay in prison may not be an effective deterrent so long as life on the street is not itself especially desirable.

Another common explanation for crime offered by the defendants — particularly for property crimes — suggested that there was a kind of excitement and satisfaction in getting away with it. Sometimes this view simply seemed to reflect a child's delight in putting something over on his parents; for other men it suggested more: an alienation from the forces of law and order. It was also, for some, the emotional thrill or sense of accomplishment in doing something that is highly dangerous — in a sense "crime" is like auto racing, mountain climbing, or skydiving. It is difficult to sort these out and more difficult to understand exactly what kind of excitement the men found in the crime, for they were often unable to describe it in detail:

> I didn't need the money in a sense, but I went in there mainly for the money — but I didn't need it, have to have it. I wasn't doing drugs like the rest of my friends. It was so easy. I can't explain it. I know I'm not crazy, cause I got good sense. But it's just that first day — all it took was people weren't home, open the window, crawled in. It was just like that, that easy, and it was open. I was scared plus excited at the same time.

> *What about the other times? Same way?*

> The same way, but you get less scared.

*   *   *

> Well, sure, there's a satisfaction out of it. It's almost like when you're winning at games — you were a sports fanatic, which I am too, you know, something like that. But I can't even say that, when I was doing these things, I got more satisfaction out of that than actually out of the money. Because I've never had trouble with money, you know. I was always a fairly good gambler when I was a kid and everything. I didn't need money that badly.

> *What was the satisfaction?*

> Just like winning. You know, maybe you were rebelling a little bit; I don't say it was that strong — I wasn't just doing it for that alone, you know.

> *If it was a game, who was the opponent?*

> Well, to tell the truth, I'm thinking now I could pull all kinds of ideas from my mind who the opponent would be. Back then I wouldn't, you know, couldn't really define anything like that.

> *What would you say now?*

Well, I'd say that I was trying to beat the police — something like that. But I think that really is — if you were to think about that — it really is just an excuse for the many reasons for doing it.

*   *   *

Did you ever think you might get sent to prison?

I didn't think that I was gonna ever get caught.

Why not?

Because I had a style. There's a style to selling drugs. And if it wasn't for a friend of mine, the informer, I wouldn't be here now. I'd still be out there selling drugs. Yeah. There's a style.

You thought you were so good at it that they wouldn't get you?

That's right. And apparently I was, you know, until he (the friend-turned-informer) got mad with me and brought two agents to me. Because as far as the blue coat was concerned, he could never touch me. They tried many a time, but they could never do anything to me. Take me to the police station, shake me down; the lieutenant say, "Let him go, he's clean." Yeah. I look at him and laugh. Make an ass of him on the way back to the street. You know? They do that. Yeah.

Why?

Why? Because I knew that he knew that I was doing wrong, but he couldn't prove it. He never had no proof. When I got arrested, they had a stack of statements this high, you know, about me and my activities, but maybe that's only hearsay, you know. You can't take me into court and convict me nowheres in the country on that hearsay. I don't know nothing about this; so I laughed. It made me feel good to know that they put up enough time and effort to try and catch me and they couldn't, they couldn't.

Why did it make you feel good?

It made me feel good to know that I was doing something and getting away with it. Yeah. Yes, that's what made me feel all right.

*   *   *

It's a strange experience — breaking into something. Your body is just sort of caterpillars running through it, and you get these strange feelings.

Is it enjoyable?

Ah, it was.

Exciting?

It was. There was no reason for me to go out and do it. I just went out and did it. I can't justify my reason. I didn't need the money that bad to go out and break into places. Ah, I just did it. I had fun doing it.

* * *

I do things like that, you know, to get back even for, you know?

Who are you getting back at?

Really you're not gettin back at nobody but yourself, you know.

Who do you feel you're getting back at?

Like on the people — you outslicked em, you know?

"Them" is the cops?

The — you know, yeah — the law. All right, so I was out there, right?
See, the man, he's not lookin at me, you know? I'm getting by, and it
makes you feel good. You're thinking maybe, I can do things. Or if you
just do it because you're just completely lost. You want a piece, you
know; you think you're bein somebody.

* * *

Did you ever think about getting caught?

Yeah. I knew I'd get caught sooner or later.

You thought you would be caught?

Sooner or later. Well, I played the game to see how long I could stay up.
Just like anybody. Boy, if you could get a rerun. I wish I had a video
tape in my pocket to show you how hard it was for them to catch me.
You'd roll in the floor laughing of all the stuff I did to get away. They
only took 'em two weeks to catch me, but they had to go through hell to
catch me in two weeks. Runnin through swamps, swimmin, and everything to catch me, and it was really bad. And it's the truth — I'm not
tryin to make it sound like a brag — "Hey, they can't catch me; I'm too
good for them" — but it's the truth. I mean they so much as went and
told the officer that brought me in to have an extra two-week vacation.
That's how much they wanted me.

Some of the men quoted above — the last two — were young (eighteen and
seventeen years old), and the "kid stuff" quality of their remarks is understandable. The others, though, were both older (from twenty to twenty-six)
and generally more mature. Still, there is the quality of a child's satisfaction
in their remarks. In part it is the child's satisfaction in simply getting away
with something, the knowledge of doing wrong without detection or
sanction. These remarks also have the quality of one who seeks *attention*
from his parent by doing wrong. Although they speak of the satisfaction in
terms of their not being "noticed," one gets the feeling that what they really
want is just the opposite. Their satisfaction seems similar to thumbing one's
nose at a powerful authority figure. The satisfaction derives not only from
demonstrating that you yourself are powerful and autonomous, but also
from getting the attention of your "superior," making him acknowledge

your existence and care about you.

Also implicit in these remarks is a set of subcultural norms that are significantly different from those suggested by the criminal code. Stealing a car or getting away with a B and E is satisfying not only because you "get away with something" but also because it indicates that you are a tough guy, a man who has been around. Even going to prison can bring some prestige to a person—as he sees his relations with his peers—and hence is not by any means an unequivocally unpleasant or bad fate. But though there is a strain of such thought expressed by these men, it is not accurate to suggest that they are simply members of another "culture," following a fairly detailed and authoritative set of norms that are at variance with the norms of society at large. Rather, they exist within a society with norms that they accept as authoritative, yet consistently violate. They long to be able to live by these norms, yet do not.

Why, if they long for these norms, do they break them so often? In part their failure to obey them stems from the fact that the norms prescribe ways of living with one another (e.g., do not steal from your neighbor; settle your disputes by discussion or, if necessary, by recourse to the legal process) which do not fit their circumstances. One is content not to steal from his neighbor, or to settle disputes without direct violence, if these ways of living serve his interests in a reasonably effective manner. One is less likely to steal if he has other ways of making a living; he will discuss things or, if necessary, call into play legal machinery if he has a reasonable expectation that he will get some satisfaction. In many ways the men interviewed do not enjoy such alternatives.

Their short time perspective is not simply the product of personal weaknesses. It is also a product of living in a society in which the material affluence they desire is *already available* to many others in a visible way. The impatience of the defendants to get things for themselves and to get them quickly, then, is the product in part of literally being able to see and feel and taste the material satisfactions that they desire.

> See, sometime I don't know what I do. Sometime I drink to make me happy; sometime I drink for things I been thinking, you know. Sometime I drink just to think, I would like to do this; I would like to do that, you know. I would like to help the people out. I would like to do the best I can. I wish I can become somebody some day. I would like to be—a man I really want to become, you know? I'm a man, but not the man I want to become. And sometime when I drink, it make me happy; sometime when I drink, it make me think. Sometime when I drink it make me do things I don't want to do. It just—things I don't want to do. Then I want to see if I can help myself, which is not good at all, because if you got a store, and I see that you got enough money—you work for that—you won't like me to go there and take your store and

get the money out, you know, and get lost, because then you're gonna feel sorry. Like I've been doing myself, you know. Most of the times I've been caught for, I get on probations. Sometime I get off free. But when I do those kind of things, I feel sorry for myself. I say to myself, Why did I doing this for? Why? How come I'm this kind of person? I don't like to do this. I say to myself, I wish I wasn't this kind of person I am. I want to change my life. I want to be somebody else. I want to be a different person than what I am. I don't like to do this to nobody. I hate to do this to the people. And sometime I think a lot of time, How come I see everybody — a lot of people with nice, nice things — nice clothes, nice shoes, nice car, good job, money all the time in the pocket. Why can I not have the same what they got? And that make me — when I think about those — that's when it come inside me: I want to be that kind of person; I want to have what he got. And that's what'll make me do what I want to get (it). I say to myself, Just working I'm not gonna get what I want right away. If I work and I do this, I might get it fast. And then I say, But I don't like to do this, no matter how. If I got a job and maybe it take a little time to get what I want, but I can get it, you know?

These remarks capture, I think, the personal and social dilemmas facing the typical defendant. He is the subject of norms prescribing how he ought to live that emanate from the middle-class society in which his own poverty-ridden life is embedded. He sees around him the things that he wants, and he longs to have them. He wants them fast because they seem so accessible. He feels himself captured by his own wants and behaves in ways that he knows are wrong. He comes to despise himself, to think that he is weak and a "bad man" — personalizing his guilt rather than attributing it to the social conditions that may have caused his poverty or violence.

When he does get caught, and "they" punish him, he discovers that they really don't care very much about him. He is a nuisance, and they treat him as though they would some incidental bother distracting them from going about their lives. His interaction with the law — in which he finds himself an object in the hands of those who simply wish to get rid of him — enforces his own image of himself as an outsider and as a "bad person."

The moral ways of living that the law symbolizes and that he himself longs for seem to have no place in the enforcement of the law. He does not learn that those rules he violated are "right," for he knows this already; he does not learn that the more "civil" ways of treating people that the law symbolizes are available to *him*, for he is not treated in a particularly civil manner. All he really learns is that he ought to be slick, that he ought to try not to make mistakes and not get caught next time. He longs for some personal attention, for someone to "fix him up" and make him capable of living the way he wants to live, but he does not find it in the legal system. What he finds is an extension of his own life on the street, an extension of the life he hates.

In this sense the criminal justice system basically serves the function of a tax on the lives of the people who encounter it. The nature of their lives is such that they often engage in a mode of behavior—fighting, stealing, taking dope—that violates the law, for such behavior is a defining characteristic of their way of coping with their lives. The society says to them that if they do so, they will have to pay a tax to the commonweal in return for their "opportunity" to engage in such activity. Middle-class and wealthy people also have to pay taxes in return for their ability to make money, raise their families, have fun. Society values their activities (is, in fact, defined by them), and hence their tax can be paid in money. The defendants cannot pay their tax in money; so they pay it in inconvenience, pain, and sometimes loss of freedom for substantial periods of time.

The nature of our society—the fact that "we" cherish a modicum of privacy and protection of citizens against the imposition of governmental power—means that the "tax" we impose on the criminal is not so onerous that he will not be willing to pay it. Moreover, even if the tax were imposed at a much steeper rate, the relative lack of other more palatable alternatives might still make him willing to pay. So the defendant pays his tax: he lives in fear of the police, is arrested periodically, spends some time in jail, and sometimes has to go to prison. His encounters with the law are the product of his own needs and of his failure to internalize the norms of the law because they do not serve his own interests very well. His encounters with the law do not teach him moral lessons about how he ought to behave; rather, they reinforce his image of himself as an outsider, as an appendage of the society of which he would so much like to be a member.

3

The Criminal Justice Non-System

Richter H. Moore, Jr.

Collectively the agencies in the United States responsible for the administration of justice have in recent years been referred to as the criminal justice system. This is a delusion. What we call a criminal justice system is merely a group of components which do not function together as a comprehensive or comprehensible whole. The report of the President's Commission on Law Enforcement and the Administration of Justice in 1967 found the system a pervasive fragmentation of police, court, and correctional agencies.

A Task Force of the National Commission on the Causes and Prevention of Violence in its report *Law and Order Reconsidered* examined in detail the absence of a single criminal justice system. It found,

> Our society has commissioned its police to patrol the streets, to prevent crime, arrest suspected criminals, "enforce the law." It has established courts to conduct trials of accused offenders, sentence those who are found guilty and "do justice." It has created a correctional process consisting of prisons to punish convicted persons and a program to rehabilitate and supervise them so they might become useful citizens.
>
> It is commonly assumed that these three components — law enforcement (police, sheriffs, marshals), the judicial process (judges, prosecutors, defense lawyers), and corrections (prison officials, probation and parole

Moore, Richter, "The Criminal Justice Non-System," from *Readings in Criminal Justice* (Moore, Marks and Barrow eds.), Indianapolis: Bobbs-Merrill, 1976, pp. 5-13.

officers) — add up to a "system" of criminal justice. The system, however, is a myth.[1]

The concept of a system carries with it the idea of a unity of purpose, and
organized inter-relationships among the component parts. In the United
States today instead of recognized connections the criminal justice
"system," be it local, state, or federal, is composed of a well defined group
of separate agency responsibilities. In other words, it is a continuum
through which each accused may pass: from the police, to the courts, to the
prison and back to the streets.

The end result is that what we call the criminal justice system does not
deter crime, does not detect crime, does not convict, and does not correct,
so concluded Lloyd Cutler, the director of the 1970 President's Commission
on Violence.

A recent survey by the Law Enforcement Assistance Administration
(LEAA) supported that assessment. It found that some 16.7 million serious
crimes had been committed in the United States during the first half of 1973
but that only 5.3 million had been reported by the victims. Of these, only
3.9 million found their way into the FBI's uniform crime statistics.[2]

Other studies indicate that only about 12 percent of the crimes committed
in the United States result in arrest and 6 percent in convictions. The
convictions include a large number of bargained pleas. Of those who
commit crimes, only about 1.5 percent are ever incarcerated.[3]

Such facts turn people off to the criminal justice system according to
LEAA administrator Richard Velde. Their cynicism is reflected in the low
faith they have that the police will solve the crimes, their frustration at the
delays in the courts, and their feeling that those convicted are prematurely
released from prison.

The public has not been alone in its dissatisfaction with such poor
performance. Members and officials of the agencies that participate in the
criminal justice process become frustrated by the apparent inefficiencies
and unfairness of the system they perceive as perpetrated by the other
components of it. Every group is the critic and target of criticism of every
other group.

The effectiveness of the system or the mission and priorites of the system
are going to be viewed differently by the policeman, the trial judge, the
prosecutor, the defense attorney, the corrections administrator, the
appellate tribunal, the slum dweller and the residents of the suburbs.
Isolated and antagonistic within their traditional responsibilities, each
component analyzes its problems from its own point of view and each vies
with the others for public funds. Each is jealous of its authority and each
proceeds according to a different set of priorities. This attitude reflects a
lack of guidance oriented toward a single criminal justice system.

All of the Presidential Commissions and advisory commissions have found not only a lack of overall direction in the criminal justice field, but have found even within the parts almost no attempt to approach tasks from the point of view of the system. One of the primary causes for these deficiencies according to the Commission on Violence is a weakness in leadership, poor management practices and a lack of information. The task force report says, "A recognized profession of criminal justice system administrators does not exist today."[4]

They found few court administrators, and the idea of court management by trained professionals taking hold very slowly. They found effective police administration to be rare. The great majority of police agencies were headed by chiefs who had started as patrolmen and had risen through the ranks without benefit of higher education and with no training in modern management, finance, personnel, communications, or community relations. Tradition and antiquated civil service concepts barred lateral entry and thereby inhibited the recruitment of police administrators from other departments or from sources outside government. The Commission found no structure for formulating cohesive crime budgets, only individual agency requests. They found no central collection and analysis of criminal justice information. Crime received high attention only as a short-term reaction to crisis.

The crime crisis of the past few years has resulted in an upsurge of support for the police by the so-called silent majority, even civil libertarian politicians have become champions of law and order. Riots, assassinations, muggings, and rapes have created major political pressures from the public, demanding a solution to the crime problem — but there seems to be no consensus as to the nature of the problem.

A part of the responsibility for the crisis lies in the nature of society today. Among the problems and conditions contributing to it are the alarming increase in narcotics, drug abuse, urban overcrowding, inability of urban government to meet the needs of citizens, the gap between affluence and poverty, overpopulation, economic recession, discrimination and an increase of revolutionary activities. Transient populations have lost their concern for community. Assimilation has become internal and intramural rather than international. Attempts to adjust to a standardized environment through racial integration have led to conflicts. The ideal of family unity has seriously declined. The responsibility for child training is frequently delegated to schools, organizations or other parent surrogates, sometimes even to movie houses and often to television sets. New attitudes toward the young have resulted in their greater freedom to participate in adult activities, without at the same time being required to assume responsibility for their actions. Alliances between criminals and ostensibly law-abiding citizens and complacency toward organized crime involving corruption, bribery, extortion and murder all contribute to crime crisis.

In an attempt to face the changing crime challenge a type of fear reactive solution has been employed. Money has been poured into impressive new equipment for local police forces. New agencies have been created to fight crime, often without proper guidelines or guidance, and without consideration of the effect they will have on the system as a whole. The public persists in the unfortunate ranking in terms of superiority-inferiority of those in the criminal justice field with the judiciary in the superior position, the police following and the prison officials at the bottom of the efficacy ladder.

This muddle has been exploited by a radical minority who attempt to discredit the criminal justice system, especially the police. At the same time, another vocal minority cries for a "super" police force that will eliminate crime, the opponents of law and order, and probably freedom as well. For their part, the police confront the problem of overcoming public opposition to their authority even while the public demands increased protection from crime.

The violence of the decade of the 60's, and the report of the 1967 President's Commission, brought a recognition that the criminal justice system was in a state of dynamic change. It said:

> The police must adapt themselves to the rapid changes and patterns of behavior that are taking place in America. This is a time when traditional ideas and institutions are being challenged with increasing insistence. The poor want an equal opportunity to earn a share of America's wealth. Minority groups want a final end put to the discrimination they have been subjected to for centuries. Young people, the fastest growing segment of the population have more freedom than they ever have had. The police must be willing and able to deal understandingly and constructively with these often unsettling, even threatening changes.[5]

Acknowledging these social and political sources of lawlessness and unrest police administrator O.W. Wilson observed:

> Police service today extends beyond mere routine investigation and disposition of complaints; it also has as an objective the welfare of the individual and of society. If society is to be effectively safeguarded against crime, the police must actively seek out and destroy delinquency inducing influences in the community and assist in providing suitable treatment for the maladjusted.[6]

The Commission found a compelling need for a new vision among all the agencies that make up the criminal justice system. This new vision requires new concepts to meet the needs of a changing crime environment. It demands recognition that the tasks of the criminal justice system have changed and that attitudes toward it, its personnel and its role in modern society must change.

Until recently few Americans perceived a need for an educated policeman or prison guard. Such jobs were considered to require only a hard head, plenty of muscle, a sadistic chracter and the favor of a local politician. To consider the law enforcement officer, corrections official or court clerk as a professional was unheard of. When the demand for professionalism in these roles began to be heard, it applied only to practitioners within the separate parts of the system, not for a criminal justice professional equally at home in its several parts.

If the pervasive fragmentation of the criminal justice system into police, court and correctional agencies is to be eliminated, these parts must be recognized as components of a whole. To achieve this, those concerned with criminal justice must look to systems management, systems analysis and systems creation for aid in integrating the parts which make up the direct delivery apparatus into one criminal justice system. To accomplish this goal a task force of the President's Commission on Violence envisioned a new office or agency to serve as a catalyst for bringing together the fragmented efforts in the criminal justice field.

The obvious instrumentality to provide the unifying force is an educational experience at the college level. This will enable criminal justice practitioners to understand the concept of a system and their role as a part of it. To fulfill this need and aid in developing a single system concept, O.W. Wilson wrote:

> Related to the need to consider the system of justice as an entity, is the urgency for a recognized discipline or field of study which encompasses the law enforcement and criminal justice systems as a whole. Until very recently no college or university in the United States offered a degree in the administration of criminal justice — that is, a generalized degree covering expertise in police, courts and corrections.[7]

The report of the 1967 President's Commission, *The Challenge of Crime in a Free Society* gave impetus for the establishment of criminal justice programs at the college level:

> Individual citizens, social service agencies, universities, religious institutions, civic and business groups and all types of governmental agencies at all levels must become involved in planning and executing changes in the criminal justice system.[8]

The report stressed the need for universities to provide the professional education essential to the development of effective personnel for the criminal justice system:

> The problem of personnel is at the root of most of the criminal justice systems problems. The system cannot operate fairly unless its personnel

are fair. The system cannot operate swiftly and certainly unless its personnel are efficient and well informed. The system cannot make wise decisions unless its personnel are thoughtful. In many places, many police departments, congested urban lower courts, the understaffed county jails, the entire prison, probation and parole apparatus, more manpower is needed...everywhere more skilled, better trained, more imaginative manpower is needed.[9]

The Commission concluded that the system of criminal justice must attract more and better people—police, prosecutors, judges, defense attorneys, probation and parole officers and correction officials—with more knowledge, expertise, initiative, and integrity. Criminal justice education can help provide these better people.

Disturbances growing out of ethnic or racial tensions can be dealt with more effectively if the persons responsible for handling them have some understanding of ethnic relations, racial politics, civil rights, and racial history. University level study of such issues may not guarantee solutions, but it can contribute to more rational reactions. A college education diminishes prejudice and reveals the falsity of racial and ethnic stereotypes. It will enable the law enforcement officer, the correctional custodian, the juvenile staffer, or the court clerk to bring greater resources to bear on their work and to react in a more rational and a more detached manner. The educated law enforcement officer may recognize a mental or physical abnormality where another might see only a drunk or disturber of the peace. An educated correctional custodian may observe danger signals and move to prevent prison riots where another would enflame the situation by treating prisoners as caged animals. A knowledgeable juvenile staffer can discriminate between criminal intent and emotional disturbance and deal with the problem accordingly.

Criminal justice students must be provided with an education that will enable them to weigh alternative courses of action when they become practitioners. They must gain insight into the effects of their actions on the persons with whom they deal and on the image of the system their performance conveys to the public. Their education must not be limited to a single area within the system but, as O.W. Wilson urges, must encompass the criminal justice system as a whole. They must be equipped to become competent systems managers and professional administrators with a broad understanding of the system and of the entire structure of government of which they are an integral part.

Such a broad education will not be possible without intensive new research into the needs and relationships of criminal justice agencies. Lack of such knowledge has slowed the development of a comprehensive approach to the criminal justice system. Partly from lack of research, the system has moved without any sense of direction, without testing its assumptions or establishing priorities. Tradition, convenience, or fashion have too often been substituted for analysis. Since less than one percent of the monies in criminal justice are spent on research, it is not surprising that relatively little work has been done to learn how best to deter crime and how to detect, apprehend, and rehabilitate criminals.[10] Even less investigation has been done on the problems faced in creating an atmosphere conducive to breaking down the separate agency syndrome and establishing recognition of a single criminal justice system.

The 1967 President's Commission's call for research into all fields of criminal justice has brought about some limited responses. The blue curtain of secrecy screening police departments from any sort of study by outsiders has parted slightly to allow researchers entree into the life and world of the police. In his book *Behind the Shield,* Arthur Niederhoffer suggested that police forces have resisted outside study for fear of learning too much about themselves,[11] but such probing is necessary for evaluation and program development.

Research has encountered suspicion at even higher levels. Findings of promising studies and successful pilot projects have been rejected out of hand, as when then President Nixon dismissed some of the recommendations offered by the national Commission on Criminal Justice Standards and Goals. Research organizations producing positive results have been discouraged by bureaucratic ineptness, sometimes exhibited even by the LEAA and its state counterparts. One very promising crime prevention project nationally acclaimed by operating agencies and professional groups ran afoul of an examiner in the state planning agency at the end of its first year. He responded to its continuation request with four pages of questions that showed he had not read the results and had no understanding of the study's potential. The university conducting the research observed that it would take nearly as much time to prepare the new proposal required by his action as to carry out the remaining work, and it withdrew from the project. Thus valuable insights have been lost, at least temporarily.

Inadequate, incompetent and insufficient planning share the responsibility for the lack of research and the mediocre strides which have been made toward the development of a homogenous criminal justice system. For only in the last eight years has any thought been given to comprehensive criminal justice planning. Even so planning has not been comprehensive and frequently has been unrealistic. Planning agencies established to develop comprehensive criminal justice plans have bowed to agency pressures and allowed planning to be done unilaterally by persons representing parts of the system without considering how the plans for that one part will affect the other parts. This has occurred partly because of a lack of personnel educated to look at the criminal justice system as a whole.

When LEAA began to pour monies into the states for planning, state authorities drew personnel largely from existing agencies, most often law enforcement. Frequently these people brought with them parochial attitudes and agency prejudices and biases, not a systems outlook. The upshot was that law enforcement agencies which at the local level are the most active and visible have tended to dominate the planning perspective. In some states, the planning agencies have been called law enforcement planning agencies.

The outcome of such unwise planning practices can be dramatically demonstrated in the consequences of attempting to strengthen part of the system unilaterally without considering the impact on the whole structure. In concentrating on law enforcement, by giving the police more manpower and equipment, the desired result will be more arrests. More arrests increase prosecutions. Cases become stalled for months and even years in the courts. To lessen the impact on the courts pleas are bargained. Serious charges are reduced to lesser ones, often to misdemeanors. Criminals are released on bond to commit other offenses before they are tried for the first. Seeing their efforts go for nothing, many police develop a negative and uncooperative attitude toward the courts. If the courts produce increased convictions the prison system, already undermanned and overcrowded, becomes even more so. The probation and parole system is innundated and case workers have far more people than they can supervise. The whole system is weakened when planning does not consider the effect of action on an agency in light of the system as a whole. It is obvious that if all the branches of the system are not strengthened, growth in one will overwhelm the others.[12]

The single agency symdrome with its historical tradition of minimum communication and virtually no cooperatin among the parts of this "non-system" must be overcome. The elements can no longer pursue their own objectives exclusively and relentlessly without regard for the rest of the system. Lines of communication must be developed between police, courts, corrections, juvenile authorities, and other agencies within the criminal justice system. Research and education in the college and universities must be urgently pursued to establish a basis for new cooperative relationships between formerly compartmentalized and jealous agencies.

Planners and administrators must be educated to consider the agencies merely as elements of a total system. The problems and special viewpoints of each part must be taken into account, of course, but any solutions will only further the present chaos if they are not related to the needs of a single comprehensive criminal justice system.

Notes

[1] James S. Campbell, Joseph R. Sahid, David P. Stang, Task Force on the Law and Law Enforcement of National Commission on the Causes and Prevention of Violence, *Law and Order Reconsidered.* New York: Bantam Books, 1970, p. 264.

[2] "Much Crime is Unreported," *The Washington Post,* Nov. 28, 1974, p. A-3.

[3] T.M. Thompson, "The Criminal Justice System: A View from the Outside," *Crime and Delinquency,* January 1972, p. 23-29.

[4] *Ibid.,* p. 267.

[5] Report of the President's Commission on Law Enforcement and Administration of Justice. *The Challenge of Crime in a Free Society.* Washington: U.S. Government Printing Office, 1967, p. 100.

[6] Wilson, O.W. and McLaren, Roy C. *Police Administration* (3rd Edition) New York: McGraw-Hill, 1972, p. 6.

[7] *Ibid.,* p. 11.

[8] Commission on Law Enforcement and Administration of Justice, p. IX.

[9] *Ibid.,* p. 12.

[10] Thompson, p. 24.

[11] Garden City, N.Y.: Doubleday Anchor, 1969.

[12] Thompson, p. 25.

Section II

Justice and Injustice in the Streets: The Police

The role of the police in American Society is undoubtedly one of the least understood aspects of the criminal justice system. Philosophical conflicts in the field of criminal justice are personified in the police officer. Handcuffed, according to crime control groups; riotous, according to due process groups, the police officer finds that the role he or she must play in the criminal justice system is wrought with conflicting expectations.

There are a variety of issues which contribute to the conflict and confusion in law enforcement. While most would agree that the police mission is to achieve "order under law," it is not always easy to apply this abstract concept to street situations. The officer does not have a lawyer by his or her side when making the decision to arrest a suspect who may have been involved in a crime. The officer may feel that probable cause exists for an arrest. However, in the days following the arrest, made perhaps in a crowded tavern after a fight in which the officer was injured, the decision will be subjected to intense scrutiny.

There are a variety of situations in which the legal basis for a decision to arrest is not always clear. In these situations the officer exercises considerable discretion. The authority to search, to arrest and to use deadly force constitute enormous responsibility for the officer. The police officer is the "gatekeeper" of the criminal justice system. The police officer who sees the victim before the blood has been washed away, must act while legal issues are unclear and must temper the use of force in the face of extreme provocation. The decision as to whether a person will become an arrest

49

statistic is ultimately left to the officer.

Study of the police role was ignored for many years. There are a number of factors that contributed to neglect of study in this area. First, considerable police behavior has low visibility. That is, the police officer is generally unsupervised in many areas of decision-making and the behavior is therefore difficult to study. Second, many persons believed that the prosecutor and the courts made the major decisions affecting the accused. Third, the "liberal bias" of academicians contributed to a focus on the offender often ignoring those responsible for initial decisions regarding the offender. Fourth, police departments in many metropolitan centers have been intensely political. Police officers have not been considered "professionals" in this environment and therefore were not considered worthy of study.

The police response to the riots of the 1960s brought to the attention of American society a host of problems in the field of law enforcement. There has been considerable research on these law enforcement problems over the past ten years. It would be impossible to summarize this research. However it is important to understand the socialization process for the individual officer as he or she moves from the status of civilian to that of police officer. It is equally valuable to understand the complexities of police work. Finally, it is important to understand what is often referred to as the "police subculture." It is in the context of this subculture that the values, attitudes and beliefs which ultimately affect police behavior are shaped. The articles in this section address these issues.

In "Observations on the Making of Policemen," John Van Maanen has presented an analysis of the processes involved in becoming a police officer. It is important to understand the expectations the police system has of the recruit and the socialization processes which bring about realization of those expectations. Van Maanen has provided a clear picture of both the expectations and the socialization process. In "A Professor's Street Lessons," George Kirkham has provided an analysis of the impact of police work on the individual and the extent to which Dr. Kirkham was himself impacted by the police role. Jonathan Rubenstein describes problems commonly encountered by the police officer in "Controlling People." Police work is complicated. There are many aspects of an officer's behavior that we do not understand and because we do not understand, we tend not to trust. Finally, in "Becoming Bent," Lawrence Sherman outlines one of the consequences of police work for some officers—corruption. It should not be inferred that many or most officers are corrupt. At the same time, it is important that we understand the complexity of the process of becoming corrupt and the extent to which corruption may be more an outcome of the nature of the work than of the character of the person.

4

Observations on the Making of Policemen

John Van Maanen*

In recent years the so-called "police problem" has become one of the more institutionalized topics of routine conversation in this society. Whether one views the police as friend or foe, virtually everyone has a set of "cop stories" to relate to willing listeners. Although most stories dramatize personal encounters and are situation-specific, there is a common thread running through these frequently heard accounts. In such stories the police are almost always depicted as a homogeneous occupational grouping somehow quite different from most other men.

Occupational stereotyping is, of course, not unknown. Professors, taxicab drivers, used-car salesmen, corporate executives all have

*I would like to gratefully acknowledge the generous cooperation and support of men like M.C., Dave, Doug, Leon, and Jim, who, like myself, learned what it means to live by the police culture. Their integrity, honesty, and defiance of popular stereotypes make this study a most enlightening and enjoyable experience. Also, I would like to thank my academic colleagues, in particular, Edgar H. Schein, Lyman W. Porter, Robert Dubin, and Mason Haire for their insightful suggestions and assistance during various phases of this research. Finally, I wish to express my appreciation to the Office of Naval Research, the Organizational Behavior Research Center at the University of California, Irvine, and the Organizational Studies Group at the Massachusetts Institute of Technology for partial support and total encouragement throughout this project.

Reproduced by permission of the Society for Applied Anthropology from *Human Organization* ³²(4): 407-418, 1973.

mythological counterparts in the popular culture. Yet, what is of interest here is the recognition by the police themselves of the implied differences.

Policemen generally view themselves as performing society's dirty work. As such, a gap is created between the police and the public. Today's patrolman feels cut off from the mainstream culture and unfairly stigmatized. In short, when the policeman dons his uniform, he enters a distinct subculture governed by norms and values designed to manage the strain created by an outsider role in the community.[1]

To classify the police as outsiders helps us to focus on several important things: the distinctive social definitions used by persons belonging to such marginal subcultures (e.g., "everybody hates a cop"); the outsider's methods for managing the tension created by his social position (e.g., "always protect brother officers"); and the explicit delineation of the everyday standards of conduct followed by the outsider (e.g., "lay low and avoid trouble"). Furthermore, such a perspective forces a researcher to delve deeply into the subculture in order to see clearly through the eyes of the studied.

Context

While observation of the police in naturally occurring situations is difficult, lengthy, and often threatening, it is imperative. Unfortunately, most research to date relies almost exclusively upon interview-questionnaire data (e.g., Bayley and Mendelsohn 1969; Wilson 1968), official statistics (e.g., Webster 1970; President's Commission on Law Enforcement and the Administration of Justice 1967), or broad-ranging attitude surveys (e.g., Sterling 1972; McNamara 1967). The very few sustained observational studies have been concerned with specific aspects of police behavioral patterns (e.g., Skolnick 1966—vice activities; Reiss 1971—police-citizen contacts; Bittner 1967, Cicourel 1967 police encounters with "skid row alcoholics" and juveniles, respectively). This is not to say these diverse investigations are without merit. Indeed, without such studies we would not have even begun to see beneath the occupational shield. Yet, the paucity of in-depth police-related research—especially from the outsider perspective—represents a serious gap in our knowledge of a critical social establishment.[2]

In particular the process of becoming a police officer has been neglected.[3] What little data we presently have related to the police socialization process come from either the work devoted to certain hypothesized dimensions of the police personality (e.g., dogmatism, authoritarianism, cynicism, alienation, etc.) or cross-sectional snapshots of police attitudes toward their public audiences. Using a dramaturgic metaphor, these studies have concentrated upon the description of the actors, stage setting, and "on stage" performance of the police production. Little attention has been paid to the orientation of the performers to their particular role viewed from "backstage" perspective. Clearly, for any performance to materialize there must be casting sessions, rehearsals, directors, stagehands, and some form(s) of compensation provided the actors to insure their continued performance. Recognizing that to some degree organizational socialization occurs at all career stages, this paradigm focuses exclusively upon the individual recruit's entry into the organization. It is during the breaking-in period that the organization may be thought to be most persuasive, for the person has few guidelines to direct his behavior and has little, if any, organizationally based support for his "vulnerable selves" which may be the object of influence. Support for this position comes from a wide range of studies indicating that early organizational learning is a major determinant of one's later organizationally relevant beliefs, attitudes, and behaviors (Van Maanen 1972; Lortie 1968; Berlew and Hall 1966; Evan 1963; Hughes 1958; Dornbush 1955). Schein (1971) suggested perceptively that this process results in a "psychological contract" linking the goals of the individual to the constraints and purposes of the organization. In a sense, this psychological contract is actually a modus vivendi between the person and the organization representing the outcomes of the socialization process.

Method

The somewhat truncated analysis that follows was based upon the observation of novice policemen in situ. The study was conducted in Union City over a nine-month period.[4] Approximately three months of this time were spent as a fully participating member of one Union City Police Academy recruit class. Following the formal training phase of the initiation process, my fully participating role was modified. As a civilain, I spent five months (roughly eight to ten hours a day, six days a week) riding in patrol units operated by a recruit and his FTO (i.e., Field Training Officer charged with imputing "street sense" into the neophyte) as a back-seat observer.

From the outset, my role as researcher-qua-researcher was made explicit. To masquerade as a regular police recruit would not only have been problematic, but would have raised a number of ethical questions as well (particularly during the field training portion of the socialization sequence).[5]

The conversational data presented below are drawn primarily from naturally occurring encounters with persons in the police domain (e.g., recruits, veterans, administrators, wives, friends, reporters, court officials, etc.) While formal interviews were conducted with some, the bulk of the data contained here arose from far less-structured situations. (See Epilogue for a further discussion of the methods employed in this study—eds.)

The Making of a Policeman: A Paradigm

For purposes here, the police recruit's initiation into the organizational setting shall be treated as if it occurred in four discrete stages. While these stages are only analytically distinct, they do serve as useful markers for describing the route traversed by the recruit. The sequence is related to the preentry, admittance, change, and continuance phases of the organizational socialization process an are labeled here as choice, introduction, encounter, and metamorphosis, respectively.

Preentry: Choice

What sort of young man is attracted to and selected for a police career? The literature notes that police work seems to attract local, family-oriented, working-class whites interested primarily in the security and salary aspects of the occupation. Importantly, the authoritarian syndrome which has popularly been ascribed to persons selecting police careers has not been supported by empirical study. The available research supports the contention that the police occupation is viewed by the recruits as simply one job of many and considered roughly along the same dimensions as any job choice.

While my research can add little to the above picture, several qualifications are in order which perhaps provide a greater understanding of the particular choice process. First, the security and salary aspects of the police job have probably been overrated. Through interviews and experience with Union City recruits, a rather pervasive meaningful work theme is apparent as a major factor in job choice. Virtually all recruits alluded to the opportunity afforded by a police career to perform in a role which was perceived as consequential or important to society. While such altruistic motives may be subject to social desirability considerations, or other biasing factors, it is my feeling that these high expectations of community service are an important element in the choice process.

Second, the out-of-doors and presumably adventurous qualities of police work (as reflected in the popular culture) were perceived by the recruits as among the more influential factors attracting them to the job. With few exceptions, the novice policemen had worked several jobs since completing high school and were particularly apt to stress the benefits of working a nonroutine job.

Third, the screening factor associated with police selection is a dominating aspect of the socialization process. From the filling out of the application blank at City Hall to the telephone call which informs a potential recruit of his acceptance into the department, the individual passes through a series of events which serve to impress an aspiring policeman with a sense of being accepted into an elite organization. Perhaps some men originally take the qualifying examination for patrolman lightly, but it is unlikely many men proceed through the entire screening process—often taking up to six months or more—without becoming committed seriously to a police career. As such, the various selection devices, if successfully surmounted, increase the person's self-esteem, as well as buttress his occupational choice. Thus, this anticipatory stage tends to strengthen the neophyte's evaluation of the police organization as an important place to work.

Finally, as in most organizations, the police department is depicted to individuals who have yet to take the oath of office in its most favorable light. A potential recruit is made to feel as if he were important and valued by the organization. Since virtually all recruitment occurs via generational or friendship networks involving police officers and prospective recruits, the individual receives personalized encouragement and support which helps sustain his interest during the arduous screening procedure. Such links begin to attach the would-be policeman to the organization long before he actually joins.

To summarize, most policemen have not chosen their career casually. They enter the department with a high degree of normative identification with what they perceive to be the goals and values of the organization. At least in Union City, the police department was able to attract and select men who entered the organization with a reservoir of positive attitudes toward hard work and a strong level of organizational support. What happens to the recruit when he is introduced to the occupation at the police academy is where attention is now directed.

Admittance: Introduction

The individual usually feels upon swearing allegiance to the department, city, state, and nation that "he's finally made it." However, the department instantaneously and somewhat rudely informs him that until he has served his probationary period he may be severed from the membership rolls at any time without warning, explanation, or appeal. It is perhaps ironic that in a period of a few minutes, a person's position vis-a-vis the organization can be altered so dramatically. Although some aspects of this phenomenon can be found in all organizations, in the paramilitary environment of the police world, the shift is particularly illuminating to the recruit.

For most urban police recruits, the first real contact with the police sub-culture occurs at the academy. Surrounded by forty to fifty contemporaries, the recruit is introduced to the harsh and often arbitrary discipline of the organization. Absolute obedience to departmental rules, rigorous physical training, dull lectures devoted to various technical aspects of the occupation, and a ritualistic concern for detail characterize the academy. Only the recruit's classmates aid his struggle to avoid punishments and provide him an outlet from the long days. A recruit soon learns that to be one minute late to a class, to utter a careless word in formation, or to be caught walking when he should be running may result in a "gig" or demerit costing a man an extra day of work or the time it may take to write a long essay on, say, "the importance of keeping a neat appearance."

Wearing a uniform which distinguishes the novices from "real" policemen, recruits are expected to demonstrate group cohesion in all aspects of academy life. The training staff actively promotes solidarity through the use of group rewards and punishments, identifying garments for each recruit class, inter-class competition, and cajoling the newcomers — at every conceivable opportunity — to show some unity. Predictably, such stactics work — partial evidence is suggested by the well-attended academy class reunions held year after year in the department. To most veteran officers, their police academy experiences resulted in a career-long identification. It is no exaggeration to state that the "in-the-same-boat" collective consciousness which arises when groups are processed serially through a harsh set of experiences was as refined in the Union City Police Department as in other institutions such as military academies, fraternities, or medical schools.[6]

The formal content of the training academy is almost exclusively weighted in favor of the more technical aspects of police work. A few outside speakers are invited to the academy (usually during the last few weeks of training), but the majority of class time is filled by departmental personnel describing the more mundane features of the occupation. To a large degree, the formal academy may be viewed as a didactic sort of instrumentally oriented ritual passage rite. As such, feigning attention to lectures on, for example, "the organization of The Administrative Services Bureau" or "state and local traffic codes" is a major task for the recruits.

However, the academy also provides the recruit with an opportunity to begin learning or, more properly, absorbing the tradition which typifies the department. The novices' overwhelming eagerness to hear what police work is really like results in literally hours upon hours of war stories (alternately called "sea stories" by a few officers) told at the discretion of the many instructors. One recruit, when asked about what he hoped to learn in the academy, responded as follows:

> I want them to tell me what police work is all about. I could care less about the outside speakers or the guys they bring out here from upstairs who haven't been on the street for the last twenty years. What I want is for somebody who's gonna level with us and really give the lowdown on how we're supposed to survive out there.

By observing and listening closely to police stories and style, the individual is exposed to a partial organizational history which details certain personalities, past events, places, and implied relationships which the recruit is expected eventually to learn, and it is largely through war stories that the department's history is conveyed. Throughout the academy, a recruit is exposed to particular instructors who relate caveats concerning the area's notorious criminals, sensational crimes, social-geographical peculiarities, and political structure. Certain charismatic departmental personalities are described in detail. Past events—notably the shooting of police officers—are recreated and informal analyses passed on. The following excerpt from a criminal law lecture illustrates some of these concerns.

> I suppose you guys have heard of Lucky Baldwin? If not, you sure will when you hit the street. Baldwin happens to be the biggest burglar still operating in this town. Every guy in this department from patrolman to chief would love to get him and make it stick. We've busted him about ten times so far, but he's got an asshole lawyer and money so he always beats the rap....If I ever get a chance to pinch the SOB, I'll do it my way with my thirty-eight and spare the city the cost of a trial.

The correlates of this history are mutually held perspectives toward certain classes of persons, places, and things which are the objective reality of police work. Critically, when war stories are presented, discipline within the recruit class is relaxed. The rookies are allowed to share laughter and tension-relieving quips with the veteran officers. A general atmosphere of comraderie is maintained. The near lascivious enjoyment accompanying these informal respites from academy routine serve to establish congeniality and solidarity with the experienced officers in what is normally a rather harsh and uncomfortable environment. Clearly, this is the material of which memories are made.

Outside the classroom, the recruits spend endless hours discussing nuances and implications of war stories, and collective understandings begin to develop. Via such experiences, the meaning and emotional reality of police work starts to take shape for the individual. In a sense, by vicariously sharing the exploits of his predecessors, the newcomer gradually builds a common language and shared set of interests which will attach him to the organization until he too has police experience to relate.

Despite these important breaks in formality, the recruits' early perceptions of policing are overshadowed by the submissive and often degrading role they are expected to play in the academy. Long, monotonous hours of class time are required, a seemingly eternal set of examinations are administered, meaningless assignments consume valuable off-duty time, various mortifying events are institutionalized rituals of academy life (e.g., each week, a class "asshole" was selected and received a trophy depicting a gorilla dressed as a policeman), and relatively sharp punishments enacted for breaches of academy regulations. The multitude of academy rules make it highly unlikely that any recruit can complete the training course unscathed. The following training division report illustrates the arbitrary nature of the dreaded gigs issued during the academy phase.

> You were observed displaying unofficerlike conduct in an academy class. You openly yawned (without making any effort to minimize or conceal the fact), (this happened twice), you were observed looking out the window constantly, and spent time with your arms lying across your desk. You will report to Sergeant Smith in the communications division for an extra three hours of duty on August 15 (parentheses theirs).

The main result of such stress training is that the recruit soon learns it is his peer group rather than the "brass" which will support him and which he, in turn, must support. For example, the newcomers adopt covering tactics to shield the tardy colleague, develop cribbing techniques to pass exams, and become proficient at constructing consensual ad hoc explanations of a fellow-recruit's mistake. Furthermore, the long hours, new friends, and ordeal aspects of the recruit school serve to detach the newcomer from his old attitudes and acquaintances. In short, the academy impresses upon the recruit that he must now identify with a new group— his fellow officers. That this process is not complete, however, is illustrated by the experience of one recruit during this last week of training before his introduction to the street. This particular recruit told his classmates the following:

> Last night as I was driving home from the academy, I stopped to get some gas. . . . As soon as I shut off the engine some dude comes running up flapping his arms and yelling like crazy about being robbed. Here I am sitting in my car with my gun on and the ole buzzer (badge) staring him right in the face. . . . Wow! . . . I had no idea what to do; so I told him to call the cops and got the hell away from there. What gets me is that it didn't begin to hit me that I WAS A COP until I was about a mile away (emphasis mine).

To this researcher, the academy training period serves to prepare the recruits to alter their initially high but unrealistic occupational expectations. Through the methods described above, the novices begin to absorb the subcultural ethos and to think like policemen. As a fellow recruit stated at the end of the academy portion of training:

> There's sure more to this job than I first thought. They expect us to be dog catchers, lawyers, marriage counselors, boxers, firemen, doctors, baby-sitters, race-car drivers, and still catch a crook occasionally. There's no way we can do all that crap. They're nuts!

Finally, as in other highly regulated social systems, the initiate learns that the formal rules and regulations are applied inconsistently. What is sanctioned in one case with a gig is ignored in another case. To the recruits, academy rules become behavioral prescriptions which are to be coped with formally, but informally dismissed. The newcomer learns that when The Department notices his behavior, it is usually to administer a punishment, not a reward. The solution to this collective predicament is to stay low and avoid trouble.

Change: Encounter

Following the classroom training period, a newcomer is introduced to the complexities of the "street" through his Field Training Officer (hereafter referred to as the FTO). It is during this period of apprenticeshiplike socialization that the reality shock encompassing full recognition of being a policeman is likely to occur. Through the eyes of his experienced FTO, the recruit learns the ins and outs of the police role. Here he learns what kinds of behavior are appropriate and expected of a patrolman within his social setting. His other instructors in this phase are almost exclusively his fellow patrolmen working the same precinct and shift. While his sergeant may occasionally offer tips on how to handle himself on the street, the supervisor is more notable for his absence than for his presence. When the sergeant does seek out the recruit, it is probably to inquire as to how many hazardous traffic violations the "green pea" had written that week or to remind the recruit to keep his hat on while out of the patrol car. As a matter of formal policy in Union City, the department expected the FTO to handle all recruit uncertainties. This traditional feature of police work — patrolmen training patrolmen — insures continuity from class to class of police officers regardless of the content of the academy instruction. In large measure, the flow of influence from one generation to another accounts for the remarkable stability of the pattern of police behavior.

It was my observation that the recruit's reception into the Patrol Division was one of consideration and warm welcome. As near as interviewing and personal experience can attest, there was no hazing or rejection of the recruit by veteran officers. In all cases, the recruits were fully accepted into the ongoing police system with good-natured tolerance and much advice. If anyone in the department was likely to react negatively to the recruits during their first few weeks on patrol, it was the supervisor and not the on-line patrolmen. The fraternal-like regard shown the rookie by the experienced officers stands in stark contrast to the stern greeting he received at the police academy. The newcomer quickly is bombarded with "street wise" patrolmen assuring him that the police academy was simply an experience all officers endure and has little, if anything, to do with real police work. Consequently, the academy experiences for the recruits stand symbolically as their rites de passage, permitting them access to the occupation. That the experienced officers confirm their negative evaluation of the academy heightens the assumed similarities among the rookies and veterans and serves to facilitate the recruit's absorption into the division. As an FTO noted during my first night on patrol:

> I hope the academy didn't get to you. It's something we all have to go through. A bunch of bullshit as far as I can tell.... Since you got through it all right, you get to find out what it's like out here. You'll find out mighty fast that it ain't nothing like they tell you at the academy.

During the protracted hours spent on patrol with his FTO, the recruit is instructed as to the real nature of police work. To the neophyte, the first few weeks on patrol is an extremely trying period. The recruit is slightly fearful and woefully ill-prepared for both the routine and eccentricities of real police work. While he may know the criminal code and the rudimentaries of arrest, the fledgling patrolman is perplexed and certainly not at ease in their application. For example, a two-day veteran told the following story to several of his academy associates.

> We were down under the bridge where the fags hang out and spot this car that looked like nobody was in it.... Frank puts the spot on it and two heads pop up. He tells me to watch what he does and keep my mouth shut. So I follow him up to the car and just kind of stand around feeling pretty dumb. Frank gives 'em a blast of shit and tells the guy sitting behind the wheel he's under arrest. The punk gets out of the car snivelling and I go up to him and start putting the cuffs on. Frank says, "just take him back to the car and sit on him while I get the dope on his boyfriend here." So I kind of direct him back to the car and stick him in the backseat and I get in the front.... While Frank's filling out a FIR (Field Investigation Report) on the other guy, the little pansy in the backseat's carrying on about his wife and kids like you wouldn't believe. I'm starting to feel sorta sorry for arresting him. Anyway, Frank finishes filling out the FIR and tells the other guy to get going and if he ever sees him again he'll beat the holy shit out of him. Then he comes back to the car and does the same number on the other fag. After we drove away, I told Frank I thought we'd arrested somebody. He laughed his ass off and told me that's the way we do things out here.

To a recruit, the whole world seems new, and from his novel point of view it is. Like a visitor from a foreign land, the daily events are perplexing and present a myriad of operational difficulties. At first, the squawk of the police radio transmits only meaningless static; the streets appear to be a maze through which only an expert could maneuver; the use of report forms seems inconsistent and confusing; encounters with a hostile public leave him cold and apprehensive; and so on. Yet, next to him in the patrol unit is his partner, a veteran. Hence, the FTO is the answer to most of the breaking-in dilemmas. It is commonplace for the rookie to never make a move without first checking with his FTO. By watching, listening, and mimicking, the neophyte policeman learns how to deal with the objects of his occupation — the traffic violator, the hippie, the drunk, the brass, and the criminal justice complex itself. One veteran reflected on his early patrol experiences as follows:

> On this job, your first partner is everything. He tells you how to survive on the job... how to walk, how to stand, and how to speak and how to think and what to say and see.

Clearly, it is during the FTO phase of the recruit's career that he is most susceptible to attitude change. The newcomer is self-conscious and truly in need of guidelines. A whole folklore of tales, myths, and legends surrounding the department is communicated to the recruit by his fellow officers — conspicuously by his FTO. Through these anecdotes — dealing largely with mistakes of "flubs" made by policemen — the recruit begins to adopt the perspectives of his more experienced colleagues. He becomes aware that nobody's perfect and, as if to reify his police academy experiences, he learns that to be protected from his own mistakes, he must protect others. One such yarn told to me by a two-year veteran illustrates this point.

> Grayson had this dolly he'd been balling for quite a while living over on the north side. Well, it seemed like a quiet night so we cruise out of our district and over to the girl's house. I baby-sit the radio while Grayson goes inside. Wouldn't you know it, we get an emergency call right away. ...I start honking the horn trying to get the horny bastard out of there; he pays me no mind, but the neighbors get kind of irritated at some cop waking up the nine-to-fivers. Some asshole calls the station and pretty soon Sparky and Jim show up to find out what's happening. They're cool but their Sergeant ain't, so we fabricate this insane story 'bout Sparky's girlfriend living there and how he always toots the horn when passing. Me and Grayson beat it back to our district and show up about 45 minutes late on our call. Nobody ever found out what happened, but it sure was close.

Critical to the practical learning porcess is the neophyte's own developing repertoire of experiences. These events are normally interpreted to him by his FTO and other veteran officers. Thus, the reality shock of being "in on the action" is absorbed and defined by the recruit's fellow officers. As a somewhat typical example, one newcomer, at the prodding of his patrol partner, discovered that to explain police actions to a civilian invited disrespect. He explained

> Keith was always telling me to be forceful, to not back down and to never try and explain the law or what we are doing to a civilian. I didn't really know what he was talking about until I tried to tell some kid why we have laws about speeding. Well, the more I tried to tell him about traffic safety, the angrier he got. I was lucky to just get his John

Hancock on the citation. When I came back to the patrol car, Keith explains to me just where I'd gone wrong. You really can't talk to those people out there, they just won't listen to reason.

In general, the first month or so on the street is an exciting and rewarding period for the recruit. For his FTO, however, it is a period of appraisal. While the recruit is busy absorbing many novel experiences, his partner is evaluating the newcomer's reaction to certain situations. Aside from assisting the recruit with the routines of patrol work, the training officer's main concern is in how the recruit will handle the "hot" or, in the contemporary language of the recruits, the "heavy" call (i.e., the in-progress, or on-view, or help the officer situation which the experienced officer knows may result in trouble). The heavy call represents everything the policeman feels he is prepared for. In short, it calls for police work. Such calls are anticipated by the patrolmen with both pleasure and anxiety, and the recruit's performance on such calls is in a very real sense the measure of the man. A Union City Sergeant described the heavy call to me as follows:

It's our main reason for being in business. Like when somebody starts busting up a place, or some asshole's got a gun, or some idiot tries to knock off a cop. Basically, it's the situation where you figure you may have to use the tools of your trade. Of course, some guys get a little shaky when these incidents come along, in fact, most of us do if we're honest. But, you know deep down that this is why you're a cop and not pushing pencils somewhere. You've got to be tough on this job and situations like these separate the men from the boys. I know I'd never trust my partner until I'd seen him in action on a hot one.

While such calls are relatively rare on a day-to-day basis, their occurrence signals a behavioral test for the recruit. To pass, he must have "balls." By placing himself in a vulnerable position and pluckily backing-up his FTO and/or other patrolmen, a recruit demonstrates his inclination to share the risks of police work. Through such events, a newcomer quickly makes a departmental reputation which will follow him for the remainder of his career.

At another level, testing the recruit's propensity to partake in the risks which accompany police work goes on continuously within the department. For example, several FTO's in Union City were departmental celebrities for their training techniques. One officer made it a ritual to have his recruit write parking citations in front of the local Black Panther Party headquarters. Another was prominent for requiring his recruit to "shake out" certain trouble bars in the rougher sections of town (i.e., check identifications, make cursory body searches, and possibly roust out customers, a la *The French Connection*). Less dramatic, but nonetheless as important, recruits are appraised as to their speed in getting out of the patrol car, their lack of hesitation when approaching a suspicious person, or their willingness to lead the way up a darkened stairwell. The required behaviors vary from event to event; however, contingent upon the ex post facto evaluation (e.g., Was a weapon involved? Did the officers have to fight the suspect? How many other patrolmen were on the spot?), a novice makes his departmental reputation. While some FTO's promote these climactic events, most wait quietly for such situations to occur. Certainly varying definitions of appropriate behavior in these situations exist from patrolman to patrolman, but the critical and common element is the recruit's demonstrated willingness to place himself in a precarious position while assisting a brother officer. In the police world, such behavior is demanded.

Although data on such instances are inherently difficult to collect, it appears that the behaviorally demonstrated commitment to one's fellow officers involved in such events is a particularly important stage in the socialization process. To the recruit, he has experienced a test and it provides him with the first of many shared experiences which he can relate to other officers. To the FTO, he has watched his man in a police work situation and now knows a great deal more about his occupational companion.

Aside from the backup test applied to all recruits, the other most powerful experience in a recruit's early days on patrol is his first arrest. Virtually all policemen can recall the individual, location, and situation surrounding their first arrest. One five-year veteran patrolman stated:

> The first arrest is really something. I guess that's because it's what we're supposedly out here for....In my case, I'd been out for a couple of weeks but we hadn't done much....I think we'd made some chippies, like stand-ups, or DWI's, but my partner never let me handle the arrest part. Then one night he tells me that if anything happens, Ive got to handle it. Believe me, I'll never forget that first arrest, even if it was only a scumbag horn (wino) who had just fallen through a window....I suppose I can remember my first three or four arrests, but after that they just start to blur together.[7]

It is such occurrences that determine the recruit's success in the department. To some extent, both the back up test and the first arrest are beyond the direct control of the newcomer. The fact that they both take place at the discretion of the FTO underscores the orderliness of the socialization process. In effect, these climactic situations graphically demonstrate to the recruit his new status and role within the department. And after passing through this regulated sequence of events, he can say, "I am a cop!"

Continuance: Metamorphosis

This section is concerned broadly with what Becker et al. (1961) labeled the final perspective. As such, the interest is upon the characteristic response recruits eventually demonstrate regarding their occupational and organizational setting. Again, the focus is upon the perspectives the initiates come to hold for the backstage aspect of their career.

As noted earlier, one of the major motivating factors behind the recruit's decision to become a policeman was the adventure or romance he felt would characterize the occupation. Yet, the young officer soon learns the work consists primarily of performing routine service and administrative tasks—the proverbial clerk in a patrol car. This finding seems well-established in the pertinent literature and my observations confirm these reports (e.g., Wilson 1968; Webster 1970; Reiss 1971). Indeed, a patrolman is predominantly an order taker—a reactive member of a service organization. For example, most officers remarked that they never realized the extent to which they would be "married to the radio" until they had worked the street for several months.

On the other hand, there is an unpredictable side of the occupation and this aspect cannot be overlooked. In fact, it is the unexpected elements of working patrol that provides self-esteem and stimulation for the officers. This unpredictable feature of patrol work has too often been understated or disregarded by students of police behavior. To classify the police task as bureaucratically routine and monotonous ignores the psychological omnipresence of the potential "good pinch." It is precisely the opportunity to exercise his perceived police role that gives meaning to the occupational identity of patrolmen. Operationally, this does not imply patrolmen are always alert and working hard to make the "good pinch." Rather, it simply suggests that the unexpected is one of the few aspects of the job that helps maintain the patrolman's self-image of performing a worthwhile, exciting, and dangerous task. To some degree, the anticipation of the "hot call" allows for the crystallization of his personal identity as a policeman. One Union City patrolman with ten years' experience commented succinctly on this feature. He noted:

> Most of the time being a cop is the dullest job in the world...what we do is pretty far away from the stuff you see on Dragnet or Adam 12. But, what I like about this job and I guess it's what keeps me going, is that you never know what's gonna happen out there. For instance, me and my partner will be working a Sunday first watch way out in the north end and expecting everything to be real peaceful and quiet like; then all of a sudden, hell breaks loose...Even on the quietest nights, something interesting usually happens.

Reiss noted perceptually the atypical routine enjoyed by patrolmen. After examining the police "straight eight" — the tour of duty — he stated:

> No tour of duty is typical except in the sense that the modal tour of duty does not involve the arrest of a person (Reiss 1971:19).

Still, one of the ironies of police work is that recruits were attracted to the organization by and large via the unrealistic expectation that the work would be adventurous and exciting. In the real world such activities are few and far between. Once a recruit has mastered the various technical and social skills of routine policing (e.g., "learning the district," developing a set of mutual understandings with his partner, knowing how and when to fill out the myriad of various report forms) there is little left to learn about his occupation which can be transferred by formal or informal instruction. As Westley (1951) pointed out, the recruit must then sit back and wait, absorb the subjective side of police work and let his experiences accumulate. The wife of one recruit noted this frustrating characteristic of police work. She said:

> It seems to me that being a policeman must be very discouraging. They spend all that time teaching the men to use the gun and the club and then they make them go out and do very uninteresting work.

It has been suggested that for a newcomer to any occupation, "coping with the emotional reality of the job" is the most difficult problem to resolve (Schein 1963). In police work, the coping behavior appears to consist of the "learning of complacency." Since the vast majority of time is spent in tasks other than real police work, there is little incentive for performance. In other words, the young patrolman discovers that the most satisfying solution to the labyrinth of hierarchy, the red tape and paperwork, the plethora of rules and regulations and the "dirty work" which characterize the occupation is to adopt the group norm stressing staying out of trouble. And the best way in which he can stay out of trouble is to minimize the set of activities he pursues. One Union City veteran patrolman explained:

> We are under constant pressure from the public to account for why we did or did not do this or that. It's almost as if the public feels it owns us. You become supersensitive to criticisms from the public, almost afraid to do anything. At the same time, the brass around here never gives a straightforward answer about procedures to anyone and that creates a lot of discontent. All communication comes down. But, try and ask a question and it gets stopped at the next level up. It gets to the point where you know that if you don't do anything at all, you won't get in trouble.

In a similar vein, another veteran officer put it somewhat more bluntly. He suggested caustically:

> The only way to survive on this job is to keep from breaking your ass...
> if you try too hard you're sure to get in trouble. Either some civic-
> minded creep is going to get outraged and you'll wind up with a com-
> plaint in your file; or the high and mighty in the department will come
> down on you for breaking some rule or something and you'll get your
> pay docked.

These quotations suggest that patrolman disenchantment has two edges. One, the police with the general public — which has been well-substantiated in the literature — and two, the disenchantment with the police system itself. In short, a recruit begins to realize (through proverb, example, and his own experience) it is his relationship with his fellow officers (particularly those working the same sector and shift — his squad) that protects his interests and allows him to continue on the job — without their support he would be lost.[8]

To summarize, the adjustment of a newcomer in police departments is one which follows the line of least resistance. By becoming similar in senti-ment and behavior to his peers, the recruit avoids censure by the depart-ment, his supervisor and, most important, his brother officers. Furthermore, since the occupational rewards are to be found primarily in the unusual situation which calls for "real" police work, the logical situa-tional solution is for the officers to organize their activities in such a way as to minimize the likelihood of being sanctioned by *any* of their audiences. The low visibility of the patrolman's role vis-a-vis the department allows for such a response. Thus, the pervasive adjustment is epitomized in the "lie low, hang loose and don't expect too much" advice frequently heard within the Union City Police Department. This overall picture would indicate that the following tip given to me by a Union City veteran represents a very astute analysis of how to insure continuance in the police world. He suggested:

> There's only two things you gotta know around here. First, forget
> everything you've learned in the academy 'cause the street's where
> you'll learn to be a cop; and second, being first don't mean shit around
> here. Take it easy, that's our motto.

The above characterization of the recruit socialization process, while necessarily a drastic condensation of a much more complex and interde-pendent process, does delineate the more important aspects of becoming a policeman. Furthermore, this descriptive narrative hints that many of the recent attempts to alter or reform police behavior are likely to meet with frustration and failure.

A Coda For Reformers

Most police reformers view the behavior of individual patrolmen as a problem for the department or society, not vice versa. I have, in a small way, tried to correct this bias by describing the point of view of the entering recruit. This emphasizes the intelligibility of the newcomer's actions as he works out solutions to his unique problems. In short, we "looked up" at the nature of the network above the recruit rather than using the usual approach which, in the past, has "looked down" on the "outsider." Perhaps this approach indicates the dilemma in which our police are indeed trapped.

In a very real sense, this article suggests a limit upon the extent to which the police can be expected to solve their own problems. Regardless of how well-educated, well-equipped, or professional the patrolman may become, his normative position and task within society will remain unchanged. From this perspective, the characteristic response of police officers to their present situation is indeed both rational and functional. Clearly, the police subculture—like subcultures surrounding bricklayers, lawyers, or social workers—will probably exist in even the most reformed of departments. To change the police without changing the police role in society is as futile as the labors of Sisyphus.

The long-range goal should be a structural redefinition of the police task and a determination of ways in which the external control principle—so central to the rule of law—may be strengthened. Of course, ways must be found to make the policeman's lot somewhat more tolerable, both to him and to the general citizenry. Organizational change can aid this process by designing training programs which place less stress on the apprenticeship relationship. However, it is doubtful that without profound alterations in the definition and structural arrangement of the police task (and in the implied values such arrangements support), significant change is possible.

Thus, plans to increase the therapeutic and operational effectiveness of police institutions by "in-house" techniques must be judged in terms of what is being done now and what might be done—and, given the features of the police institution as described here, the difference is painfully small. The particular pattern of police practices is a response to the demands of the larger complex and, as such, reflects the values and norms prevalent throughout the society. The extent to which the police system undermines the rule of law; the extent to which the public is willing to alter the crime fighter image of police; the extent to which the police bureaucracy will allow change; and ultimately, the extent to which the police system as presently constructed can operate under strict public accounting—these are the major issues confronting the police, not the degree to which the individual policeman can be professionalized.[9]

Notes

[1]The use of the term "outsider" in the above context is not intended to invidiously portray the police. Rather, the term simply connotes the widespread conviction carried by the police themselves that they are, of necessity, somehow different, and set-off from the larger society. To most police observers, isolationism, secrecy, strong in-group loyalties, sacred symbols, common language, and a sense of estrangement are almost axiomatic subcultural features underpinning a set of common understandings among police in general which govern their relations with one another as well as with civilians (Bayley and Mendelsohn, 1969; President's Commission, 1967; Skolnick, 1966). Such a perspective emphasizes the necessity to view the world from the eyes of the outsider — a perspective which ideally is empathetic but neither sympathetic or judgmental.

[2]If one takes seriously research findings regarding esoteric subcultures, social scientists interested in police behavior are limited in their choice of methodological strategy. If we are to gain insight into the so-called police problem, researchers must penetrate the official smoke screen sheltering virtually all departments and observe directly the social action in social situations which, in the last analysis, defines police work.

[3]One exception is Westley's (1951) insightful observational study of a midwestern police department. However, his research was devoted mainly to the description of the more salient sociological features of the police occupation and was concerned only peripherally with the learning process associated with the police role.

[4]Union City is a pseudonym for a sprawling metropolitan area populated by more than a million people. The police department employs well over 1,500 uniformed officers, provides a salary above the national average, and is organized in the classic pyramidal arrangement (see Van Maanen, 1972). Based on interviews with police personnel from a number of different departments and, most importantly, critical readings of my work by policemen from several departments, the sequence of events involved in recruit socialization appears to be remarkably similar from department to department. This structural correspondence among recruit training programs has been noted by others (see Ahern, 1972; Berkeley, 1969; Neiderhoffer, 1967).

[5]While it cannot be stated categorically that my presence had little effect upon the behavior of the subjects, I felt I was accepted completely as a regular group member in my particular police academy class and little or no behavior was (or, for that matter, could be) altered explicitly. Furthermore, the lengthy, personal, and involving nature of my academy experiences produced an invaluable carry-over effect when I moved to the street work portion of the study. The importance of continuous observation and full participation as an aid for minimizing distortions and behavior change on the part of social actors has been strikingly demonstrated by a number of social scientists (e.g., see Whyte, 1943; Becker, 1963; Dalton, 1964; and, most recently, Schatzman and Strauss, 1973).

[6]Significantly, a recruit is not even allowed to carry a loaded weapon during the classroom portion of his academy training. He must wait until graduation night before being permitted to load his weapon. To the recruit, such policies are demeaning. Yet, the policies "stigmatizing" the recruits-as-recruits (e.g., different uniforms, old and battered batons, allocation of special parking spaces, special scarfs, and name plates) were exceedingly effective methods of impressing upon recruits that they were members of a particular class and were not yet Union City Police Officers.

[7]By "chippies," the officer was referring to normal arrests encountered frequently by patrolmen. Usually, a chippie is a misdemeanor arrest for something like drunkenness. The chippie crimes the officer noted in the quotation, "stand-up" and "DWI's" refer to drunk-in-public and driving-while-intoxicated, respectively.

[8]In most ways, the patrolmen represent what Goffman (1959) calls a team. In Goffmanesque, a team is "a set of individuals whose intimate co-operation is required if a given projected

definition of the situation is to be maintained" (1959:104). The situational definition to be sustained in the patrol setting is that "all-is-going-well-there-are-no-problems." The covert rule for patrolmen is to never draw attention to one's activities. An analysis I conducted on written weekly FTO progress reports illustrates this point convincingly. Of over 300 report forms, only one contained an even slightly negative evaluation. Uniformly, all forms were characterized by high praise for the recruit. The topics the FTO's chose to elaborate upon were typified by such concerns as the recruit's driving skill, the recruit's pleasing personality, the recruit's stable home life, and so on. The vast majority of reports contained no reference whatsoever to the types of activities engaged in by the recruits. The point is simply that in no case was an FTO Report filed which might result in departmental attention. It should be clear that such behavior does not pass unnoticed by the recruit. Indeed, he learns rapidly the importance and value of his team as well as the corresponding definition of the police situation. [9]I have attempted to suggest in this article that the intelligibility of social events requires they be viewed in a context which extends both spatially and in time. Relatedly, social actors must be granted rationality for their behavior. Given the situational imperatives faced by patrolmen, is it any wonder our police recoil behind a blue curtain? Perhaps we have reached what R.D. Laing (1964) calls the "theoretical limit of institutions." According to Laing, this paradoxical position is characterized by a system which, when viewed as a collective, behaves irrationally, yet is populated by members whose everyday behavior is eminently rational.

References Cited

Ahern, J.F., (1972) *Police in Trouble.* New York: Hawthorn Books.

Bayley, P.H., and H. Mendelsohn, (1969) *Minorities and the Police.* New York: The Free Press.

Becker, H.S. (1963) *Outsiders: Studies in the Sociology of Deviance.* New York: The Free Press.

Becker, H.S., B. Greer, E.C. Hughes, and A. Strauss (1961) *Boys in White: Student Culture in Medical School.* Chicago: University of Chicago Press.

Berkeley, G.E. (1969) *The Democratic Policeman.* Boston: Beacon Press.

Berlew, D.E., and D.T. Hall, (1966) The socialization of managers; effects of expectations on performance. *Administrative Science Quarterly* 11:207-23.

Bittner, E., (1967) The police on skid row. *American Sociological Review* 32:699-715.

Cicourel, A.V., (1967) *The Social Organization of Juvenile Justice.* New York: John Wiley and Sons.

Dalton, M., (1964) Preconceptions and methods in men who manage. In *Sociologists at Work,* P. Hammond, ed. New York: Doubleday.

Dornbush, S.M., (1955) The military academy as an assimilating institution. *Social Forces* 33:316-21.

Evan, W.M., (1963) Peer group interaction and organizational socialization: a study of employee turnover. *American Sociological Review* 28:436-40.

Goffman, E., (1959) *The Presentation of Self in Everyday Life.* New York: Doubleday.

Greer, B., (1964) First days in the field. In *Sociologists at Work,* P. Hammond, ed. New York: Doubleday.

Hughes, E.C., (1958) *Men and their Work* Glencoe, Illinois: The Free Press.

Laing, R.D., (1964) The obvious. In *Dialectics of Liberation,* D. Cooper, ed. London: Institute of Phenomenological Studies.

Lortie, D.C., (1968) Shared ordeal and induction to work. In *Institutions and the Person,* H.S. Becker, B. Greer, D. Riesman, and R.T. Weiss, eds. Chicago: Aldine.

McNamara, J., (1967) Uncertainties in police work: the relevance of police recruits' background and training. In *The Police: Six Sociological Essays,* D.J. Bordura, ed. New York: John Wiley and Sons.

Neiderhoffer, A., (1967) *Behind the Shield.* New York: Doubleday.

President's Commission on Law Enforcement, *(1967)* Task Force Report: The Police. Washington, D.C.: Government Printing Office.

Reiss, A.J., (1971) *The Police and the Public.* New Haven: Yale University Press.

Schatzman, L., and A. Strauss, (1973) *Field Research: Strategies for a Natural Sociology.* Englewood Cliffs, New Jersey: Prentice-Hall.

Schein, E.H., (1963) Organizational socialization in the early career of industrial managers. Paper presented at the New England Psychological Association. Boston, Massachusetts. (1971) Organizational socialization and the profession of management. *Industrial Management Review* 2:37-45.

Skolnick, J., (1966) *Justice Without Trial: Law Enforcement in a Democratic Society.* New York: John Wiley and Sons.

Sterling, J.W., (1972) Changes in Role Concepts of Police Officers. Washington, D.C.: International Association of Chiefs of Police.

Van Maanen, J. (1972) Pledging the police: a study of selected aspects of recruit socialization in a large, urban police department. Ph.D. Dissertation, University of California, Irvine. (1976) Breaking-in: socialization to work. In *Handbook of Work, Organization, and Society,* R. Dubin, ed. Chicago: Rand-Mcnally.

Webster, J.A. (1970) Police task and time study. *Journal of Criminal Law, Criminology and Police Science* 61:94-100.

Westley, W.A., (1951) The police: a sociological study of law, custom and mortality. Ph.D. Dissertation, University of Chicago, Chicago, Illinois.

Whyte, W.F., (1943) *Street Corner Society.* Chicago: University of Chicago Press.

Wilson, J.Q., (1968) *Varieties of Police Behavior.* Cambridge, Massachusetts. Harvard University Press.

5

A Professor's "Street Lessons"

George L. Kirkham

As policemen have come under increasing criticism by various individuals and groups in our society in recent years, I cannot help but wonder how many times they have clenched their teeth and wished they could expose their critics to only a few of the harsh realities which their job involves.

Persons such as myself, members of the academic community, have traditionally been quick to find fault with the police. From isolated incidents reported in the various news media, we have fashioned for ourselves a stereotyped image of the police officer which conveniently conforms to our notions of what he is. We see the brutal cop, the racist cop, the grafting cop, the discourteous cop. What we do not see, however, is the image of thousands of dedicated men and women struggling against almost impossible odds to preserve our society and everything in it which we cherish.

For some years, first as a student and later as a professor of criminology, I found myself troubled by the fact that most of us who write books and articles on the police have never been policemen ourselves. I began to be bothered increasingly by many of my students who were former policemen. Time and again, they would respond to my frequently critical lectures on

From *FBI Law Enforcement Bulletin,* March, 1974, pp. 14-22. Reprinted by permission.

the police with the argument that I could not possible understand what a police officer has to endure in modern society until I had been one myself. Under the weight of this frustration, and my personal conviction that knowledge has an applied as well as a theoretical dimension, I decided to take up this challenge: I would become a policeman myself as a means of establishing once and for all the accuracy of what I and other criminologists had been saying about the police for so long.

From Professor to Cop

Suffice it to say that my announced intention to become a uniformed patrolman was at first met with fairly widespread disbelief on the part of family, friends, and colleagues alike. At 31, with a family and an established career as a criminologist, I was surely an unlikely candidate for the position of police recruit. The very idea, it was suggested to me, was outrageous and absurd. I was told that no police administrator in his right mind would allow a representative of the academic world to enter his organization. It had never been done and could not be done.

Fortunately, many of my students, who either had been policemen or were at the time, sounded a far more optimistic and enthusiastic note. Police administrators and officers alike, they said, would welcome the opportunity to expose members of the academic community to the problems of their occupation. If one of us were really willing to see and feel the policeman's world from behind a badge and blue uniform, instead of from the safe and comfortable vantage point of a classroom or university office, police officers themselves would do everything in their power to make the opportunity available. Despite these assurances from my police-men-students, I remained skeptical over my chances of being allowed to do such an unorthodox thing.

This skepticism was, however, soon to be overcome. One of my better criminology students at the time was a young police officer on educational leave from the Jacksonville, Fla., Sheriff's Office. Upon learning of my desire to become a police officer in order to better understand the problems of policemen, he urged me to contact Sheriff Dale Carson and Undersheriff D.K. Brown of his department with my proposal. I had earlier heard other police officers describe the consolidated 800-man force of Jacksonville-Duval County as one of the most progressive departments in the country. I learned that Sheriff Carson and Undersheriff Brown, two former FBI Agents, had won considerable respect in the law enforcement profession as enlightened and innovative administrators.

The size and composition of Jacksonville, as well as its nearness to my university and home, made it appear to be an ideal location for what I wished to do. Numbering just over one-half million residents, Jacksonville impressed me as being the kind of large and rapidly growing American city which inevitably experiences the major social problems of our time: crime and delinquency, racial unrest, poverty, and mental illness. A seaport and industrial center, Jacksonville offered a diversity of urban, suburban, and even rural populations in its vast land area. I took particular note of the fact that it contained a fairly typical inner-city slum section and black ghetto, both of which were in the process of being transformed through a massive program of urban redevelopment. This latter feature was espeically important to me insofar as I wanted to personally experience the stresses and strains of today's city policeman. It was, after all, he who had traditionally been the subject of such intense interest and criticism on the part of social scientists such as myself.

Much to my surprise, both Sheriff Carson and Undersheriff Brown were not only supportive but enthusiastic as well over my proposal to become a city patrolman. I made it clear to them at the outset that I did not wish to function as an observer or reserve officer, but rather wanted to become a fully sworn and full-time member of their department for a period of between 4 and 6 months. I further stated that I hoped to spend most of this period working as a uniformed patrolman in those inner city beats most characterized by violence, poverty, social unrest, and high crime rates. They agreed to this, with the understanding that I would first have to meet the same requirements as any other police candidate. I would, for example, have to submit to a thorough character investigation, a physical examination, and would have to meet the same training standards applied to all other Florida police officers. Since I was to be unpaid, I would be exempted from departmental civil service requirements.

Restyling an Image

Both Carson and Brown set about overcoming various administrative and insurance problems which had to be dealt with in advance of my becoming a police officer. Suppose, for example, I should be injured or killed in the line of duty, or should injure or kill someone else. What of the department and city's liability? These and other issues were gradually resolved with considerable effort on their part. The only stipulation set forth by both administrators was one with which I strongly agreed: for the sake of morale and confidence in the department, every officer must know in advance exactly who I was and what I was doing. Other than being in the unusual position of a "patrolman-professor," I would be indistinguishable from other officers in every respect, from the standard issue .38 Smith and Wesson revolver I would carry to the badge and uniform I would wear.

The biggest and final obstacle which I faced was the necessity that I comply fully with a 1967 Florida Police Standards law, which requires that every police officer and deputy sheriff in the State complete a minimum of 280 hours of law enforcement training prior to being sworn in and assigned to regular duty. Since I had a full-time university job nearly 200 miles from Jacksonville, this meant that I would be unable to attend the regular sheriff's academy. I would have to attend a certified academy in my own area, something which I arranged to do with Sheriff Carson's sponsorship.

For 4 months, 4 hours each evening and 5 nights a week, I attended the Tallahassee area police academy, along with 35 younger classmates. As a balding intellectual, I at first stood out as an oddity in the class of young men destined to become local law enforcement officers. With the passage of time, however, they came to accept me and I them. We joked, drank coffee, and struggled through various examinations and lessons together. At first known only as "the professor," the men later nicknamed me "Doc" over my good-natured protests.

As the days stretched into weeks and the weeks into months, I took lengthy notes on the interviewing of witnesses at crime scenes, investigated imaginary traffic accidents, and lifted fingerprints. Some nights I went home after hours of physical defense training with my uniformly younger and stronger peers with tired muscles, bruises, and the feeling that I should have my head examined for undertaking such a rugged project.

As someone who had never fired a handgun, I quickly grew accustomed to the noise of 35 revolvers firing at the cardboard silhouettes which our minds transformed into real assailants at the sound of the range whistle. I learned how to properly make car stops, approach a front door or darkened building, question suspects, and a thousand other things that every modern police officer must know. After what seemed an eternity, graduation from the academy finally came, and with it what was to become the most difficult but rewarding educational experience of my life: I became a policeman.

The School of Hard Knocks

I will never forget standing in front of the Jacksonville police station on that first day. I felt incredibly awkward and conspicuous in the new blue uniform and creaking leather. Whatever confidence in my ability to "do the job" I had gained during the academy seemed to evaporate as I stood there watching other blue figures hurrying in the evening rain toward assembly. After some minutes, I summoned the courage to walk into the station and into my new career as a core city patrolman.

That first day seems long ago now. As I write this, I have completed over 100 tours of duty as a patrolman. Although still a rookie officer, so much has happened in the short space of 6 months that I will never again be either the same man or the same scientist who stood in front of the station on that first day. While it is hard to even begin to describe within a brief article the many changes which have occurred within me during this time, I would like to share with fellow policemen and colleagues in the academic community a few of what I regard as the more important of what I will call my "street lessons."

I had always personally been of the opinion that police officers greatly exaggerate the amount of verbal disrespect and physical abuse to which they are subjected in the line of duty. During my first few hours as a street officer, I lived blissfully in a magic bubble which was soon to burst. As a college professor, I had grown accustomed to being treated with uniform respect and deference by those I encountered. I somehow naively assumed that this same quality of respect would carry over into my new role as a policeman. I was, after all, a representative of the law, identifiable to all by the badge and uniform I wore as someone dedicated to the protection of society. Surely that fact would entitle me to a measure of respect and cooperation — or so I thought. I quickly found that my badge and uniform, rather than serving to shield me from such things as disrespect and violence, only acted as a magnet which drew me toward many individuals who hated what I represented.

I had discounted on my first evening the warning of a veteran sergeant who, after hearing that I was about to begin work as a patrolman, shook his head and cautioned, "You'd better watch yourself out there, Professor! It gets pretty rough sometimes!" I was soon to find out what he meant.

Several hours into my first evening on the streets, my partner and I were dispatched to a bar in the downtown area to handle a disturbance complaint. Inside, we encountered a large and boisterous drunk who was arguing with the bartender and loudly refusing to leave. As someone with considerable experience as a correctional counselor and mental health worker, I hastened to take charge of the situation. "Excuse me, Sir," I smiled pleasantly at the drunk, "but I wonder if I could ask you to step outside and talk with me for just a minute?" The man stared at me through bloodshot eyes in disbelief for a second, raising one hand to scratch the stubble of several days' growth of beard. Then suddenly, without warning, it happened. He swung at me, luckily missing my face and striking me on the right shoulder. I couldn't believe it. What on earth had I done to provoke such a reaction? Before I could recover from my startled condition, he swung again — this time tearing my whistle chain from a shoulder epaulet. After a brief struggle, we had the still shouting, cursing man locked in the back of our cruiser. I stood there, breathing heavily with my hair in my eyes as I surveyed the damage to my new uniform and looked in bewilderment at my partner, who only smiled and clapped me affectionately on the back.

Theory vs. Practice

"Something is very wrong," I remember thinking to myself in the front seat as we headed for the jail. I had used the same kind of gentle, rapport-building approach with countless offenders in prison and probation settings. It had always worked so well there. What was so different about being a policeman? In the days and weeks which followed, I was to learn the answer to this question the hard way. As a university professor, I had always sought to convey to students the idea that it is a mistake to exercise authority, to make decisions for other people, or rely upon orders and commands to accomplish something. As a police officer myself, I was forced time and again to do just that. For the first time in my life, I encountered individuals who interpreted kindness as weakness, as an invitation to disrespect or violence. I encountered men, women, and children who, in fear, desperation, or excitement, looked to the person behind my blue uniform and shield for guidance, control, and direction. As someone who had always condemned the exercise of authority, the acceptance of myself as an unavoidable symbol of authority came as a bitter lesson.

I found that there was a world of difference between encountering individuals, as I had, in mental health or correctional settings and facing them as the patrolman must: when they are violent, hysterical, desperate. When I put the uniform of a police officer on, I lost the luxury of sitting in an air-conditioned office with my pipe and books, calmly discussing with a rapist or armed robber the past problems which had led him into trouble with the law. Such offenders had seemed so innocent, so harmless in the sterile setting of prison. The often terrible crimes which they had committed were long since past, reduced like their victims to so many printed words on a page.

Now, as a police officer, I began to encounter the offender for the first time as a very real menace to my personal safety and the security of our society. The felon was no longer a harmless figure sitting in blue denims across my prison desk, a "victim" of society to be treated with compassion and leniency. He became an armed robber fleeing from the scene of a crime, a crazed maniac threatening his family with a gun, someone who might become my killer crouched behind the wheel of a car on a dark street.

Lesson in Fear

Like crime itself, fear quickly ceased to be an impersonal and abstract thing. It became something which I regularly experienced. It was a tightness in my stomach as I approached a warehouse where something had tripped a silent alarm. I could taste it as a dryness in my mouth as we raced with blue lights and siren toward the site of a "Signal Zero" (armed and dangerous) call. For the first time in my life, I came to know — as every policeman knows — the true meaning of fear. Through shift after shift it stalked me, making my palms cold and sweaty, and pushing the adrenalin through my veins.

I recall particularly a dramatic lesson in the meaning of fear which took place shortly after I joined the force. My partner and I were on routine patrol one Saturday evening in a deteriorated area of cheap bars and pool halls when we observed a young male double-parked in the middle of the street. I pulled alongside and asked him in a civil manner to either park or drive on, whereupon he began loudly cursing us and shouting that we couldn't make him go anywhere. An angry crowd began to gather as we got out of our patrol car and approached the man, who by this time shouting that we were harassing him and calling to bystanders for assistance. As a criminology professor, some months earlier I would have urged that the police officer who was now myself simply leave the car double-parked and move on rather than risk an incident. As a policeman, however, I had come to realize that an officer can never back down from his responsibility to enforce the law. Whatever the risk to himself, every police officer understands that his ability to back up the lawful authority which he represents is the only thing which stands between civilization and the jungle of lawlessness.

The man continued to curse us and adamantly refused to move his car. As we placed him under arrest and attempted to move him to our cruiser, an unidentified male and female rushed from the crowd which was steadily enlarging and sought to free him. In the ensuing struggle, a hysterical female unsnapped and tried to grab my service revolver, and the now angry mob began to converge on us. Suddenly, I was no longer an "ivory-tower" scholar watching typical police "overreaction" to a street incident — but I was part of it and fighting to remain alive and uninjured. I remember the sickening sensation of cold terror which filled my insides as I struggled to reach our car radio. I simultaneously put out a distress call and pressed the hidden electric release button on our shotgun rack as my partner sought to maintain his grip on the prisoner and hold the crowd at bay with his revolver.

How harshly I would have judged the officer who now grabbed the shotgun only a few months before. I rounded the rear of our cruiser with the weapon and shouted at the mob to move back. The memory flashed through my mind that I had always argued that policemen should not be allowed to carry shotguns because of the "offensive" character and the potential damage to community relations as a result of their display. How readily as a criminology professor I would have condemned the officer who was now myself, trembling with fear and anxiety and menacing an "unarmed" assembly with an "offensive" weapon. But if circumstances had dramatically changed my perspective, for now it was *my* life and safety that were in danger, *my* wife and child who might be mourning. Not "a policeman" or Patrolman Smith—but *me,* George Kirkham! I felt accordingly bitter when I saw the individual who had provoked this near riot back on the streets the next night, laughing as though our charge of "resisting arrest with violence" was a big joke. Like my partner, I found myself feeling angry and frustrated shortly afterward when this same individual was allowed to plead guilty to a reduced charge of "breach of peace."

Loud Defendants and Silent Victims

As someone who had always been greatly concerned about the rights of offenders, I now began to consider for the first time the rights of police officers. As a police officer, I felt that my efforts to protect society and maintain my personal safety were menaced by many of the very court decisions and lenient parole board actions I had always been eager to defend. An educated man, I could not answer the questions of my fellow officers as to why those who kill and maim policemen, men who are involved in no less honorable an activity than holding our society together, should so often be subjected to minor penalties. I grew weary of carefully following difficult legal restrictions, while thugs and hoodlums consistently twisted the law to their own advantage. I remember standing in the street one evening and reading a heroin "pusher" his rights, only to have him convulse with laughter halfway through and finish reciting them, word for word, from memory. He had been given his "rights" under the law, but what about the rights of those who were the victims of people like himself? For the first time, questions such as these began to bother me.

As a corrections worker and someone raised in a comfortable middle class home, I had always been insulated from the kind of human misery and tragedy which became part of the policeman's everyday life. Now, the often terrible sights, sounds, and smells of my job began to haunt me hours after I had taken the blue uniform and badge off. Some nights I would lie in bed unable to sleep, trying desperately to forget the things I had seen during a particular tour of duty: the rat-infested shacks that served as homes to those far less fortunate than I, a teenage boy dying in my arms after being struck by a car, small children clad in rags with stomachs bloated from hunger playing in a urine-spattered hall, the victim of a robbery senselessly beaten and murdered.

In my new role as a police officer, I found that the victims of crime ceased to be impersonal statistics. As a corrections worker and criminology professor, I had never given much thought to those who are victimized by criminals in our society. Now the sight of so many lives ruthlessly damaged and destroyed by the perpetrators of crime left me preoccupied with the question of society's responsibility to protect the men, women, and children who are victimized daily.

For all the tragic victims of crime I have seen during the past 6 months, one case stands out above all. There was an elderly man who lived with his dog in my apartment building downtown. He was a retired bus driver and his wife was long deceased. As time went by, I became friends with the old man and his dog. I could usually count on finding both of them standing at the corner on my way to work. I would engage in casual conversation with the old man, and sometimes he and his dog would walk several blocks toward the station with me. They were both as predictable as a clock: each evening around 7, the old man would walk to the same small restaurant several blocks away, where he would eat his evening meal while the dog waited dutifully outside.

One evening my partner and I received a call to a street shooting near my apartment building. My heart sank as we pulled up and I saw the old man's mutt in a crowd of people gathered on the sidewalk. The old man was lying on his back, in a large pool of blood, half trying to brace himself on an elbow. He clutched a bullet wound in his chest and gasped to me that three young men had stopped him and demanded his money. After taking his wallet and seeing how little he had, they shot him and left him on the street. As a police officer, I was enraged time and again at the cruelty and senselessness of acts such as this, at the arrogance of brazen thugs who prey with impunity on innocent citizens.

A Different Perspective

The same kinds of daily stresses which affected my fellow officers soon began to take their toll on me. I became sick and tired of being reviled and attacked by criminals who could usually find a most sympathetic audience in judges and jurors eager to understand their side of things and provide them with "another chance." I grew tired of living under the ax of news media and community pressure groups, eager to seize upon the slightest mistake made by myself or a fellow police officer.

As a criminology professor, I had always enjoyed the luxury of having great amounts of time in which to make difficult decisions. As a police officer, however, I found myself forced to make the most critical choices in a time frame of seconds, rather than days: to shoot or not to shoot, to arrest or not to arrest, to give chase or let go—always with the nagging certainty that others, those with great amounts of time in which to analyze and think, stood ready to judge and condemn me for whatever action I might take or fail to take. I found myself not only forced to live a life consisting of seconds and adrenalin, but also forced to deal with human problems which were infinitely more difficult than anything I had ever confronted in a correctional or mental health setting. Family fights, mental illness, potentially explosive crowd situations, dangerous individuals—I found myself progressively awed by the complexity of tasks faced by men whose work I once thought was fairly simple and straightforward.

Indeed, I would like to take the average clinical psychologist or psychiatrist and invite him to function for just a day in the world of the policeman, to confront people whose problems are both serious and in need of immediate solution. I would invite him to walk, as I have, into a smoke-filled pool room where ·five or six angry men are swinging cues at one another. I would like the prison counselor and parole officer to see their client Jones—not calm and composed in an office setting, but as the street cop sees him—beating his small child with a heavy belt buckle, or kicking his pregnant wife. I wish that they, and every judge and juror in our country, could see the ravages of crime as the cop on the beat must: innocent people cut, shot, beaten, raped, robbed, and murdered. I would, I feel certain, give them a different perspective on crime and criminals, just as it has me.

Humaneness in Uniform

For all the human misery and suffering which police officers must witness in their work, I found myself amazed at the incredible humanity and compassion which seems to characterize most of them. My own stereotypes of the brutal, sadistic cop were time and again shattered by the sight of humanitarian kindness on the part of the thin blue line: a young patrolman giving mouth to mouth resuscitation to a filthy derelict; a grizzled old veteran embarrassed when I discovered the bags of jelly beans which he carried in the trunk of his car for impoverished ghetto kids—to whom he was the closest thing to an Easter Bunny they would ever know; an officer giving money out of his own pocket to a hungry and stranded family he would probably never see again; and another patrolman taking the trouble to drop by on his own time in order to give worried parents information about their problem son or daughter.

As a police officer, I found myself repeatedly surprised at the ability of my fellow patrolmen to withstand the often enormous daily pressures of their work. Long hours, frustration, danger, and anxiety—all seemed to be taken in stride as just part of the reality of being a cop. I went eventually through the humbling discovery that I, like the men in blue with whom I worked, was simply a human being with definite limits to the amount of stress I could endure in a given period of time.

I recall in particular one evening when this point was dramatized to me. It had been a long, hard shift—one which ended with a high-speed chase of a stolen car in which we narrowly escaped serious injury when another vehicle pulled in front of our patrol car. As we checked off duty, I was vaguely aware of feeling tired and tense. My partner and I were headed for a restaurant and a bite of breakfast when we both heard the unmistakable sound of breaking glass coming from a church and spotted two long-haired teenage boys running from the area. We confronted them and I asked one for identification, displaying my own police identification. He sneered at me, cursed, and turned to walk away. The next think I knew I had grabbed the youth by his shirt and spun him around, shouting, "I'm talking to you, punk!" I felt my partner's arm on my shoulder and heard his reassuring voice behind me, "Take it easy, Doc!" I released my grip on the adolescent and stood silently for several seconds, unable to accept the inescapable reality that I had "lost my cool." My mind flashed back to a lecture during which I had told my students, "Any man who is not able to maintain absolute control of his emotions at all times has no business being a police officer." I was at the time of this incident director of a human relations project designed to teach policemen "emotional control" skills. Now here I was, an "emotional control" expert, being told to calm down by a patrolman!

A Complex Challenge

As someone who had always regarded policemen as a "paranoid" lot, I discovered in the daily round of violence which became part of my life that chronic suspiciousness is something that a good cop cultivates in the interest of going home to his family each evening. Like so many other officers, my daily exposure to street crime soon had me carrying an off-duty weapon virtually everywhere I went. I began to become watchful of who and what was around me, as things began to acquire a new meaning: an open door, someone loitering on a dark corner, a rear license plate covered with dirt. My personality began to change slowly according to my family, friends, and colleagues as my career as a policeman progressed. Once quick to drop critical barbs about policemen to intellectual friends, I now became extremely sensitive about such remarks—and several times became engaged in heated arguments over them.

As a police officer myself, I found that society demands too much of its policemen: not only are they expected to enforce the law, but to be curbside psychiatrists, marriage counselors, social workers, and even ministers, and doctors. I found that a good street officer combines in his daily work splinters of each of these complex professions and many more. Certainly it is unreasonable for us to ask so much of the men in blue; yet we must, for there is simply no one else to whom we can turn for help in the kind of crises and problems policemen deal with. No one else wants to counsel a family with problems at 3 a.m. on Sunday; no one else wants to enter a darkened building after a burglary; no one else wants to confront a robber or madman with a gun. No one else wants to stare poverty, mental illness, and human tragedy in the face day after day, to pick up the pieces of shattered lives.

As a policeman myself, I have often asked myself the questions: "Why does a man become a cop?" "What makes him stay with it?" Surely it's not the disrespect, the legal restrictions which make the job increasingly rough, the long hours and low pay, or the risk of being killed or injured trying to protect people who often don't seem to care.

The only answer to this question I have been able to arrive at is one based on my own limited experience as a policeman. Night after night, I came home and took off the badge and blue uniform with a sense of satisfaction and contribution to society that I have never known in any other job. Somehow that feeling seemed to make everything—the disrespect, the danger, the boredom—worthwhile.

An Invaluable Education

For too long now, we in America's colleges and universities have conveyed to young men and women the subtle message that there is somehow something wrong with "being a cop." It's time for that to stop. This point was forcibly brought home to me one evening not long ago. I had just completed a day shift and had to rush back to the university with no chance to change out of uniform for a late afternoon class. As I rushed into my office to pick up my lecture notes, my secretary's jaw dropped at the sight of the uniform. "Why, Dr. Kirkham, you're not going to go to class looking like *that*, are you?" I felt momentarily embarrassed, and then struck by the realization that I would not feel the need to apologize if I appeared before my students with long hair or a beard. Free love advocates and hate-monger revolutionaries do not apologize for their group memberships, so why should someone whose appearance symbolizes a commitment to serve and protect society? "Why not," I replied with a slight smile, "I'm proud to be a cop!" I picked up my notes and went to class.

Let me conclude this article by saying that I would hope that other educators might take the trouble to observe firsthand some of the policeman's problems before being so quick to condemn and pass judgment on the thin blue line. We are all familiar with the old expression which urges us to refrain from judging the worth of another man's actions until we have walked at least a mile in his shoes. To be sure, I have not walked that mile as a rookie patrolman with barely 6 months' experience. But I have at least tried the shoes on and taken a few difficult steps in them. Those few steps have given me a profoundly new understanding and appreciation of our police, and have left me with the humbling realization that possession of a Ph.D. does not give a man a corner on knowledge, or place him in the lofty position where he cannot take lessons from those less educated than himself.

6

Controlling People

Jonathan Rubenstein

A policeman's principal concern is to physically control the people he is policing. While he sometimes wants to hurt or humiliate them, that is not nearly so often his purpose as it is the consequence of his efforts to control them. When he intervenes in a person's life, his attitude is basically instrumental. He mainly wants to place himself as quickly as possible in a position that will allow him to control the person, if that is required, or hopefully to discourage any inclinations to resist him or his orders. That is why he ignores the risks he takes in driving and violates departmental regulations by refusing to use the safety belt provided for him. The idea of being confined and prevented from moving quickly out of his car terrifies him.

Policemen act as though all people are right-handed. If he has any choice in the matter, the patrolman tries to move in a leftward direction toward a person in order to control his fighting arm. This allows him to stand at the person's right, at a slight angle, when he is facing him, which keeps his gun away from the man he is seeking to dominate. He consistently violates the normal distances which people seek to maintain when they are engaged in friendly conversation, causing discomfort and nervousness when he does not mean to. He is not formally trained to do this, nor does he do it consciously, but an understanding of his actions would not deter him, since his objective is the maintenance of his personal security and not the discomfort of others. By constantly crowding people, he reduces their opportunities for kicking and punching him effectively. When he can, the patrolman stands slightly at an angle to the person he is confronting to avoid a crippling blow to the groin. Naturally he can be grabbed and wrestled with; this is the main reason why most policemen wear clip-on ties and hate any gear that offers someone a handhold on them.

The first and sometimes the only thing a policeman looks at when approaching someone is his hands. Recruits are warned repeatedly to train themselves to check people's hands first ("If the guy's got a brick, he better be building a house"). But he must do more than just look—he must learn to expect to see things. A policeman is frequently called into the presence of people who are distressed, depressed, angry, or fearful. It is not surprising that many of them are holding some kind of weapon, which they do not necessarily intend for use against him. He must be prepared to disarm them swiftly without resorting to force. Often he sees boys walking down the street carrying sticks or boards; he usually disarms them and sends them on their way, unless there has been a specific call or an order to bring them in. Anyone who comes into his presence is unceremoniously disarmed. A boy carrying a bow and arrow has the toy taken from him, and given to his mother after the policeman finishes talking with them. A woman opens her door for an officer taking a meet complainant, and he quickly grabs a butcher knife and pistol. He enters the house, unloads the gun, places the knife in a drawer, sits down for a cup of coffee and a little conversation, and leaves after the woman has had a good cry and he is reasonably sure she will not commit suicide. People often tell him of weapons in their houses and offer to get them, but the experienced patrolman will not let anyone handle a gun in his presence. People holding paper bags are looked at carefully, because every policeman knows that it is not an elegant manner of transporting a gun but it is one that is used often enough. He is not concerned about hurting the feelings of the people whom he handles unceremoniously in these moments. He only cares about disarming them for there are occasions when the door opens and he is looking directly into the barrel of a shotgun, and then is stripped of everything he is but his blue suit.[1]

Anyone whose hands are concealed, wittingly or not, risks serious injury or worse when he attracts the attention of a policeman. Hidden hands imply danger to a policeman, and he must decide in a few seconds what course of action to take. Whatever he decides to do, he must continue until he has succeeded or failed, because there is no possibility of mediation with a policeman intent on assuring his security, and he will be satisfied only by seeing empty hands.

A young white officer noticed a man standing near a street corner turn away as the patrol car approached. He stopped his car and rolled down the window to look at the elderly Negro man. Instead of getting out of the car, he yelled across the deserted street to him, "Take your hand out of your coat." The man had turned back toward the car when it stopped, and he had his right hand jammed inside. He did not react to the command. They were frozen for several seconds; then the patrolman repeated his demand. When the man remained silent, the officer drew his pistol, continuing to remain seated in his car. He placed his gun in plain view and again ordered the man to show his hand. The man was very agitated but he remained silent. Slowly he began to extract his hand, but he gave the appearance of concealing some intention which threatened the patrolman, who cocked his gun and pointed it directly at the man. Suddenly the old man drew out his hand and threw a pistol to the ground. He stood trembling. The patrolman uncocked his gun with a shaking hand and approached. He was on the verge of tears, and in a moment of confusion, fear, and anxiety, he struck the man with the butt of his pistol. "Why didn't you take your hand out when I told you? I almost shot you, you dumb bastard." The man protested the treatment he had received, complaining that there was no reason to hit him. He said he had had no intention of using the gun but was carrying it for self-protection. The patrolman recovered from his fright, but despite his regret for striking the man in anger, he refused to acknowledge any responsibility. "Are you wearing a sign? How the fuck am I supposed to know what you're gonna do?"

From a purely technical point of view, the patrolman had initially made an error by failing to close the distance between himself and the suspect, allowing himself no alternative but to leave or use his gun. If he had charged the man immediately upon suspecting him of some misdeed, any passer-by might have "seen" an elderly black man being "assaulted" by a policeman, but the patrolman would have avoided the chance of a much more serious incident. The presumption here is that the policeman was behaving correctly in having suspicions about the man and stopping to make any kind of investigation. Nobody obliged him to stop the man, and if he had continued on his patrol, his superiors and colleagues would not have known. But the patrolman makes these stops because they are his job. He knows colleagues who do not make them, or seldom do so, to avoid moments like the ones he had passed through, but if his morale is high and if he treats his job in a serious way, he has little choice but to exercise the skills he has developed. Whether these stops should be allowed is a political issue. They have tactical value to the police, but the use of suspicion stops as a police tactic cannot be decided from a simple, technical viewpoint but must be made in terms of the political values of the people who pay the police.

The positioning and distance of a patrolman in relation to the person he is seeking to control are absolutely critical. When they are separated by many feet, the chances of the policeman drawing his gun are considerable. But even if he is in close proximity to the suspect, the policeman can still fail unless he positions his body to do what he wants to. He uses his gun infrequently when he is close to a suspect, relying instead on his hand weapons and his physical assets. When he commits himself to this kind of action and fails, he is in serious trouble.

Consider the predicament of the patrolman turning off his fifteenth hydrant on a hot, steamy day. He approached the gushing hydrant, wrench in hand, watching the children splashing and a young man washing his Irish setter. He asked them to stand back, but the man continued to wash his dog, splashing water freely about and entirely ignoring the presence of the officer. He was told again to move, this time forcefully but without insult. The fellow looked up and said, "Fuck you, pig!" In that split second the patrolman committed himself. He lunged in anger, but trying to avoid the water, he arched his body and limited his reach. The fellow leaped back into the middle of the street and taunted the policeman with obscene gestures and remarks. If the policeman gave chase, he might capture him, but the chances were not good. Every time he took a step forward, the fellow sprang back, yelling louder and attracting larger and larger numbers of onlookers. The policeman grew angrier by the moment and was very reluctant to withdraw, although he realized his situation was untenable. He concluded the incident by vowing to "get" the fellow.

The policeman had every intention of settling the "score" with the young man and mentioned him to his sergeant and several colleagues, who urged that he remain away. The policemen did not find the young man, although one night he found them. When they were answering a call at another house, the fellow allegedly dropped a jug of water out of a second-floor window, narrowly missing a patrolman. The officer called an assist, broke into the man's house, and arrested him after an altercation. A number of law suits erupted out of this event, and the fellow moved out of the district.

The policeman's intense concern with position, his ability to see a suspect's hands and to make some judgment about his physical capactiy and inclinations combine to make all car stops potentially explosive moments. A policeman usually stops a car because he thinks that it is stolen, that the occupants are trying to avoid him, or that there has been some kind of traffic violation. He has used his power to stop the car. He can see the driver and the other occupants, but he cannot make any judgments about what they are doing. He cannot see their hands or how big they are, or determine what they might do. All the unknowns he fears are present as he proceeds to investigate.

The patrolman is under orders—often disregarded—not to make suspicious car stops when he is working alone. Each time he makes a car stop, he is supposed to inform his dispatcher and, before getting out of his car, give his location and the color, make, and license number of the car. If he is alone and his stop is on suspicion, he is supposed to await the arrival of a back-up before proceeding. If his suspicion is strong and the stop is made at night, the patrolman tries to blind the driver by shining his spotlight directly onto the car's rear-view mirror. He does not take his eyes off the car once he has signaled the stop. He counts the number of occupants he sees and makes sure that they all remain visible. If he is alone and waiting for another officer, he will stay in his car and order anyone trying to get out to remain seated.

If two men are making a suspicion stop, they use speed and position to overcome the deficiencies in their situation. Both patrolmen emerge quickly, stepping out with one leg so that their bodies do not turn away from the car they are going to approach. The recorder stations himself at the right rear of the car, looking through the back windows to make sure nobody is hiding on the floor or concealing something under the seat. The driver approaches the front of the car and positions himself to maximize his advantage over the occupants. He stands to the rear of the front door and well away from it, to avoide the possibility of someone opening the door and knocking him down. By standing back, he obliges the person to turn around to him, an awkward and uncomfortable position. Policemen are urged to adopt this posture whenever they stop a car, but when a patrolman is issuing a traffic ticket, he finds it difficult to maintain a hostile posture without seeming aggressive. Few policemen walk directly to a car window without first making some judgment about the driver.

There is no way for the policeman completely to settle his anxieties when making a car stop. The people he is seeking to control are right before him; he is close to them, but he cannot get near enough to place them under his physical control. His personal estimate of his own vulnerability greatly increases his tension. Many patrolmen not only unlatch the strap on their holsters before approaching a car but actually pull their guns. At night it is not uncommon to see policemen unholster their guns and conceal them behind a thigh as they approach a suspicious car. There is relatively little the occupants of a car can do to ease the situation. Occasionally people who have considerable experience with the police place their hands on top of the steering wheel to indicate their peaceful intentions. But this does not calm him; rather it tells the officer that he is approaching someone who is cop-wise and his wariness increases.

The policeman's unease does not result from the attitudes of the people but from the constraint of the situation. Even when he sees people who give every appearance of peace, he is unlikely to relax his wariness. Two patrolmen approached a parked car with a running motor. It was very early on a frosty Sunday morning. The white policeman walked directly toward the driver, but his black partner restrained him. "Sleeping like a baby, right? Made a load and can't get home, so he pulls over and parks. Well, you want to check 'em out, see he ain't dead. But before you open the door or knock on the window, look inside first. You gotta make sure the car is in park and the guy don't have a knife in his hand. A lot of these dudes have been rolled so many times they keep an open knife on their lap before they doze off, for protection, you know. That's O.K., you know, but you don't want no surprises when you wake him up. Some of 'em been rolled by guys in blue suits, too, and you can't forget that neither.''

A car stop combines the anxieties of entry into an enclosed space where concealment is possible with the frustrations of being unable to control people who are visible and in some sense publicly available. The policeman must try to balance his need to give a stern and forceful appearance, his "I mean business" manner, with a recognition that most stops turn into nothing, that they are false alarms that can get out of hand if he acts too aggressively or, in his desire to control the people, is insulting. In moments of extreme tension, when the police are mobilized in search of "cop killers" or feel that the department is being beseiged and threatened, some men cast caution to the wind and openly use their guns to control car stops. A faultlessly polite patrolman pointed his revolver directly at a person's head, saying, "Sir, would you please stand out of your car?" But even having a gun ready is not always a guarantee of success.

Two patrolmen stopped a car they knew to be stolen. The plate was listed on the hot sheet and they had checked it with the dispatcher before moving. They were on special patrol in search of some men who the day before had murdered a policeman. Both policemen had their revolvers out as they approached the car, which held two men. The driver had his hands on the steering wheel and was looking back over his shoulder at the advancing officer. According to the patrolman, the fellow smiled and said to him, "Shit, man, you don't need that." He suckered the officer, who hesitated and then holstered his gun. He later claimed that he knew he had made an error the moment he did it. The man dropped his hand and came up with a .45, shooting the policeman twice, while the other man wounded the second officer. The two men were captured a short while later. There is no point in a policeman having his gun out unless he is prepared to shoot someone, and the police cannot be allowed to think of shooting except in defense. Their assailant must be allowed the first move, however slight, but the police have to be able to protect themselves. If they are not allowed to approach people closely, carefully controlling their movements and even violating their bodies, the only way they can make suspicion stops is with their guns unhooked and their sticks ready to hit.

A patrolman with twenty year's experience had recently arrested two robbery suspects on a car stop. He recalled that although he had drawn his gun several times, he had never shot anyone. "I don't know, they were just bad, the way they were acting. The detectives found a gun under the seat. I was real close to them, working alone. I had my gun pointed right at the driver's head. If one of them had bent down, I would have shot him. It would have been too bad for me if it had been a handkerchief under there, but I would have shot him."

The policeman knows that he does not have an unrestricted right to interfere with people's privacy, but his decision to violate their bodies is not made with regard either to their feelings or to their rights. At the police academy the distinctions between a frisk and a search are carefully explained to him, and the limitations of his authority are defined as clearly as the law allows, but his instructors stress that he should not hesitate to frisk anyone if he feels it is necessary.[2] "Any judgment you make is gonna have to be backed up in court, but if you think you should, do it." Body control is treated as a technical issue; considerable time is spent teaching recruits how to efficiently violate the privacy of fellow citizens.

Several recruits at the academy were arbitrarily selected to enact a stop and frisk in class. They were given a situation; first one and then the other played the officer and the suspect. Almost everyone failed. They spoke in muffled tones, asked politely for some identification, and muttered questions about why he was loitering in the alley at so late an hour. "You just gonna stand there and ask him to put his hand in his coat pocket? Hey, boy, you're up an alley, it's dark, and we ain't here," the instructor piped in. Everyone, including a few ex-policemen back for a refresher, failed badly and knew it. How do you frisk someone? How do you not violate him? He's your friend and buddy.

The instructor concealed several guns and knives on a student collaborator and arranged to demonstrate frisking. "O.K., it ain't so easy. Half you guys would be on your ass by now and this guy's gonna play football with your head, remember that. So now, we learn how to frisk." The collaborator and another student were called to the front of the room. Two others were called up to frisk them. "O.K. Put 'em on the wall and frisk 'em down," the black instructor ordered. The recruits mumbled their orders, and without using their hands or stepping in close to the men, they positioned "suspects" on the wall. Both men used their feet to kick at the subjects' legs, spreading them to keep the man off balance. "Hey, wait a minute. Why all this kickin'? Everybody starts kickin' the guy's legs. Why all the rough stuff?" The men finished their frisk and were followed by two other recruits. Throughout the hour nobody found any of the weapons, and each man commenced his frisking by kicking or roughing up his classmate.

The instructor exhibited his mock displeasure (his students rarely find any weapons the first time) and demonstrated a proper frisk on his collaborator. "When you frisk someone, it is for your own protection. You don't have to kick him. You have to put him under your control and frisk him systematically.'' The instructor used his entire body, placing the man in the position he wanted him, feet back and spread wide, every muscle tensed to keep his head, which was far forward, from slipping down and causing him to fall. "You want to stand right in there. Don't be afraid of him. You gonna be afraid when he ain't in this position. Now you got him. Put your leg inside his, and if he moves you can trip him up. If he takes a few bumps, that's resisting. Frisk him systematically. Don't use your fingertips. Use your palms. Start with the palms on his head and work one side of his body and then the other. Look at his hair, and don't be afraid to put your hands in his crotch, it won't bite. And if the guy gives you any shit, why you can give him a little shot to remember you while you're there.''

The instructor showed them the concealed knives and guns and told them, "They were hardly hidden. But you are gonna learn. And listen, the rough stuff is for nothing. It doesn't help you find anything. If you're nervous, the guy out there is gonna know it. He may have more experience at this than you. You give him a chance, he'll take it. Don't talk to him or let him distract you, just frisk him. Then if he don't stand still, you make him, but don't get tough just because you're nervous and don't like the guy's color or looks or whatever.''

After several weeks of practicing and discovering the many places a weapon can be concealed (one student sliced open his finger on a razor blade stuck behind a belt), the students' admiration for their instructor was unbounded and their efficiency at frisking vastly improved. Most of the kicking had disappeared, and the recruits were beginning to use their bodies to place people on the wall and to control them while they were there. But even using loaded guns (with blanks) and switchblades did not create the necessary ingredients to make it all real—fear and anger.

Most frisking is actually done casually and in an offhand manner. When a policeman is working alone, he is reluctant to bend down, which he must do in a full frisk from the rear, and he will forgo it unless he has strong reasons to believe the person is armed. A decision to frisk is also affected by the relative size of the people involved. Few policemen frisk youngsters (unless they are quite large), because an officer assumes that if he gets any trouble from a kid, he can put him down. He contents himself with casually feeling the outer pockets of his jacket and his waist area. But the experienced man does not waste these few motions. He is not delicate in polking his hands about while he is making conversation.

A frisk usually occurs after a stop is made, and the patrolman has made some determination about his initial suspicions, but there are numerous occasions when the frisk and stop occur almost simultaneously.

Two patrolmen were searching an area for suspects in the shooting of a police officer. There was little information about the killers except that they were young. Driving slowly down an almost deserted street, they passed a young man walking in the opposite direction. "Did he turn away? Yeah, let's get him. Shit, I hate backin' up on these dudes," he muttered to his recorder, throwing the car into reverse. He jumped out, ran between two parked cars, grabbed the man, and turned him about. He was frisking his midriff when the man said, "Hey, Hank, what's the matter, man?" The patrolman, surprised at hearing his name, looked up and noticed that he had stopped the brother of a close friend. He stopped the frisk and apologized. They smoked a cigarette, chatted, and parted. He had been so intent on quickly approaching the suspect without losing sight of the man's hands that he did not even look at his face. He was not embarrassed but considered the action an excellent example of how to do his job properly. "He might have been a killer. When you go up on someone like that, you got no business lookin' at his face," he said.

If the policeman has not stopped a person on suspicion or encountered him under circumstances that suggest involvement in disorder on crime, he will not frisk him unless in the course of conversation something is said suggesting violence or resistance. He does not search everyone he meets or everyone he stands next to on a dark street. He is never relaxed in the presence of strangers, and he assumes that his alertness and readiness are sufficient to handle surprises, but if there is a hint of a weapon present, his entire manner changes abruptly.

The patrolmen were interviewing a man who claimed that two acquaintances had robbed him of a thousand dollars. "Wow, that's like a million bucks in this neighborhood. You must be a number writer, pal," one officer said, with a grin. The alleged victim did not think it funny, and the more he talked of his loss, the angrier he became. He was quite vague in giving a description of the robbers, and the patrolmen began to think the man was just another drunk. "I'm gonna kill them motherfuckers!" he mumbled, and in a second one officer had grabbed him by the arm, twisted him about, and started frisking him. From inside the man's overcoat he extracted an ice pick. "I didn't like the way he said 'kill.' You hear that kinda shit all the time, but he really meant it. An ice pick is the worst, too, because there's no hole when you pull it out. All the bleeding is on the inside," he said to his inexperienced partner.

Whenever he is making a suspicion stop, the patrolman conducts some kind of frisk. How he proceeds depends on whether he is working alone or with a partner. If he is alone, he will not bother to back-frisk anyone he thinks has no chance of overpowering him. But if the person appears to be strongly built and willing to "give it a go," he will turn him about, often accompanying his commands with a few threats, but he will not bend down to do a thorough search. Instead he uses his stick to feel the man's legs or, if he has no stick, does not bother to do a complete job. If he bends down, the policeman is vulnerable, and while the man may not hurt him, he has a chance to "make it"; no policeman wants to give anyone the opportunity of involving him in a chase.

When patrolmen work in pairs, their approach alters completely. Two men who work together regularly come to understand each other's attitudes and routines. They divide responsibilities, and each knows what he is going to do when they make a stop or go into a place where there is some kind of trouble. Whether they are stopping one man or five, one officer conducts his interrogation and the frisk, and the other stands back and controls the scene. If they have stopped a group of men, the patrolman does not hesitate to unholster his gun in order to make them more responsive to his commands. Working in pairs, one man can focus his attention on the frisk and does not have to worry about the chances of assault or flight.

Working alone, the patrolman's control of the situation is slight and tenuous. If he is working one to one, only fear prevents the person he has stopped from proceeding. The degree of force the policeman must use to make him obey depends as much on his willingness to appear forceful as it does on the actual use of force. There are many policemen who rarely use force for the simple reason that they appear willing (and possibly are) to do almost anything to subdue resistance. Other patrolmen, who misjudge their power (or like to abuse it), often find themselves in situations where they are risking serious danger for little reward.

A young, aggressive patrolman told of a problem he had encountered when he stopped six men outside a bar. "I had all six on the wall, you know, and I was gonna search the one on the end when one guy said they should rush me. I cocked my gun and nobody moved, and I told him if they came, I'd burn him. What else could I do? I started to frisk the one guy when the guys at the other end started drifting around the corner. I lost two, but I finished the other four." If he had expected solace and comfort from his colleagues, he was disappointed. "Carl, you are a dumb motherfucker. You keep up that crazy shit, you are gonna be in the hospital or dead."

Even if the policeman is careful not to exceed the limits of his capacity to safely control suspects, he cannot focus his attention closely on what he is doing when he frisks someone. Most frisks are done quickly and informally to assure the officer that the suspect does not have anything on him which might be used against the policeman. Patrolmen who fancy themselves specialists in gun pinches frisk people very thoroughly, but they are exceptional. Every time a person is arrested he is usually frisked twice, first by the arresting officer and then by the wagon crew, before he is transported to the station, but weapons are still overlooked, concealed behind belt buckles, in armpits, and even in a folded wallet.

A patrolman recalled a time when he was working plainclothes and was arrested during a raid on a speakeasy. The police missed the small revolver he had stuck behind his belt buckle. "I was sittin' on the bench in the station, waitin', you know, to tell 'em who I was when we was in private, but I was worried if they noticed the gun they'd kick the shit outta me. So I called a cop over and real quiet I told him I was still carryin'. He almost shit." On another occasion, a young man was sitting in a station, handcuffed, waiting for some detectives to come for him. He acted quite nervous, kept looking about and fidgeting. Finally a patrolman approached and told him to keep quiet. He apologized and said he was very nervous because he had a gun in his pocket that the policeman had not taken from him. The patrolman seized him by the lapels, twisted him about as he raised him from the bench, and grabbed the gun.

Frisking is much more common in some parts of the city than in others, and it is not an activity engaged in exclusively by the police. There are bars and restaurants where regular patrons "bump" into strangers, checking whether or not they are armed. Prostitutes who work out of bars frequently seek to protect themselves from entrapments by plainclothesmen by holding hands and pretending affection for a potential client while actually checking to see if the man's hands match what he claims to do for a living and if he is carrying a small gun or a jack somewhere about his middle. These people frisk for protection, as a policeman does. An officer is forbidden by regulation to frisk a woman except in an extreme emergency; he must turn her over to a matron or a policewoman. Undoubtedly the number of complaints against the police would increase if this restriction were lifted, but so, too, would the number of stops and arrests. There are many reasons why a policeman does not look with suspicion on women in public places (except in areas where prostitutes work), but one of them certainly is his inability to protect himself. Not only can he not frisk a woman, a policeman is reluctant to hit a woman, and even when he has justification (from his point of view), he recalls doing so with regret and chagrin.

Although a policeman views frisking as a defensive act devoid of personal comment, those he stops cannot help but feel angered by their powerlessness, if for no other reason. Regardless of how the policeman behaves or what he says, he is compelling the person to submit to him and to turn his body over for examination. Younger men in some parts of the city are so familiar with the routine that when they are hailed by the police, they stop and spread their arms to the side before the officer has asked a question or even approached. They understand that this signal of submission will gain them more gentle and circumspect treatment. Sometimes a patrolman runs his hands absentmindedly over a man's pockets while engaging in conversation, not really meaning to frisk him but just letting him know that he is in control, that for the moment the man belongs to the patrolman. It is not a consciously hostile or aggressive act. It is an expression of the policeman's belief that regardless of the momentary tone of the interaction, his place in that relationship is supported ultimately by his personal will and readiness to exercise all of the authority invested in him. There is no way he can make this point without causing discontent, because the authority given to him can be exercised only by restraining the liberty of some persons and violating their autonomy. A policeman does not enjoy frisking people. During a busy tour he may wash up several times because many of the people he stops are filthy. He constantly grumbles about the dirt and the odors, but they do not cause him to keep his distance or to avoid intimate contact. He knows that when he is on the street, it is only his readiness to demonstrate his power that maintains the edge necessary for him to do his work and come home safely each day.

[1] "A 26-year-old man armed with a Luger pistol and a rifle disarmed three policemen early today and held them at bay for nearly two hours.... The man finally gave up his weapons and surrendered after having a cup of coffee with two of the policemen. The drama started when police received a report of a 'disturbance.'...The first officer to respond was Policeman Robert Patrick...who said he saw Hansen standing at the front door, his back toward the street. 'Did you call, sir?' Patrick asked. Hansen turned around and according to Patrick, "The next thing I knew I had a rifle to my head.'" *Philadelphia Daily News,* July 27, 1971 (footnotes renumbered—eds.).

[2] A policeman may examine the outer clothing of any person he stops on suspicion if he feels the person means him harm or may be concealing a weapon. If he feels anything that might be a weapon, he may go into the person's clothing and extract the object for examination. If in the course of the frisk he discovers any contraband or evidence implicating the person in some crime, it is not considered to be legally seized since the policeman has conducted what amounts to a search without reasonable grounds. The distinctions between stop and frisk are discussed in Lawrence P. Tiffany, Donald M. McIntyre, Jr., and Daniel L. Rotenberg, *Detection of Crime* (Boston: Little, Brown, 1967), pp. 44-57. The general issue is still under intense legal review, and the recent Supreme Court and federal court decisions will be amended and refined in upcoming cases. The most recent decisions are *Terry vs. Ohio.* 88 S. Ct. 1868 (1968); *Sibron vs. New York.* 88 S. Ct. 1889 (1968); *United States vs. McMann,* 370 F.2d 757 (2d Cir. 1967). The stop-and-frisk authority of the police in a number of other countries is discussed in Sowle, *Police Power and Individual Freedom.* In no country do the police appear to have less formal power than they do in America, although the actual practices may differ. A cursory discussion of police frisking in London and the negative response of people is in Peter Laurie, *Scotland Yard* (London: Bodley Head, 1970), pp. 62-65.

7

Becoming Bent:
Moral Careers of Corrupt Policemen

Lawrence W. Sherman

> *I came finally to understand what corruption is and
> how it gets a man...rogues outside, but inside,
> honest men.*
>
> Lincoln Steffens
>
> *Even a bent policeman has a conscience.*
>
> Frank Williamson, Q.P.M.
> *H.M. Inspector of Constabular (retired)*

My task here is to describe the process by which policemen become
corrupt in two specific ways: how they come to accept bribes, and how they
come to commit burglary. The central argument of this paper is that police
grafters and burglars only "get that way" through a painful process of
choices, and not because they are pathological "rotten apples." Though
which choices will be taken cannot be predicted, the process should become
clearer through a picture of how the choices are presented to policemen. As
we rely totally on the available literature, we are unfortunately long on
concepts and short on data.

Reprinted by permission of the author from *Police Corruption: A Sociological Perspective.*

Data on the general moral careers of policemen is provided by Westley (1970), Wambaugh (1970), and Niederhoffer (1969), but they make little specific mention of corruption. Maas (1973) describes the moral career of an honest policeman, Frank Serpico. But with one exception, the life histories of *corrupt* policemen have been compiled exclusively by journalists. Steffens (1931) describes the moral career of a nineteenth-century New York policeman, Max Schmittberger, an extraordinary grafter who turned straight and became chief of police. Wittels (1949) describes a grafter's career in an eastern U.S. police department from 1930 to 1948. Stern (1962) and Smith (1965) interviewed policemen involved in the 1961 burglary scandal in Denver. Stoddard (1968), the lone social scientist, interviewed a convicted police burglar from another midwestern city.

The concepts used to explain police corruption in the past have relied upon *affinity* and *affiliation,* in Matza's (1969) terms. Vollmer (1936), Tappan (1960), and Sutherland and Cressey (1960) all stress that police recruitment attracts men who are predisposed to corruption, since they already have an *affinity* for deviance. Attacking that view, Stoddard (1968) (and Wilson, 1963) stresses the *affiliation* of the honest police recruit with a dishonest police subculture. Nowhere has the *signification*, or labeling, processes in police corruption been explicitly discussed.

This paper will ignore the affinity argument, since much data and experience suggest police recruits have a conception of police work as honest at the time they apply (see also McNamara, 1966). The focus will be on the process of affiliation with other policemen, and with other corrupt policemen, and with the way a corrupt policeman signifies, or defines, his behavior in relation to himself and others. For that, we shall look to those Matza (1969) calls the neo-Chicagoans.

The Concepts of a Moral Career

Howard Becker, Erving Goffman, and William Westley were all graduate students together at the University of Chicago's Department of Sociology, thirty years after the heyday of the Chicago School. Thus, it is not surprising that they have all reformulated the early Chicago work on deviant careers in a similar fashion. The crucial difference between their work and such studies as Shaw's (1930) *Jack Roller,* is that Shaw et al. looked for careers *of deviants* from a correctional view-point, whereas the neo-Chicagoans look for careers *in diviance* from an appreciative stand-point. They have disentangled, though not very carefully, the *moral* career from the *occupational* career.[2]

Goffman (1961) defines career in a broad sense of "any social strand of any person's course through life" and a *moral* career as the "regular sequence of changes...in the person's self and in his framework of imagery for judging himself and others." Thus, the moral career is influenced by the occupational career, but does not *depend* on it; a businessman may begin to smoke pot and stop after intense usage while his business career progresses without interruption. Or a businessman may gradually compromise his ethics and enter into restraint of trade, then find his occupational career ended in prison. Moral careers and occupational careers *may* converge, but they do not *have* to.

The fundamental notion in a moral career is that of social process. Compare Becker's discussion of Mead's concepts with Steffens' similar discussion of Captain Schmittberger's life:

> George Herbert Mead...tells us that the reality of social life is a conversation of significant symbols, in the course of which people make tentative moves and then adjust and reorient their activity in the light of responses (real and imagined) others make to those moves. The formation of the individual act is a *process* in which conduct is continually reshaped to take account of the expectations of others, as these are expressed in the immediate situation and as the actor supposes they may come to be expressed. [Becker, 1966, italics added.]

> The *process* of corruption had begun so quietly with that first tip and proceeded so gradually in an environment where it was all a matter of course that [Schmittberger] never realized what he was doing till the Lexow Committee's exposure...exposed him to himself. "I didn't know how it looked...till I saw the other Lexow witnesses telling things." [Steffens, 1931, italics added.]

And as both Becker and Steffens suggest, the process of a moral career involves different *stages* of becoming bent. Goffman (1961) builds on that framework with the notions of moral career *contingencies, moral experiences,* and an equilibrium career stage of *apologia. Contingencies* are circumstances or problems which a person must face, often for purely accidental reasons. The *moral experience* is a reaction to contingencies, often involving an ethical decision of action, that alters the "framework of imagery" in which a person evaluates himself and others. The moral experience is a benchmark between the *stages* in a moral career, which usually culminate (for the deviant) in an *apologia*: a distorted image of one's life course that brings it into alignment with the basic values of his society (Goffman, 1961, pp. 139-40).

Thus, the moral career is a process of self-labeling that takes place, for the policeman, within a context of affiliation. As Matza (1969) notes, affiliation with a deviant group does not preordain deviance, it only invites it: but the invitation may be quite strong. Westley (1970) describes four strong mechanisms of group social control which affect a man who becomes affiliated as a policeman: expediency, categorical reactions, sanctions, and personal integrity.

Expediency is simply the path of least resistance to finding definitions of complex situations: following the prescriptions of older policemen and adopting the rules of the group. Categorical reaction is the policeman's discovery that he has been socially stereotyped: society has labeled him with the reputation engendered by the actions of all other policemen. (As a "cop" he is just as categorically defined as a "con" or a "nigger.") The sanctions most often used against policemen violating group norms are the refusal to share information and the refusal to work with the wayward officer. The maintenance of personal integrity (self-esteem) in the face of a conflict between police group values and those of the larger society creates a pressure to break with one or the other value-sets; for the man who accepts the invitation to police affiliation, he must largely break with, or redefine, societal values. Goffman's apologia is a means of excusing that break, but Westley (1970) notes that a policeman's value conflict is never wholly resolved (see also Chwast, 1965).

Both Goffman's subjective view of the moral career and Westley's objective view of the forces that shape it may easily be misread as determinism, but they did not mean that. As Cohen (1955) notes, behavior is determined both by the facts of the situation (Goffman's contingencies) *and* by the individual's frame of reference for interpreting those facts: "the interests, preconceptions, stereotypes and values [he brings] to the situation" (p. 53). Cohen also notes that in order to deal effectively with many situations, the frame of reference, or values, of the individual must change. But that does not explain why one solution to a situation (one outcome of Goffman's moral experience) is chosen rather than another: "Different individuals *do* deal differently with the same or similar problems and these differences must likewise be accounted for" (Cohen, 1955, p. 55).

We cannot account for those individual differences with the available data. All we can do here is follow the careers of a few policemen to extreme forms of corruption while stressing that many other policemen drop out along the way. The interrelatedness of moral decisions about corruption to home life, sexual relationships, and other nonoccupational factors may be glimpsed in Chinua Achebe's novel, *No Longer at Ease* (1960).[3] But with the available data we can only focus on the situational contingencies and the changes in frame of reference which result from dealing with such decisions, without fully understanding the frame of reference the individuals *initially* brought to the situation.

A final note on the situations of these moral careers is that there are wide differences in the values of police subcultures and opportunities for police corruption. Thus, each moral career described and analyzed below will be prefaced by a description of its organizational context.

Becoming a Policeman

The most important context for police moral careers, both in terms of situation and frame of reference, is of course the fact that the individual has become a policeman. Perhaps a key contingency in a policeman's moral careers is the system of appointment he must deal with. Wittels (1949) describes the great disillusionment of a young police applicant when he was visited by the ward (political) boss and told his application stood no chance without a six-hundred-dollar "contribution" to the party and the reregistration of his entire family to the "right" party. Few cities maintain such a system today, but Royko (1971) suggests it may persist in Chicago.

Recruit school, when there is one—and in half of our cases there was not—is usually an experience of great idealism and anticipation of an exciting career. Westley (1970) describes the recruit school as a *rite de passage* which detaches a man from his old experience and prepares him for the new by teaching the rough outlines of the job as it appears on the books (p. 156). But Niederhoffer (1969) describes the New York recruit school's "unrealistic" stress on ethics and professionalism as the first source of cynicism about the job.

Both Westley and Niederhoffer agree that contact with older police officers in the first day on duty teaches the recruit that the formal rules are largely a sham—a situation which is true for virtually all police departments and many bureaucracies (see Gouldner, 1954). From the older officers, the recruit learns what the *real* rules of the police subculture are, often in apocryphal form. While these rules vary widely, one universal rule of police departments is secrecy and not reporting the misdeeds of brother officers (Westley, 1970; Vollmer, 1930).

Though taking on this new peer definition of police work is something of a reality shock, more traumatic is the first contact with hostility from the public. As he begins to take responsibility for his actions, the rookie becomes emotionally involved in maintaining respect for his authority. From bitter experience, he sees that his lot is with other policemen, and that nonpolicemen are enemies. As Westley notes, "The rookie has then become a cop, and the group has gained a new member."

Thus, *allowing for individual differences,* the process of becoming a policeman is one of facing a set of contingencies that produce moral experiences which change a man's frame of reference. With his new uniform and group membership, he feels society has labeled him an "outsider"—and he in turn labels nonpolicemen as outsiders (Becker, 1963). As Becker's dance musicians hate "squares," so policemen hate "civilians." Since not very long ago the police recruit was a civilian himself, he has undergone a radical redefinition of self in a very short time. That change is even reflected in his life outside the job, which often relies exclusively on other police families for social contact.

Becoming a Grafter

While the process of becoming a policeman is fairly universal to police work, the process of becoming a grafter is not. The key contingency for entering a moral career of grafting—i.e., accepting bribes—is the extent to which grafting already occurs in the work group the rookie is assigned to. This is not the place to explain why grafting subcultures arise in some police departments and not others, but we should again note that there are wide differences in the phenomena. Our two case studies of grafters both took place within a context of well-organized police graft, run by a corrupt political machine. The first is Max Schmittberger of the nineteenth century New York police, as told by Steffans (1931). The second is "Gus Blawker," a composite character of policemen known by Wittles (1949) between 1930 and 1949. Summaries of their cases follow:

Case No. 1.

Max Schmittberger was a tall, handsome, but naive baker's apprentice in the 1880s when some Tammany (political) leaders offered to get this fine specimen on the police force—free! Without understanding, Max joined up and was soon directing traffic on Broadway. Since he pleased his superiors, he was transferred to the "fat" Tenderloin precinct, the major vice market of New York.

One night a brothel owner pressed ten dollars in his hand. Confused, he presented it to his captain. Angered by Max's honesty, the captain explained graft to him and began to assign him to posts more and more crucial to the graft system. He moved from liaison with the hack thieves to regulation of the brothels, finally to be promoted to the job of "bagman"—collecting twenty thousand dollars a month for the captain.

When the Lexow investigation began (1894), he was jarred back to honesty. As the star witness, he told the commission all of the details of the graft system. Though punished by his peers for years after, the forces of reform eventually had him appointed chief of police.

Case No. 2.

Gus Blawker had an idealistic conception of police work in 1930 when the ward boss told him the conditions of appointment to the force. Disillusioned, but desperately needing a job, he borrowed the necessary money.

In the first days on the beat, he witnessed the vice squad shake down a speakeasy that had skipped a payment. His attempts to arrest politically influential men for traffic violations were severely reprimanded, and he was assigned to a boring suburban beat.

Through luck he made a much publicized arrest of a famous robber, for which he was promoted to detective. But his zeal in raiding a protected gambling house was rewarded with demotion to his old beat.

When his son needed an expensive operation, he appealed to the ward leader for a promotion with a promise to "play the game." As head of a detective squad, he took no graft until the machine required him to fix an important case. When his payoff arrived, he stared at the envelope for an hour before taking out the money. When his son needed another operation, he shook down a gambling joint.

From that point on he collected regularly from gamblers. The next step was to shake down brothels and then drug pushers. When he was arrested ten years later, he was rich enough to fix the case against him and retire in luxury.

Though Blawker's experience is probably more representative than Schmittberger's, we may derive similar conclusions from both. Most important is the process of increased involvement by which they became grafters. That is, they became more accustomed to taking graft as the graft organization tested them with first petty graft, then graft for allowing more serious offenses. Most people would agree that drug pushing is a more serious crime than gambling; we may assume that neither Gus Blawker's morality (self-definition) nor the policies of the graft organization would let him begin his grafting career with drug pushers. Rather, he worked up a ladder of increasing self-perceived social harm of offenses, neutralizing any moral objection to the (crime-specific) graft at each rung of the ladder—each stage of his moral career. The same seemed to happen with Schmittberger.

If we generalize these cases to all possible sources of graft, we may hypothesize a continuum of graft stages which follows a policeman's initial frame of reference about the social harm of each source of graft. The first stage is police "perks"—free coffee and meals from restaurants on his beat. The moral experience about accepting these perks usually occurs in the recruit's first days on duty, and the peer pressure to accept them is great. If he does accept the minor perks, he then has a different image of self to contend with when a bar owner operating after closing hours offers him a drink. Again a moral experience; a decision to accept the drink and let the place stay open redefines the policeman's self, if only slightly.

The third step in the grafting career may be another regulative bribe—a motorist handing him a driver's license with a five-dollar bill in it or a construction foreman giving him ten dollars to overlook materials left illegally on the sidewalk. He may either accept or reject the bribe, but acceptance is made easier if he is used to taking gifts from restaurants and bars.

If there are regular payoffs made by a local gambling operation, and if the rookie has passed the tests of accepting minor graft, the other policemen receiving the gambling payoffs may offer to cut him in. This moral experience is particularly difficult, because it is an invitation to solidarity with his, by now, *only* "significant others," an invitation he is loath to reject. Indeed, policemen I knew in New York who rejected the offer soon transferred out of the work unit to graft-free "inside" jobs. But most New York policemen seem to accept the offer (Knapp, 1972).

The fifth step in a grafting career may be prostitutes' bribes, either from pimps, lone streetwalkers, or more regularly, brothel operators. The relationships established in prostitution graft can lead easily into narcotics graft, since drug traffic is often closely linked with prostitution (Knapp, 1972). Accepting narcotics graft, however, is the most difficult moral experience of all, since the initial frame of reference of most policemen would abhor the thought of helping drug pushers. If that graft is accepted, though, it is not unknown for policemen to go on to selling drugs themselves.

To summarize the hypothetical stages of the moral career of a grafter:

1. Minor "perks"
2. Bar closing hours
3. Regulative crimes (traffic, construction)
4. Gambling
5. Prostitution
6. Narcotics

Again, the hypothesis is only that this career will be followed when situational contingencies make it available and then *only if the policeman accepts the invitation to bribery.* Even when all of the graft sources are available, a policeman may stop at a middle rung of his self-perceived ladder of social harm. The stage at which he stops can become a key element in his apologia: "I might take money from gamblers, and whores, 'cause they don't hurt anybody—but I won't mess around with pushers!" Put another way: "I might be bad, but I'm not *that* bad."

Stoddard (1968) suggests that most policemen stop at a certain stage of deviance on the basis of group definition of "limits." An English police official told me that Manchester constables in the 1930s might brag about bribes from pub owners and gamblers, but they would never mention bribes from prostitutes. Cook (1971) notes that the 1950s clean graft (gamblers, prostitutes) and dirty graft (drugs) in the New York police (that gradually disappeared during the 1960s).

Assuming there are group limits to bribery, some policemen go beyond them. A characteristic of deviance from group bribery norms is the switch from pure bribery to extortion, or from "reactive" to proactive" graft (Reiss, 1971). The Knapp Commission has labeled the two kinds of grafters as "grass-eaters" (reactive) and "meat-eaters" (proactive). One possible explanation of the shift from grass to meat is that of secondary deviance (Lemert, 1967). In this case, the agent defining the individual as deviant is the individual himself, without the intervention of (another) agent of social control. Assuming the initial frame of reference of the grafter was morally opposed to graft, one of the moral experiences may be so severe that, if resulting in a decision for more graft, it may produce a "What the hell, I'm a crook, so I'll make the most of it" reaction. Subsequent career stages will then become proactive. Blawker, on the day that he received "the envelope," sought out a friend in tears and got very drunk. From then on he was a proactive grafter.

Individual differences in the initial frame of reference are important, since the switch from reactive to proactive graft does not occur at any particular stage of the grafting career. Policemen in vice-ridden Harlem have progressed to the extreme stages of grafting on an entirely reactive basis (virtually just standing on the corners and holding out their hands). Those more given to personality explanations of crime would of course suggest that individual differences are paramount: some policemen join the force with an entrepreneurial affinity for proactive graft. But the data available so far suggest that secondary deviation is a more likely explanation.

One final contingency in the moral career of a grafter should be checked in future case study research. Both Schmittberger and Blawker (as well as the burglars described below) experienced a negative social reaction in their work group to acts of honesty or honest enforcement. This moral experience tends to occur early in the police career, and it clearly redefines the self in terms of perceived definitions of being a policeman. Future research should examine the extent to which such an experience is a necessary element in a grafting career.

Becoming a Burglar

If individual differences and choice was important to stress in the moral careers of the grafter, it is an even more important caveat in the moral career of the police burglar. And as important as different individual frames or reference are the differences in situational contingencies.

Police burglary is not nearly as persistent a phenomenon as police graft. This is not the place to explain differences in the extent of burglary (see Wilson, 1963), but we should note that there was (1) a series of police burglary scandals all over the United States in the early 1960s, with few reports of it since, and (2) a police burglary group discovered in London in the mid-1960s, with no reports of it since.

Cook (1966), reviewing the 1961 Denver scandal, suggests a pattern that fits Cohen's (1955) description of the evolution of deviant subcultures. To restate Cook's analysis in Cohen's terms, policemen collectively face a status problem that can best be solved by acquiring more money. Many alternative means of supplementing a salary are available, but an easy route is to pick up "lying around" loot at the scene of a burglary. "Exploratory gestures" among the policemen are made at the scene of a burglary, and some goods or money is also pocketed. Further gestures (suggestions) are made, and if well received, a burglary is planned. A successful burglary makes the idea more attractive to other policemen who are invited to join in. In Denver, when a transfer program inadvertently broke up the initial burglary subculture, its members spread the innovation to other patrol districts—making the exploratory gestures that established new subcultures.

Seen in this context, we may summarize the moral careers of two police burglars: the first from Denver, interviewed by Smith (1965), the second from another midwestern city, interviewed by Stoddard (1968).

Case No. 3.

> Patrolman Hastings joined the Denver police to be an "eager beaver" cop, but discovered two policemen committing a burglary while he was still a probationary patrolman. Keeping his mouth shut, he stayed with honest, good police work.
>
> His slated promotion to detective fell through when he arrested a politically influential man, who was immediately let off by the court.
>
> Disillusioned, he agreed to his partner's suggestion one night to pick up "lying around" loot at the scene of a burglary, and his sergeant later took a cut of the loot.
>
> A few nights later, they were called to a fur warehouse burglary, which turned out to be an insurance fraud done by the owner. The lieutenant's presence and the owner's offer of a free mink stole induced Hastings to "go along."
>
> From then on he committed burglary on a regular basis, often at the request of insurance swindling businessmen.

Case No. 4.

> Patrolman Smith began his police career with free meals at Sam Paisano's restaurant and immediately learned that Paisano was virtually immune from any kind of protection.
>
> While still a rookie, he observed his partner steal candy bars from a supermarket. Refusing to share the loot, he was advised he should "go along" or face the consequence—social isolation.

When he did pass his "test," he joined in on picking up "lying around" loot. Eventually, his group began planning burlaries. When he was finally caught, he was surprised how alone he was, and he realized that "lying around" loot was the limit of theft by police standards; planned burglary was deviant.

A key contingency in Hastings' moral career was that he entered a police subculture of planned burglary and was invited to join it. In Smith's case, he was invited to join a subculture of "shopping" (picking up lying-around loot) and participated in the evolution of a subculture that exceeded the general group limits of theft. In both cases, they learned, while still rookies, that certain people had immunity from arrest and that other policemen committed criminal acts.

Whether a policeman joins an external burglary subculture or helps to form one, the case studies suggest the following stages in the moral career of the police burglar:

1. Learning the fallacy of impartial enforcement of the law
2. Learning that other policemen are dishonest
3. Picking up lying-around loot at the scene of a burglary ("shopping")
4. Joining in a planned burglary
5. Committing planned burglary on a regular basis

Evidence from the original case studies suggest that, just as in graft, the progression to each new stage in a burglary career depends upon a change in the frame of reference that allows a consistency with basic societal values. After the Denver scandal, several police burglars stressed in public interviews that "only the big chains and insurance companies, institutions that could afford it, had been hurt." And in Smith's case, where the peer influence had been stronger than rationalizations about insurance companies, his apologia was a perception of more policemen involved in planned burglary than was in fact the case. The societal value he used for justification of burglary was solidarity with his brother officers.

Again, individual differences are important. Some policemen may refuse even to "shop"; others may shop without ever planning a burlary; still others might pull off one planned burglary and then turn honest. As in the switch from reactive to proactive grafting, the switch from occational to regular planned burglary may possibly be explained as *secondary* deviation. Whatever the individuals moral experiences are, however, any progression is along the sequence of stages outlined here.

Social Policy Implications

The central argument of this paper is, again, that police burglars and grafters become deviant only through a gradual process of confronting contingencies and making moral decisions. The social policy implications of that argument are clear for police graft, and not so clear for police burglary.

All of the contingencies of a grafter's moral career involve nonenforcement of what Schur (1965) calls "victimless crimes." Thus, police graft could be ended tomorrow if legislatures enacted Norval Morris's dictum (1970) that "everyone has a right to go to hell any way they please." But since modern Western society is ambiguous about that dictim, and clearly opposed to it in the area of opiate selling, this paper implies a less radical solution as well.

If a moral career must be a *gradual* process of redefining one's self to accept ever more serious deviance (as defined by the intial frame of reference), then grafting might be inhibited by making the process less gradual. If the graft steps from perks, to gambling, to prostitution, then to drugs, are small, a single step from perks to drugs is quite large. If gambling and prostitution were legalized, the narcotics pusher would not face policemen accustomed to taking large bribes; the moral experience of a policeman offered a large narcotics bribe would tend to decide against acceptance, since it would require too great a redefinition of self all at once. Thus, a society concerned with police *narcotics* graft is well advised to legalize gambling and prostitution.

Police burglary, a phenomenon we know much less about, seems to be an extension of the basic business ethics of American society: theft from large institutions doesn't hurt anybody in particular, so it's all right. Smigel (1956) found this attitude to exist generally in one American town, and Steffens (1931) suggests it permeates American business. Even though the police and the wider society seem to come to this value judgment gradually, the key question is what contingencies shape the formation of such attitudes. The "neo-Chicagoan" approach would seem to lose its explanatory power here, for what is at stake is no less than a critique of Western society. For that, one should turn to the macro-level concerns of a critical sociology, perhaps analyzing theft in terms of such basic institutions as private property itself (Birnbaum, 1972).

Notes

[1] Paper presented to the National Deviancy Conference, University of York, England, April 15, 1973.

[2] I am indebted to John Gagnon for this point.

[3] See also Colin McInnes, *Mr. Love and Justice* (London: MacGibbon and Kee, 1960) for the moral careers of both a policeman and a pimp, in novel form.

References

Becker, Howard L. (1963). *Outsiders.* Glencoe, Ill.: Free Press.

——— (1966). Introduction to Shaw, Clifford, *The Jack Roller.* Chicago: University of Chicago Press.

Birnbaum, Norman (1972). *Toward a Critical Sociology.* New York: Oxford University Press.

Chwast, Jacob (1965). "Value Conflicts in Law Enforcement." *Crime and Delinquency,* 11.

Cohen, Albert K. (1955). *Delinquent Boys: The Culture of the Gang.* New York: Free Press.

Cook, Fred J. (1966). *The Corrupted Land.* London: Jonathan Cape, 1967.

——— (1971). "The Pusher Cop: The Institutionalization of Police Corruption." *New York,* August 16, 1971.

Goffman, Erving (1961). *Asylums.* Garden City, N.Y.: Anchor Books.

Gouldner, Alvin (1954). *Patterns of Industrial Bureaucracy.* New York: Free Press.

Knapp, Whitman, et al. (1972). *Report of the Commission to Investigate Alleged Police Corruption* (City of New York). New York: George Braziller.

Lemert, Edwin (1967). *Human Deviance, Social Problems, and Social Control.* Englewood Cliffs, N.J.: Prentice-Hall, Inc.

Maas, Peter (1973). *Serpico.* New York: The Viking Press, Inc.

McNamara, John H. (1966). "Uncertainties in Police Work: The Relevance of Police Recruits' Background and Training." In *The Police,* edited by David J. Bordua. New York: John Wiley & Sons, Inc.

Matza, David (1969). *Becoming Deviant.* Englewood Cliffs, N.J.: Prentice-Hall, Inc.

Morris, Norval, and Hawkins, Gordon (1970). *The Honest Politicians Guide to Crime Control.* Chicago: University of Chicago Press.

Niederhoffer, Arthur (1969). *Behind the Shield: The Police in Urban Society.* Garden City, N.Y.: Anchor Books.

Reiss, Albert J., Jr. (1971). *The Police and the Public.* New Haven, Conn.: Yale University Press.

Royko, Mike (1971). *Boss.* London: Paladin, 1972.

Schur, Edwin (1965). *Crimes Without Victims.* Englewood Cliffs, N.J.: Prentice-Hall, Inc.

Shaw, Clifford (1939). *The Jack Roller.* Chicago: University of Chicago Press.

Smigel, Erwin (1956). "Public Attitudes Towards Stealing as Related to the Size of the Victim Organization." *American Sociological Review,* 21.

Smith, Ralph L. (1965). *The Tarnished Badge.* New York: T.Y. Crowell.

Steffens, Lincoln (1931). *The Autobiography of Lincoln Steffens.* New York: Harcourt, Brace.

Stern, Mort (1962). "What Makes a Policeman Go Wrong?" *Journal of Criminal Law, Criminology and Police Science* 53.

Stoddard, Ellwyn R. (1968). "'The Informal Code' of Police Deviancy: A Group Approach to 'Blue-coat Crime.'" *Journal of Criminal Law, Criminology and Police Science* 59, no. 2.

Sutherland, Edwin H. and Cressey, Donald R. (1960). *Principles of Criminology.* Philadelphia: J.B. Lippincott Company.

Tappan, Paul (1960). *Crime, Justice and Correction.* New York: McGraw-Hill, Inc.

Vollmer, August (1936). *The Police and Modern Society.* Berkeley, Calif.: University of California Press.

——— (1930). To the U.S. National Committee of Law Observance and Enforcement. *Report on the Police.* Washington, D.C.: U.S. Government Printing Office.

Wambaugh, Joseph (1970). *The New Centurions.* New York: Dell Books.

Westley, William (1970). *Violence and the Police.* Cambridge, Mass.: Massachusetts Institute of Technology Press.

Wilson, James Q. (1963). "The Police and Their Problems: A Theory." *Public Policy.*

Wittels, David J. (1949). "Why Cops Turn Crooked." *Saturday Evening Post,* April 23, 1949.

Section III

Confrontation and Compromise: The Courts

The criminal courts are steeped in myth and surrounded by controversy. Myths abound because many citizens have ignored their rights and neglected their duties in regard to the courts. Ignored has been the right of access, recognized in the U.S. Constitution, which extends to each citizen the opportunity to observe the criminal process in open court. Neglected has been the duty to participate in and contribute to a more efficient and effective court system through service on grand and petit juries. The notice to appear for jury duty often results in the development of a host of excuses why one cannot serve. Without first hand experiences then, we should not be surprised that most Americans have relied on the media for information about the court process. For the most part, contributions made by movies, television and popular novels have not been positive and constructive in that reality is often distorted. Although "Perry Mason" and "Kaz" have entertained us, they have deceived us as well.

We have been led to believe that the criminal trial is a frequent and highly dramatic event which takes place in an emotion-filled courtroom packed by spectators and the press. We are surprised when we learn that most cases do not go to trial. Courtrooms are often empty or are utilized by a very few individuals engaged in the tedious business that makes up everyday reality for judges and lawyers. Contrary to popular conception most cases are plea bargained, a somewhat complex process through which a charge against the defendant is reduced in exchange for a plea of guilty thereby avoiding a costly and time consuming trial. Nothing in our media experience has prepared us for the attorney who is incompetent or so terribly disinterested in a case that justice is denied. The wise and dispassionate judge we see on television cannot always be found in the courtroom. Sometimes the judge we observe seems to be ignorant and prejudiced. Finally, we often overlook the fact that it is the prosecutor who ultimately determines what will happen in a criminal proceeding. It is the prosecutor who establishes the actual charges the defendant must respond to. It is the prosecutor who accepts or rejects a plea bargain and decides whether a case will go to trial.

Given the gravity of the tasks performed by the criminal courts, we should not be surprised that court operations are surrounded by controversy. Our courts function in an adversary setting and are subjected to intense and conflicting pressures. The need to protect individual rights often appears to collide with society's legitimate demand for protection. The volume of litigation has increased considerably over the past ten years and persons accused of crimes have an increased number of rights. The result is delay in the court process and crowded dockets which judges must eventually clear while providing both the substance and appearance of justice. Because many citizens are suspicious of the courts, there is an unwillingness to invest the needed financial allocations in this aspect of the criminal justice system. Courts have enjoyed autonomy for many years. They have been ignored and in their isolation have developed a host of problems which defy simple solutions. In the following section a number of these problems have been addressed.

In "The Behavior of Grand Juries," Robert Carp focuses on what is perhaps the most frequently misunderstood aspect of the judicial process. The grand jury, once thought to be a guardian of individual rights, is now under attack and is considered by some to be the tool of conviction-oriented prosecutors. The grand jury faces an uncertain future in some jurisdictions. An evaluation of the grand jury and its role as an investigative tool rather than a due-process safeguard seems likely.

Marvin Frankel's article, "Individualized Judges," focuses on the sentencing decision. Frankel, himself a federal judge, has outlined a number of problems judges must be prepared to confront in the sentencing process. Judge Frankel reminds us that his colleagues have been given enormous discretion and are then expected to function in accord with images of fairness and justice. The fact that judges often act in accord with their unique predispositions, prejudices and idiosyncracies shocks us. We have ignored the fact that judges are human first and jurists second.

In "The Practice of Law as a Con Game," Abraham Blumberg focuses on the role of the defense attorney. Blumberg contends that the image of an aggressive defense attorney fighting for the protection of his or her client's rights is a myth. The defense attorney is very much a part of the informal court organization. As a result he or she tends to be cooperative with the prosecutor. By contributing to the negotiated plea both parties benefit — the defense attorney receives a fee for very little work and the prosecutor avoids an expensive trial. The right to counsel established by the United States Supreme Court becomes meaningless as a result of these informal relationships.

Donald Newman addresses a related issue in his article "Plea Bargaining." Plea bargaining is central to the operation of our criminal courts. It is the final plea bargain agreed upon by the prosecutor and the defense attorney that will determine the sentence, a fact often ignored by those who focus solely on the judiciary in studying the sentencing process. In the final article in this section, Franklin Zimring examines problems in "Making the Punishment Fit the Crime." Zimring touches on a number of issues involved in the sentencing process as well as problems which have been ignored in the trend toward determinate sentencing. Barriers to sentencing reform identified by Zimring have been ignored by a number of reform advocates who have failed in their efforts.

8

The Behavior of Grand Juries

Robert A. Carp

For several decades students of the judicial process have had measured success in parting the veil of secrecy which surrounds the deliberations and internal dynamics of American trial juries. The classic study of Kalven and Zeisel of jury behavior in Chicago[1] and other related projects[2] have provided keen insights into the types of psychological, institutional, and sociological variables which influence the "output" of trial jury deliberations. In addition, psychologists, and sociologists have generated numerous theories about the behavior patterns of small groups,[3] and many of these theories have served as the basis of highly sophisticated studies of the interpersonal relations and voting behavior of small groups of judicial decision-makers.[4] Many of these latter studies have obvious application to the study of trial juries as small groups.

While the literature on petit jury behavior has increased, both in quantity and in theoretical and methodological sophistication, such research has not been extended to the subject of grand juries. Even though the grand jury is a vital aspect of the federal judicial process and is part of the due process guarantee in half of the state constitutions, it has received scant and generally unsophisticated treatment by judicial scholars. Grand jury literature tends to fall into three general categories: (1) studies of the

Robert A. Carp, "The Behavior of Grand Juries: Acquiescence or Justice?," *Social Science Quarterly,* March, 1975, Vol. 55, No. 4, pp. 853-870. Published by The University of Texas Press. Reprinted with permission.

history and evolution of the grand jury;[5] (2) analyses of the legal powers and prerogatives of grand juries vis-a-vis the rights and immunities of the accused;[6] and (3) critiques of the grand jury system and/or proposals for reform.[7] Although there are a few studies which purport to analyze the process of recruitment to grand juries and to speculate on the possible effects on grand jury "output" of one form of recruitment over another, these studies are neither based on quantitative data nor performed with much methodological rigor.[8]

This study is intended to help remedy the paucity of empirical data on the recruitment and internal dynamics of grand juries by reporting the results of a case study of grand jury operations in Harris County (Houston), Texas. The study may be distinguished from the existing grand jury literature, first, because the author had access to data which has not heretofore been available to judicial scholars, and, second, because the data permitted the researcher to respond concretely to questions which until this time were only subjects of speculation among students of the judicial process. The study is concerned with two major substantive questions. (1) What are the distinguishing characteristics of grand jury behavior? It is suggested that the basic behavioral traits include an excessively rapid processing of cases with little deliberation, a high level of internal agreement on the resolution of cases, and an overwhelming acquiescence in the district attorney's recommendations. (2) How are the basic behavioral characteristics of the grand jury to be accounted for? It is then argued that grand jury behavior is explained by the type of people who become grand jurors, by the grand jurors' inadequate training and preparation for their duties, by the pressures of a very heavy caseload, and by a variety of institutional and legal factors which ensure the prosecutor's domination of the grand jury.[9] Finally, some suggestions for future research on the subject of grand juries are offered.

Methodology

Data for this study derive from three principal sources. First, as a participant-observer on the 177th District Court Grand Jury (which met in Houston, Texas, between November, 1971, and February, 1972), the author had the opportunity to perform a case-by-case content analysis of the 918 cases considered by that grand jury. This analysis includes a complete record of all votes taken, the amount of time spent deliberating on the various cases, and extensive notes on the discussions among the grand jury and the district attorneys. Because of the oath of grand jury secrecy to which the author is bound, the information here provided must deal with the cases in the aggregate—not individually—and great care has been taken not to divulge specific information about sensitive or confidential subject matter.

Second, in-depth interviews were conducted with former members of Harris County grand juries. The interviewees were not selected at random but rather with an eye toward including as many *recent* grand jury members and jury foremen as possible. Twenty-three such persons in all were contacted (including six jury foremen) and all of them agreed to be interviewed. The primary purpose of these interviews was to compare the grand jury experiences of this author with those of others who have similarly served so as to detemine how typical was the performance of the 177th Grand Jury from which the hard data were drawn. No attempt was made to quantify the results of the in-depth interviews, and therefore the information they provide is anecdotal although frequently interesting and insightful.

Third, the study contains data from a questionnaire mailed to all persons who served on Harris County grand juries between 1969 and 1972. Of the 271 questionnaires mailed to the grand jurors, 156 (58 percent) were returned and included in the analysis. The questionnaire solicited information about the socioeconomic characteristics of the grand jurors and about the nature of their grand jury deliberations and experiences. The results are used throughout the study to supplement the other sources of research data and to provide a comparison and contrast between the data of the 177th Grand Jury and the other grand juries which immediately preceded and followed it.

Behavioral Characteristics of the Grand Jury

In principle the grand jury is supposed to carefully determine whether the evidence presented to it by the prosecutor is sufficient to warrant the time and expense of placing a person on trial for a felony offense. Ideally the grand jury serves as a check against an over-zealous district attorney to protect the citizen against unwarranted harrassment and prosecution by the state. How well such a function is performed in practice may be ascertained by examining the real, observable defining characteristics of grand jury behavior. First, it will be shown that the grand jury spends an extremely small amount of time deliberating on the vast majority of its cases. Second, the data will indicate a surprisingly low level of internal conflict in the grand jury decision making process. Finally, the grand jury's overwhelming approval of (or acquiescence in) the district attorney's recommendations will be demonstrated.

Time Allotted to Each Case: The Failure to Deliberate Adequately

To determine whether or not the grand jury sufficiently deliberates its cases it seems logical to begin by asking this question: how much *time* does the average grand jury spend with each case to determine whether there is enough evidence to place a man on trial for a felony offense? Although there is considerable variation in the amount of time spent deliberating on the various categories of cases, the evidence reveals that the typical grand jury spends only five minutes per case. (In 1971, twelve Harris County grand juries spent an estimated 1,344 hours deliberating on 15,930 cases.)[10] This average time of five minutes includes the assistant district attorney's summary of the case and his recommendation as to how the case should be decided (about one minute per case), the hearing of testimony by whatever witnesses are called, and the actual secret deliberations by the grand jury on each case individually. By any man's standards, "justice" is indeed swift!

Does the grand jury become more efficient as its term progresses, that is, is it able to deal with a larger number of cases per hour toward the end of its term than at the beginning? Eighty-four percent of the questionnaire respondents indicated that this was their impression. Table I (panel a) suggests that such was also the case with the 177th Grand Jury despite a slight initial increase in the amount of time spent per case.

This grand jury spent an average of 7.4 minutes per case during its first six working sessions while spending but 5.9 minutes per case during the final six working days.

Another question about the deliberation process is how many (and what types of cases) are actually discussed by the grand jury and how many are simply voted on without any discussion at all after the district attorney's one minute summary of the facts of the case. For the 177th Grand Jury a full 80 percent of the cases were voted on with no discussion whatsoever.[11] This percentage is probably even greater for most other Harris County grand juries since the 177th Grand Jury spent a mean time of seven minutes per case, whereas the average figure for the other grand juries between 1969 and 1971 was five minutes.

Table I (panel 6) also suggests that after a slight initial increase the percentage of cases discussed by the grand jury tends to decrease as the term progresses.[12] For instance, during its first nine sessions (November 3rd through December 6th) the 177th Grand Jury chose to discuss 27 percent of its cases, whereas it decided to discuss only 12 percent during its final nine meetings (January 3rd through the 31st). Why this is so is explained in part in this statement by a former grand jury foreman:

> As time went on fewer and fewer of the cases were actually discussed.
> Toward the end of the term someone would say he wanted to discuss a

particular case, and then when someone else would pop up and say 'What's the point of discussing this case? We had a case like it a couple weeks ago. You know where I stand on cases like this, and I know where you stand. Why discuss this all over again? Let's just vote on it and get on to the next case.' And more often than not, nothing more would be said. We would just vote without discussing the case.''

The phenomenon of discussing fewer and fewer cases as the term progresses probably explains the increasing grand jury "efficiency" as outlined in panel a of Table I.

The evidence also suggests that grand juries do discriminate in the amount of time allotted to specific categories of cases, that is, while a grand jury might spend several hours investigating and discussing a prominent murder or rape case, it might spend less than a minute dealing with the average robbery or drunken driving case. When asked on the questionnaire about which types of cases his grand jury spent the most time deliberating, the frequency distribution of responses was in the following rank order: (1) drug cases, 29 percent; (2) crimes of passion, e.g., murder, rape, 27 percent; (3) burglary, 9 percent; (4) forgery and embezzlement, 9 percent; (5) theft, 8 percent; (6) victimless sex crimes, e.g., sodomy, 8 percent; (7) robbery, 5 percent; and (8) driving while intoxicated, 5 percent.

The 177th Grand Jury likewise gave differential treatment to certain types of cases at the expense of others. This panel chose to discuss two-thirds of its victimless sex crimes cases while deciding to talk about only 5 percent of the driving while intoxicated cases. Crimes of passion and drug cases were discussed about a third of the time while 28 percent of the theft cases and 19 percent of the burglary cases were talked about. This was followed by robbery cases and the cases involving forgery and embezzlement which were discussed respectively 9 and 6 percent of the time.

The High Level of Unanimity in Grand Jury Decision Making

The most striking feature of grand jury voting patterns is the exceptionally high degree of unanimity. This is confirmed by interviews with former grand jury members and by examining the voting record of the 177th Grand Jury: of the 918 cases decided by that Grand Jury, a non-unanimous vote occurred in a mere 42 cases (5 percent). The evidence further indicates that as the grand jury term progresses, there is a tendency toward increased unanimity in its voting patterns. This is in accord with one of Bales' conclusions about small group decision-making behavior: as the small group continues to deliberate on a matter (or on a series of questions), there is an increased tendency toward group solidarity.[13]

The results in panel c of Table I show that during its first nine working days the 177th Grand Jury cast less than unanimous votes in 6 percent of its cases, whereas during its last nine sessions there was a divided vote in only 3

Table I

Behavioral Characteristics of the 177th Grand Jury
(Number of Cases in Parentheses)

	Time Periods[1]							
	Nov. 3-10	Nov. 15-22	Nov. 29-Dec. 6	Dec. 8-29	Jan. 3-10	Jan. 12-19	Jan. 24-31	Overall Average
Average number of minutes per case spent deliberating on cases by the 177th Grand Jury	7.3	7.5	8.0	7.6	6.5	6.0	5.6	7.0
Percentage of cases discussed by the 177th Grand Jury	24	26	33	25	5	20[2]	6	20
Percentage of divided votes for the 177th Grand Jury	9	3	6	3	2	6[2]	1	5
Percentage of cases on which the 177th Grand Jury did not follow the district attorney's recommendations	11	10	11	5	4	5	2	7
Total (N)	(148)	(112)	(135)	(146)	(111)	(154)	(112)	(131)

[1]Each of these time periods includes three working sessions except the period December 8 through the 29th, which includes five working sessions. The three month session is divided into seven time periods each of which includes an average of 131 cases.

[2]Time period six tends to deviate from the overall tendency. This was primarily because one grand juror suddenly insisted on discussing all of the usually routine driving-while-intoxicated cases. This was the result of an unpleasant personal encounter he had had with law enforcement officials relating to a drunken driving charge during the New Year's holiday.

percent of its decisions. This excerpt from a journal kept by one former grand jury member is insightful:

> In general there is a fairly united spirit among us, and I think we all feel that pressure to "dissent only when absolutely necessary," as Chief Justice Taft used to urge. I myself today felt inclined to bring a T.B. (true bill) in a case this afternoon, but I could see no one else agreed with my position, and so when the vote was taken I held my peace.

Victimless sex crimes was the only category of cases which served to create disharmony on the 177th Grand Jury; a divided vote resulted in one-third of all such offenses. Disagreement on the other types of cases did not exceed the 6 percent level.[14] As for the former grand jurors who were asked in the questionnaire to cite cases on which their respective panels had the largest amount of internal dissension, drug cases led the way with 40 percent, followed by crimes of passion at 25 percent. No other category of cases was cited more than 9 percent of the time.[15]

Thus the evidence suggests that grand jurors most frequently divide on drug cases, crimes of passion, and victimless sex crimes while being significantly more unified on the other categories of cases. Such findings are not too surprising when one considers that cases in the three aforementioned categories are not only likely to be the most serious and complex, but they are also cases about which society in general seems to be most divided as to whether such offenses are really crimes at all or merely the actions of social dissidents and psychopaths.

The Grand Jury's Acquiescence to the Demands of the Prosecutor

A third defining characteristic of grand jury behavior is the almost total approval of the district attorney's recommendations. Although the interview data suggest that grand jurors are often critical of the prosecutor for inadequate and careless preparation of cases, for insensitivity to the inequities of our legal system, and for presenting the grand juries with inordinately heavy caseloads, the evidence also reveals that most grand juries tend (or are forced by circumstances) to rely heavily on the skill and integrity of the district attorney in deciding whether or not to bring an indictment. When asked on the questionnaire about the *usual* practice of the grand jury in bringing an indictment, 47 percent of all grand jurors indicated that their grand juries indicted (or refused to indict) solely on the basis of what the district attorney said the file of the accused contained. Another 21 percent noted that their grand jury usually did examine the file of the accused while about a third claimed that their grand jury usually required proof "sufficient to convict, including the calling of witnesses."[16]

What is perhaps most significant, then, is that nearly half of all grand juries (and the author believes this is to be a highly conservative figure) usually take action on cases solely on the basis of what the district attorney says the defendant's file contains without the grand jury even bothering to examine the file or to require full demonstration by the district attorney.

On which categories of cases is the grand jury most likely to refuse to follow the recommendations of the district attorneys?[17] The response to this query by the questionnaire recipients generated the following frequency distribution: (1) drug cases, 44 percent; (2) crimes of passion, 18 percent; (3) victimless sex crimes, 11 percent; (4) driving while intoxicated, 9 percent; (5) forgery and embezzlement, 6 percent; (6) theft, 5 percent; (7) burglary, 3 percent; and (8) robbery, 3 percent. Thus the crimes which were likely to cause the greatest amount of dissension among the grand jurors are the very felonies which were likely to result in the most disagreements between grand juries and the district attorneys; viz., drug cases, crimes of passion, and victimless sex crimes.

The above results parallel exactly the data emanating from the 177th Grand Jury. That Grand Jury, which refused to follow the district attorney's recommendations only 6 percent of the time, disagreed with the district attorneys in 28 percent of the drug cases, 27 percent of the victimless sex crimes cases, and 17 percent of the crimes of passion.[18]

Panel d of Table I suggests that the longer the grand jury is in session the more its decisions are likely to be in accord with the district attorney's recommendations. More careful analysis reveals, however, that this is not necessarily the case. For the 177th Grand Jury the evidence indicates that the district attorneys were less and less likely to present to the Grand Jury cases with which they believed the Jury would go against their recommendations. For example, of the first 137 cases presented to the Grand Jury, 25 (18 percent) were drug cases, whereas only 3 (2 percent) of the following 123 cases dealt with drug crimes. Apparently the district attorneys had determined after a few weeks that they would be more successful taking their drug cases to one of the other two grand juries sitting at the same time. In fact this was conceded by one of the district attorneys during one of the working sessions when a grand juror asked, "Why aren't you giving us any more drug cases?" The candid reply was, "Well, you folks are requiring so much (proof) of us with those cases, that we've had to take them to the other grand juries or we're going to get way behind." Therefore, a phenomenon which may well occur in Harris County is for the district attorneys to "size up" the grand juries during their first several working sessions and then to present cases to the grand jury which is most likely to act in accordance with the district attorneys' wishes. To what extent this occurs is unknown, but that it does occur to some degree is beyond doubt.

A Partial Explanation of Grand Jury Behavioral Characteristics

The evidence presented to this point suggests the following portrait of grand jury behavior. Burdened with an inordinately heavy caseload, the grand jury rapidly processes almost all of its myriad of cases, according full and adequate deliberation to only a select few which arbitrarily manage to pique the interest of the jury panel. The expedition of the huge caseload is facilitated by a very low level of internal conflict as evidenced by a record of unanimous voting on approximately 95 percent of the cases. Such internal harmony extends to the relations between the grand jury and the district attorney's staff, the former following the latter's recommendations without so much as a question about 94 percent of the time.

If such are the behavioral characteristics of the grand jury, the next logical question is: how are such behavioral patterns to be accounted for? Why doesn't the grand jury deliberate with greater thoroughness on its cases? Why is there so little internal dissension on the resolution of the many issues confronting the grand jury? And why is the public prosecutor able to so effectively dominate grand jury behavior? Partial answers to these questions have already been suggested in the preceding material, but it is the purpose of this segment of the article to provide a more systematic explanation for grand jury behavior.

The Type of People Who Become Grand Jurors

One possible explanatory factor accounting for some of the behavior patterns lies in the selection and composition of the individual members of the jury panel. This is based on the reasonable assumption that a grand jury composed of a truly random cross-section of the community might well exhibit different behavior from a jury composed largely of upper-middle class whites, or of radical members of the black community, or of a combination of poor whites and Mexican Americans. Therefore, we must explore the grand jury selection process and provide a profile of its members.

The process of selecting grand jurors in Texas is as intricate as it is arbitrary. Unlike many of its sister states which nondiscriminately select the names of grand jurors from a lottery wheel containing the names of hundreds of potential jurors, Texas grants jury commissioners almost unlimited discretion to compile a small list of names from which the grand jury is impaneled. Very little is known about these jury commissioners and about the criteria by which these officers of the court select prospective grand jurors. However, preliminary evidence suggests, first, that a significant disproportion of the commissioners are upper-middle class Anglo-Saxon white males; and, second, that the commissioners tend to select as grand jurors their friends and neighbors who have similar socioeconomic characteristics.[19] Historically most jurists have argued, and the courts have officially determined, that grand juries, like trial juries, should be representative of the population of the community as a whole. Although there is still considerable uncertainty about how this goal is to be achieved, the U.S. Court of Appeals for the Fifth Circuit has determined that the Constitution requires that members of Texas grand juries represent "a fair cross section...[of the]...community's human resources...."[20] In light of this judicial determination it is fair then to ask the question: how representative are Texas grand juries of the county populations from which they are selected? This is largely an empirical question, and for a partial answer we may compare the results of the mailed questionnaire sent to former grand jurors in Harris County with the 1970 census figures for this same county.

Table II shows that the typical Harris County grand juror is an Anglo-Saxon male college graduate about 51 years of age who is quite likely to earn about $25,000 per year while working either as a business executive or as a professional man. How does this profile compare with what the 1970 census data indicates about the "typical citizen of the county? A brief summary of these data reveals the following about the residents of Harris County: 49 percent are male and 51 percent are female; the median adult age is 39; 69 percent are Anglo-Saxon, 20 percent are black, and 11 percent are Mexican American; the median eduction is 12 years (a high school degree); and the median family income is $10,348.[21] These figures clearly demonstrate that even by rudimentary standards Harris County grand juries do not meet the judicial criterion of a "fair cross section...[of the]...community's human resources." Grossly underrepresented are women, young people, Negroes, Mexican Americans, the poor, and those with less extensive educational backgrounds.[22]

The evidence suggests that the highly non-representative composition of the grand jury manifests itself in several of the jury's behavior patterns. First, it is probably responsible to a large degree for the low level of internal conflict among the grand jurors. Jury members with highly similar backgrounds of education, income, employment, sex, age, and race are more likely to think alike and disagree less than a panel composed of individuals with highly dissimilar — or even randomly distributed — background characteristics.

Second, the upper middle class white bias of the grand jury is undoubtedly reflected in the selection of that small 5 percent of the cases which the jury does choose to deliberate on at length. The evidence reveals that the vast majority of those cases in the 5 percent category are those which include the bizarre, unusual, or "important" cases which are covered by the news media and which frequently involve the names of well-known local personages, businesses, organizations, etc. The murder of a prominent socialite, corruption in the local fire department, alleged immoral conduct

Table II

Socioeconomic Characteristics of Harris County Grand Jurors
Compared with 1970 County Census Figures for Adult Population
in Percentages (N = 156 for the Questionnaire Sample)

Characteristic	Grand Jury	County
Sex		
Male	78	49
Female	22	51
Age		
21-35 years	10	23
36-50 years	43	18
51-65 years	37	8
Over 65	10	5
Median juror age, 51	—	Median adult age, 39
Income		
Under $5,000	1	16
$ 5,000-$10,000	3	31
$10,000-$15,000	25	29
$15,000-$20,000	16	9
Over $20,000	55	15
Median juror income, $25,000 — Median family income in County, $10,348		
Race		
Anglo	82	69
Negro	15	20
Mexican American	3	11
Education		
Less than high school	0	24
Some high school	3	23
High school degree	8	25
Some college	34	13
College degree	32	
Graduate degree	23	
Median juror education, 16 years — Median County resident education, 12 years		
Employment		
Business executive	35	
Proprietor	7	
Professional	20	
Employed worker	13	Comparable data
Retired	13	not available
Housewife	11	
Other	1	

by professors at a local state university have all been subjects of extensive and exhaustive grand jury investigations in the county under study. Cases such as these are regarded as significant by upper-middle class grand juries because the subject matter has a special appeal to the moral, ethical, or even salacious instincts of the middle class mentality. On the other hand, the robbery of a liquor store, the stabbing death of a derelict in a ghetto bar, or the forgery of a credit card tend to be regarded as routine, boring, and worthy of little interest by most grand jurors. As one grand juror said in this candid jest, "We kind of looked forward to the rape and sodomy cases and stuff like that because they broke the routine. I meant if you've heard one bad check case, you've heard them all. But the unusual cases were a little more interesting, and we kind of took our time with them." The result of all this may be that the more bizarre, infamous, or salacious the case, the greater the likelihood that it will be among the small percentage of cases on which the grand jury gives careful and exhaustive investigation. And, conversely, the more routine and uninteresting the case, the greater the likelihood that it will be passed over with scant attention, the grand jury being willing to follow the often-heard advice of the district attorney: "If we make a mistake here, they'll catch it when the cases come to trial." Since 46 percent of all grand jury indictments end in either dismissals or acquittals, one may well assume that many mistakes are indeed passed over by bored, unresponsive, and overworked grand juries.[23]

Finally, the data reveal that some of the complex social problems which divide society as a whole, such as marijuana and hard drug laws, the possible pathology of the murderer and the rapist, the permissibility of "abnormal" sexual relations between consenting adults, all manifest themselves in the give-and-take of grand jury deliberations. This is evidenced by the comparatively high level of disagreement on the resolution of cases dealing with these subjects, not only among individual members of the grand jury but also between the grand jury and the district attorney's staff. Moreover, the inordinant amount of time the grand jury spends deliberating on these cases and the level of dissension which these discussions evoke are also a probable reflection of the upper-middle class composition of the grand jury. It is now common knowledge among social scientists that concern with reform of the narcotic laws, revision of the criminal code pertaining to sexual mores, etc., are almost exclusively middle and upper middle class phenomena.

The Grand Jury's Inadequate Training and Preparation for Their Duties

A second reason to account for some of the grand jury's behavior patterns is found in the process by which newly-selected jurors are trained and socialized. In Harris County all new grand jurors are provided with a training program of sorts which entails three different aspects: a *voluntary* one-day training seminar conducted primarily by police and sheriff's department officials; two booklets pertaining to grand jury procedures and instructions, one composed by the district attorney and the other prepared by the Harris County Grand Jury Association; and, finally, an in-depth, give-and-take discussion between the grand jury and an experienced member of the district attorney's staff. Let us examine each aspect of the program separately.

First, the series of lectures by law enforcement officials seems to be of limited utility for the novice grand juror. Not only do these lectures come several days *after* the formal work of the grand jury has begun, but most grand jurors tend to agree with an evaluation which was included in a recent grand jury report: "The day-long training session was interesting, but for the most part the lectures were irrelevant to the primary functions of a Grand Jury, and many of us noted rather unsubtle political overtones in the formal presentations."[24] Interviews with more than a score of former grand jurors and a content analysis of grand jury reports reveal that the primary function of the law enforcement lectures is to explain and to "plug" the work of the respective departments rather than to provide the grand juror with substantive insights into what his grand jury duties entail.

The pamphlets prepared separately by the county Grand Jury Association and by the district attorney are well-written and provide a good summary of the formal duties and functions of the grand jury. However, since these booklets are not provided until the first day of jury service, the earliest they could be read is after the grand jury has put in one full day of work, which usually means hearing at least 50 cases. More important, however, is the fact that interviews with former grand jurors indicate that very few jurors bother to read and study these booklets. This comment by one former grand juror is typical:

> Yes, I took the books home with me that first night and I glanced through them, but I can't say I really read them. I figured that we'd meet our problems as we came to them, and that's about what happened. If we had a question during our deliberations, one of us would usually say, "Let's see if the booklet says anything about this." That's how we used the books when I was on the jury. I don't think any of us actually read them as such.

The give-and-take discussion between the grand jury and an assistant district attorney is usually scheduled for the first working session, and it is the final aspect of the grand juror's formal on-the-job training. When such a discussion does indeed occur, it appears to be of some utility in acquainting grand jurors with their new duties. However, this comment by a recent member of a grand jury was far from atypical:

Yes, we were supposed to meet with one of the D.A.'s at the end of the first day, and he was supposed to explain to us what the hell was going on. But can you believe this? They [the assistant district attorneys] presented us with so many cases on our first day, it got to be five o'clock and we didn't have time for anyone to explain to us what we were supposed to be doing. We heard dozens of cases that first day, and when I got home that night I was just sick. I told my wife, "I sure would hate to be one of those guys who had his case brought before us today."

How long does it take, then, for the average grand juror to understand substantially what the duties, powers, and functions of a grand jury are? The results of the questionnaire survey reveal that the typical grand juror does not claim to fully understand his basic purpose and function until well into the third full working session of the grand jury.[25]

Using the average daily workload of 1971 as a base (58 cases per working session), this means that the grand jury hears a minimum of 116 cases before its members even claim to understand their primary duties and functions. Since the average grand jury in 1971 considered 1,328 cases,[26] the data suggests that most grand jurors stumble through the first 8 percent of their cases without fully knowing what is incumbent upon them.

The inadequate training and socialization of the grand jury is clearly one factor accounting for many of its behavioral characteristics. Since grand jurors do not learn systematically from an independent source the full measure of their duties, functions, and prerogatives, there exists the strong potential that they will become "rubber stamps" of the district attorney's staff. This is not to suggest that all grand juries become mere tools of the district attorney, but the potential for this result is by no means minimal. Jurors who do not fully understand their functions, who do not comprehend the meaning of "probable cause," and who do not know how to conduct careful, complete investigations of each case are prime candidates to be "led by the nose" by artful and experienced public prosecutors. Moreover, the evidence indicates that the district attorneys do indeed take advantage of ignorant grand juries to accomplish their desired ends. This is primarily so because the prosecutors frequently keep significant pieces of information from grand jury purview and because they occasionally deliberately route cases to the grand jury which is expected to act most favorably in accordance with their wishes.

The Pressure to Decide Cases Quickly

A third explanatory variable for grand jury behavior is found in the enormous size of the caseload with which both the prosecutor and the grand jury are forced to deal. Just as the heavy caseload at the trial court level produces pressures sustaining the plea-bargaining system, so, too, the huge workload of the grand jury has generated pressures to find alternatives to comprehensive review of each case. As indicated previously, the average grand jury, meeting but two days per week, is presented with approximately 1,328 cases during the three-month term. Since Texas law guarantees to all persons charged with a felony the right to a grand jury indictment, the district attorney is required to process all of these cases through the machinery of the grand jury. Given the small number of grand juries and the limited number of days they can work, there is little wonder that cases are processed with such careless speed. If each case were to receive adequate deliberation, the grand jury would fall hopelessly behind in its workload: if Harris County grand juries were to spend so much as an average of 20 minutes per case, their output of cases would drop by 75 percent! Thus, the sheer size of the caseload precludes careful, serious discussion of the cases.

Besides forcing the grand jury to work much too rapidly, the heavy workload is also partially responsible for the grand jury's excessive reliance on the expertise and good faith of the district attorney. To question the prosecutor's judgment, to make him "do his homework," are luxuries which efficiency-conscious grand juries cannot afford. The district attorney is hardly ignorant of this fact since he frequently admonishes the grand jury that requiring too much evidence of the prosecutor causes the grand jury "to fall behind the other grand juries" or that "grand jury delays result in innocent persons languishing in jail because they can't get their cases heard."

Factors Resulting in the District Attorney's Domination of the Grand Jury

In spite of the considerable legal powers and independence of the grand jury and despite the wishes of most grand jurors to the contrary, it is clear that the district attorney dominates the behavior of the grand jury. Why this is so has already been discussed and implied throughout the article, but it seems useful at this point to put all of the major reasons into summary perspective.

First, it is the prosecutor who has the primary role in training and indoctrinating the grand jurors. It is his office which writes the grand jury handbook, which plans the training seminars, and which instructs the jurors about their primary powers and responsibilities. Given the considerable ignorance of most grand jurors about their proper role and duties, the district attorney has the first and only real opportunity to write on this blank slate that the primary function of the grand jury is to expedite the work of the prosecutor's office with a minimum of time and obstruction.

Another factor resulting in the prosecutor's dominance is his continuing control over the sources of information throughout the three-month term. Perceived as an expert, as a professional, the district attorney is constantly looked to for guidance and information as to the proper disposition of cases and as to the legitimate functions of the grand jury. The prosecutor is fully aware of the grand jury's reliance on him in this regard and his subsequent behavior fully verifies the maxim that knowledge is power. The phenomenon is further heightened by the extremely heavy workload which forces the grand jury to trust the competence and judgment of the district attorney since the alternative is to throw sand in the gears of the judicial machinery and risk bringing it to a virtual halt.

Besides his control over the socialization of the grand jury, the prosecutor possesses some additional powers and prerogatives which ensure his dominant role. The district attorney's ability to control the agenda, that is, the sequence in which cases are presented, is worthy of mention. This power enables the prosecutor, if he is so inclined, to do such things as: (1) initially present the grand jury with a wide variety of cases to determine which ones the jury processes without question and on which cases the grand jury challenges the district attorney, thus enabling the prosecutor to channel subsequent cases to those grand juries which give him the least trouble; and/or (2) increase the size of the agenda for a grand jury which is causing him difficulty, thereby pressuring that grand jury into spending less time with its cases in order to complete the daily agenda. In addition, the district attorney has the right to take a case that has already been voted on by a grand jury to a second such jury for its consideratin. This is done whenever the prosecutor is unsatisfied with the vote of the first grand jury, and it enables him to keep trying until his will ultimately prevails in the vote of a more compliant grand jury.

Summary and Suggestions for Future Research

In sum, grand jury behavior is characterized by a rapid processing of cases with little deliberation (except for a small handful of cases of special interest to upper middle class citizens), by low internal conflict in reaching decisions, and by overwhelming approval of the district attorney's recommendations. Such behavior patterns are largely accounted for by the kind of people who become grand jurors, by the inadequacy of the grand jury training process, by the heavy caseload which requires speedy processing of cases for adequate system maintenance, and by a variety of institutional and legal factors which give the district attorney's office a monopoly on the sources of vital information and which insure his capacity to manipulate grand jury activities.

This study cannot end without making some general and specific suggestions for future research on grand juries. First, much more needs to be learned about the selection of grand jurors. We need specific answers to questions such as these: who are the jury commissioners and on what basis are they selected? What standards does the judge use in designating grand jury foremen?

Second, studies must acquire more knowledge about the grand jurors themselves. What are their values and what are their attitudes toward the police, the judicial system, and those arrested for a variety of crimes? The additional use of questionnaires and in-depth interviews with a large cross-section of grand jurors is necessary before we can draw an accurate profile of the typical grand juror.

More evidence is also needed about the internal dynamics of grand jury deliberations. Which types of grand jurors are likely to have more influence in the deliberations than others? Some evidence in this study suggests that the profession or race of the individual grand juror may cause other members of the jury to defer to him in cases which hinge on matters tangent to the grand juror's specific background. For example, on the 177th Grand Jury the lone black member was usually listened to with great attention in cases where an obviously black defendant was charging police harrassment, and the only lawyer on the jury was given considerable deference in cases which hinged on highly technical legal questions. Do grand juries develop a form of *stare decisis* as their terms progress (as was clearly the case with the 177th Grand Jury)? That is, are grand jurors, well into their term, likely to say about a case, "We had a case like this last month and we did such and such with it. We must then do the same with this case so we'll be consistent with ourselves." Also, is the grand jury foreman more likely to be on the winning side of divided votes than other grand jurors?

Finally, we need more data on the influence and role of the assistant district attorneys vis-a-vis the grand jury. Are some district attorneys more successful than others in obtaining the desired results from the grand jury? What tactics and strategies do district attorneys employ in preparing and presenting cases to grand juries? To what extent do district attorneys divert specific cases (or types of cases) from a grand jury to which the case(s) would routinely go to a grand jury which is more likely to resolve the case(s) in accordance with the district attorneys' wishes?

If answers to the above questions are found, we will be well on our way to understanding an institution and a process which at this time remains largely unexplored by students of the judicial process.

Notes

[1]Harry Kalven, Jr. and Hans Zeisel, *The American Jury* (Boston: Little, Brown and Co., 1966).

[2]*Ibid.,* see bibliographic references on pp. 541-545.

[3]Robert F. Bales, *Interaction Process Analysis: A Method for the Study of Small Groups* (Cambridge, Mass.: Addison-Wesley Press, 1950); "The Equilibrium Problem in Small Groups," Chp. 4 in Talcott Parsons, Robert F. Bales, and Edward A. Shils, eds., *Working Papers in the Theory of Action* (Glencoe, Ill.: Free Press, 1953); R.F. Bales, "Task Status and Likeability as a Function of Talking and Listening in Decision-Making Groups." in Leonard D. White, ed., *The State of the Social Sciences* (Chicago: University of Chicago Press, 1956), pp. 148-161; R. F. Bales, "Task Roles and Social Roles in Problem-Solving Groups," in Eleanor E. Maccoby, Theodore M. Newcomb, and Eugene L. Harley, *Readings in Social Psychology* (New York: Holt, 1958), pp. 437-447; R.F. Bales, *Personality and Interpersonal Behavior* (New York: Holt, Rinehart and Winston, 1970). Also, Philip E. Slater, "Role Differentiation in Small Groups," *American Sociological Review,* 20 (June, 1955), p. 300.

Also, Leonard Berkowitz, *Some Effects of Leadership Sharing in Small, Decision-Making Conference Groups,* unpublished Ph.D. Diss., Department of Psychology, University of Michigan, 1951; Leonard Berkowitz, "Sharing Leadership in Small, Decision-Making Groups," *Journal of Abnormal and Social Psychology,* 48 (April, 1953), p. 231.

[4]For example, see Thomas P. Jahnige and Sheldon Goldman, eds., *The Federal Judicial System* (New York: Holt, 1968), Part 3, Sec. C. Also, see Glendon Schubert, ed., *Judicial Behavior: A Reader in Theory and Research* (Chicago: Rand McNally, 1964), Chaps. 3, 4, and 5.

[5]For example, see Richard D. Younger, *The People's Panel: The Grand Jury in the United States, 1634-1941* (Providence, R.I.: Brown University Press, 1963); John Van Voorhis, "Note on the History in New York State of the Powers of Grand Juries," *Albany Law Review,* 26 (Jan., 1962), p. 1; and George J. Edwards, Jr., *The Grand Jury* (Philadelphia: George T. Bisel Co., 1906).

[6]For example, see Stuart A. MacCorkle, *The Texas Grand Jury* (Austin, Texas: Institute of Public Affairs, The University of Texas, 1966); S.A. MacCorkle, "Grand Jury—evidence obtained from testimony of prospective defendant cannot be used as basis of indictment," *Fordham Law Review,* 30 (Dec., 1961), p. 365; S.A. MacCorkle, "Rule of evidence as a factor in probable cause in grand jury proceedings and preliminary examinations," *Washington University Law Quarterly* (Feb., 1963), p. 102; and S.A. MacCorkle, "Criminal procedure—pretrial disclosures—defendant indicted for sub-orning witness to testify falsely before grand jury may inspect transcript of witness' testimony before grand jury," *University of Pittsburgh Law Review,* 23 (June, 1962), p. 1024.

[7]For example, see Walton Coates, "Grand jury, the prosecutor's puppet. Wasteful nonsense of criminal jurisprudence," *Pennsylvania Bar Association Quarterly,* 33 (March, 1962), p. 311; W. Coates, "California grand jury—two current problems," *California Law Review,* 52 (March, 1964), p. 116; Harold S. Russell, "Cook County grand jury: some problems and proposals," *Chicago Bar Record,* 43 (Oct., 1961), p. 9; and Arthur H. Sherry "Grand jury minutes: the unreasonable rule of secrecy," *Virginia Law Review,* 48 (May, 1962), p. 668.

[8]For example, see Frederick W. Burnett, Jr., "The Texas Grand Jury Selection System— Discretion to Discriminate," *Southwestern Law Journal,* 21 (Summer, 1967), p. 545.

[9]A very well-written study discussing phenomena similar to these in the U.S. House of Representatives Ways and Means Committee; see John F. Manley, "The House Committee on Ways and Means; Conflict Management in a Congressional Committee," *American Political Science Review,* 59 (Dec., 1965), pp. 927-939.

[10]The statistics are based on figures prepared by the Grand Jury Division of the Harris County District Attorney's Office in a report to District Attorney Carol Vance.

[11]The usual procedure in Harris County is for the assistant district attorney to present his cases for the day and then to leave the jury room. Then the foreman asks each grand juror which

cases he feels should be discussed. With the 177th Grand Jury even if only one of the jurors wished to discuss a particular case, discussion occurred. The interviews suggested that other grand juries follow a similar practice.

[12]An additional explanation of why there is an initial increase followed by a gradual long-term decrease is found in the discussion surrounding Table IV. In brief, the hypothesis is that the grand jury slowly begins to gain confidence and to challenge the work and judgement of the prosecutor — especially on the resolution of certain types of cases. Resenting such challenges, the district attorney then removes these types of cases from subsequent grand jury consideration. Thus the percentage of cases discussed by the grand jury drops after the first month because many controversial cases considered worthy of discussion are simply removed from the agenda.

[13]Bales, *Interaction Process Analysis*, esp. p. 138.

[14]Percentage of cases on which divided votes occurred for the 177th Grand Jury: (1) victimless sex crimes, 33 percent; (2) crimes of passion, 6 percent; (3) drug cases, 6 percent; (4) theft, 5 percent; (5) burglary, 4 percent; (6) robbery, 4 percent; (7) driving while intoxicated, 4 percent; and (8) forgery and embezzlement, 0 percent.

[15]Percentage of grand jurors who cited cases on which their respective grand juries had the largest amount of internal dissension: (1) drug cases, 40 percent; (2) crimes of passion, 25 percent; (3) victimless sex crimes, 9 percent; (4) forgery and embezzlement, 7 percent; (6) theft, 5 percent; (7) burglary, 4 percent; and (8) robbery, 2 percent.

[16]Given the average time of five minutes per case, the third claim could not possibly have been the *usual* practice of any of the grand juries.

[17]Disagreement with the district attorney was defined as cases where at least one of the following conditions occurred: the district attorney recommended a true bill and the grand jury voted a no bill; the district attorney sought a no bill and the grand jury brought a true bill; the grand jury indicted for a crime other than the one recommended by the district attorney; the grand jury required the district attorney to collect additional evidence for a particular case before they would consider it.

[18]Cases on which the 177th Grand Jury refused to follow the recommendations of the district attorney: (1) drug cases, 28 percent; (2) victimless sex crimes, 27 percent; (3) crimes of passion, 17 percent; (4) theft, 7 percent; (5) burglary, 5 percent; (6) forgery and embezzlement, 2 percent; (7) robbery, 1 percent; and (8) driving while intoxicated, 1 percent.

[19]This evidence is taken from an ongoing research project on the grand jury selection process conducted by myself and a graduate assistant, Claude Rowland.

[20]*Brooks v. Beto,* 366 F. 2d, 14 (5th Circuit, 1966).

[21]Census Tracts (Houston, Texas): *Standard Metropolitan Statistical Area* (Washington: U.S. Department of Commerce, 1972), pp. 1, 34, and 100.

[22]For comparative data on jury composition, see the bibliographic citations in Herbert Jacob, "Judicial insulation — elections, direct participation, and public attention to the courts in Wisconsin, *Wisconsin Law Review* (Summer, 1966), pp. 801-819.

[23]This figure is taken from a report prepared by the Grand Jury Division of the Harris County District Attorney's Office for District Attorney Carol Vance.

[24]177th Criminal District Court Grand Jury, *Report of the November 1971 Grand Jury for the 177th Criminal District Court* (Houston, Texas, 1972), p. 1.

[25]Percentage of grand jurors who indicated the length of time required before they claimed to substantially understand the duties, powers, and functions of a grand jury: (1) Understood prior to or immediately after first session, 22 percent; (2) Understood after second session, 27 percent; (3) Understood after fourth session, 32 percent; and (4) Understood after sixth session or longer, 19 percent. Median time is somewhat more than the third session.

[26]The statistics in this paragraph are based on figures prepared by the Grand Jury Division of the Harris County District Attorney's Office in a report to District Attorney Carol Vance.

9

Individualized Judges

Marvin Frankel

The absurdities of our sentencing laws would remain aesthetically repulsive, but might be otherwise tolerable, if our judges were uniformly brilliant, sensitive, and humane. Though I yield only to numerous judges in my admiration for those on the bench, I must acknowledge that we do not, in fact, approach any such state of affairs. Judges, I think, tend to be like people, perhaps even some cuts above the mine run but, unfortunately, less than gods or angels. And how, after all, could we dream it might be otherwise? Consider whence we acquire our judges, how we select them, how they are trained before and after they don robes.

To start near the beginning, most of our judges have been trained as lawyers. (There is a disappearing breed of petty magistrates for whom this is not necessarily true, and the picture is more bleak with respect to them.) Substantially nothing in the law curriculum is relevant to problems of sentencing. Indeed, until the last decade or so, the entire field of criminal law, being neither lucrative nor prestigious, occupied only a small and disfavored corner of our law schools' attention. While that state of neglect has undergone extensive repairs, these have scarcely grazed the area of interest here. Law students learn something about the rules of the criminal law, about the trial of cases, and increasingly, about the rights of defendants before and during trial. They receive almost no instruction pertinent to sentencing. They may hear some fleeting references to the purposes of criminal penalites—some generalities about retribution, deterrence, etc. But so far as any intentional consequences of their legal education are concerned, they are taught by people and exposed to curricula barren of even food for thought about sentencing.[1]

From among the total supply of law graduates who have not studied sentencing, there emerges in twenty or thirty years the narrower group from which we select the bulk of our judges. The most notable thing about this group for present purposes is that its members have mostly remained unencumbered by any exposure to, or learning about, the problems of sentencing. Characterized by their dominant attributes, our judges are men (mostly) of no longer tender years who have not associated much with criminal defendants, who have not seemed shrilly unorthodox, who have not lived recently in poverty, who have been modestly or more successful in their profession. They are likely to have had more than an average lawyer's amount of experience in the courtroom, though it is a little remarkable how large a percentage of those who go on the bench lack this credential.[2] They are unlikely to have defended more than a couple of criminal cases, if that many. They are more likely to have done a stint as prosecutors, usually as a brief chapter in the years shortly after law school. However much or little they have been exposed to the criminal trial process, most people ascending (as we say) the bench have paid only the most fleeting and superficial attention to matters affecting the sentences of convicted defendants. In this respect the pattern set in the law school is carried forward and reenforced. The professional show ends with the verdict or the plea. The histrionics later on at the sentencing proceeding may be moving or embarrassing, even effective on occasion, but are no part of the skills the average lawyer prizes and polishes as special tools of his trade.

Whatever few things may be said for them, our procedures for selecting judges do not improve the prospects of sensitive, knowledgeble sentencing. It may happen sometimes, but I do not recall ever hearing anything relevant to that subject in discussions of the qualifications of prospective judges. I put to one side for this purpose the disgraceful process, widely used, of political nominations, where the candidates are too often selected without concern for any of the qualities supposedly wanted in suitable judges. Even where relevant questions are asked, the professional criteria, reflecting the training and the profession at work, simply do not include meaningful inquiries as to whether the prospective judge is fit to wield the awesome sentencing power. Apart from elementary, and usually superficial, glances at vague qualities of "temperament," we would not know really where to look or what to ask on a subject destined to loom so large among the prospective judge's impacts upon his fellow citizens.

The judges fetched up in the process are a mixed bag, without many surprises. Some grow to be concerned and spend substantial time brooding about their sentencing responsibilities. Most, I think, are not so preoccupied. Judges are commonly heard to say that sentencing is the grimmest and most solemnly absorbing of their tasks. This is not exactly hypocrisy. It is, however, among the less meaningful things judges report about their work. Measured by the time devoted to it, by the amount of deliberation and study before each decision, and by the attention to the subject as a field of intellectual concern in general, the judges' effective expenditures of themselves in worries over sentencing do not reflect a profound sense of mission. Judges don't talk much, to each other or to anyone, about the issues and difficulties in sentencing. They don't read or write about such things. Because strictly "legal" problems are rare in this area, and appeals are normally not allowed to attack the sentence the reading pile rarely contains anything pertinent. The judge is likely to read thick briefs, hear oral argument, and then take days or weeks to decide who breached a contract for delivery of opinions. The same judge will read a presentence report, perhaps talk to a probation officer, hear a few minutes of pleas for mercy—invest, in sum, less than an hour in all—before imposing a sentence of ten years in prison.

Some judges, confronting the enormities of what they do and how they do it, are visited with occasional onsets of horror or, at least, self-doubt. Learned Hand—to some, the greatest of our judges; to all, among the small handful of the greatest—reflected such sentiments. Never accounted soft toward criminals among any who knew his work, he said of his role in sentencing: "Here I am an old man in a long nightgown making muffled noises at people who may be no worse than I am." A distinguished committee of federal judges, with Hand among its members, acknowledged "the incompetency of certain types of judges to impose sentence." It spoke of judges "not temperamentally equipped" to learn this task acceptably, of judges who compensate for their own inadequacies by "the practice of imposing severe sentences," of judges "who crusade against certain crimes which they feel disposed to stamp out by drastic sentences."[3] Other judges have expressed similar misgivings—about their own and (perhaps more strongly) about their colleagues' handling of powers so huge and so undefined over the lives of their fellow men.

Self-criticism, uncertainty, and a resultant disposition toward restraint are useful qualities in judges—for sentencing and for other aspects of the job. They are not, however, in oversupply. The kinds of people who make their way onto the bench are not by and large given to humility. If there are seeds of meekness to begin with, the trial bench is not the most fertile place for their cultivation. The trial judge may be reversed with regularity; he may be the butt of lawyers' jokes and an object lesson in the law schools; but the incidents of his daily life—the rituals of deference, the high bench, the visible evidences of power asserted directly and face-to-face—are not designed to shrink his self-image. It should be said in all fairness that the Hamlets of this world are not suited to the business of presiding over trial courts. Scores of things must be decided every day. It is often more important, as Brandeis taught, that the decisions be made than that they be correct. Both the volume and the nature of the enterprise—the regulation of the flow of evidence, the predictable eruption of emergencies, the endless stream of cloudy questions demanding swift answers—generate pressures for decisive action. And so the trial judge, who starts his career well along the course of a life in which self-effacement has not been the key thing, is encouraged to follow his assertive ways.

Conditioned in the direction of authoritarianism by his daily life in court, long habituated as a lawyer to the stance of the aggressive contestant, and exercising sentencing powers frequently without practical limits, the trial judge is not discouraged from venting any tendencies toward righteous arrogance. The books and the reliable folklore are filled with the resulting horror stories—of fierce sentences and orgies of denunciatory attacks upon defendants. One need not be a revolutionist or an enemy of the judiciary to predict that untrained, untested, unsupervised men armed with great power will perpetrate abuses. The horrible cases may result from moral or intellectual or physical deficiencies—or from all together. But we can be sure there will be some substantial number of such cases.

Everyone connected with this grim business has his own favorite atrocity stories. James V. Bennett, the enlightened former Director of the Federal Bureau of Prisons, wrote this often-quoted passage, which appears in a 1964 Senate Document:

> That some judges are arbitrary and even sadistic in their sentencing practices is notoriously a matter of record. By reason of senility or a virtually pathological emotional complex some judges summarily impose the maximum on defendants convicted of certain types of crimes or all types of crimes. One judge's disposition along this line was a major factor in bringing about a sitdown strike at Connecticut's Wethersfield Prison in 1956. There is one judge who, as a matter of routine, always gives the maximum sentence and who of course is avoided by every defense lawyer. If they have the misfortune of having their case arise before him they lay the ground for appeals since experience has indicated the appeals court is sympathetic and will, if possible, overturn the sentencing court. I know of one judge who continued to sit on the bench and sentence defendants to prison while he was undergoing shock treatments for a mental illness.[4]

Forgoing the temptation to parade more lurid instances, I think a couple of mild, substantially colorless cases within my own ken give some sense of the unchained sentencing power in operation. One story concerns a casual anecdote over cocktails in a rare conversation among judges touching the subject of sentencing. Judge X, to designate him in a lawyerlike way, told of a defendant for whom the judge, after reading the presentence report, had decided tentatively upon a sentence of four years' imprisonment. At the sentencing hearing in the courtroom, after hearing counsel, Judge X invited the defendant to exercise his right to address the court in his own behalf. The defendant took a sheaf of papers from his pocket and proceeded to read from them, excoriating the judge, the "kangaroo court" in which he'd been tried, and the legal establishment in general. Completing the story, Judge X said, "I listened without interrupting. Finally, when he said he was through, I simply gave the son of a bitch five years instead of the four." None of the three judges listening to that (including me) tendered a whisper of dissent, let alone a scream of outrage. But think about it. Not the relatively harmless, if revealing, reference to the defendant as a son of a bitch. But a year in prison for speaking disrespectfully to a judge.[5] Was that, perhaps, based upon a rapid, subtle judgment that a defendant behaving this way in the courtroom showed insufficient evidence of remorse and prospects of reform? I confidently think not. Should defendants be warned that exercise of their "right" to address the court may be this costly? They are not.[6] Would we tolerate an act of Congress penalizing such an outburst by a year in prison? The question, however rhetorical, misses one truly exquisite note of agony: that the wretch sentenced by Judge X never knew, because he was never told, how the fifth year of his term came to be added.

That short story epitomizes much that prompts me to be writing this: the large and unregulated character of the sentencing power, the resulting arbitrariness permitted in its exercise, the frightening chanciness of judicial tempers and reactions. Whatever our platonic vision of the judge may be, this subject, like others, must be considered in the setting of a real world of real, mixed, fallible judicial types.

Let me turn here to my second, somewhat more appalling, anecdote. I happened a few years ago to preside at a widely publicized trial of a government official charged with corrupt behavior and perjury, convicted finally on a perjury count. While the conviction was for perjury only, the aura of corruption tended to overhang the case. In the weeks between the verdict and the sentence, as sometimes happens, I received some unsolicited mail, often vindictive in tone, not infrequently anonymous. One letter was from a more august source. A state trial judge, from Florida, wrote as follows:

> Dear Judge Frankel:
>   I have read with interest the proceedings in the case involving above Defendant and his influence peddling, perjury, etc. . . .
>   One of the more serious problems confronting Judges in the State Courts, such as the one in which I preside, is the leniency extended by

the Federal Judiciary and the pampering of prisoners and parolees by the Federal Penal and Parole Systems. It is difficult for me to justify giving an invidiaul 10, 15, 20 years or life for armed robberies involving a few dollars when persons in the Federal Judicial System are usually given much smaller sentences and are paroled after having served a few months or years of their sentences, and then are proceeded to be loosely supervised by an overly compassionate and headturning parole system.

Accordingly, as an individual, as a Judge in the State Court, as a father of a young man serving upon the High Seas of the country as an enlisted man, and as the step-father of a drafted Army Private on Asiatic soil, and as an individual who has served honorably for five years in the service of the United States Navy in wartime, let me strongly urge upon you that you impose the maximum sentence as provided by law upon the above Defendant, and upon any other individuals who would tend to destroy and demoralize our nation's government from within.

The author of that letter was deeply in earnest. What he wrote was not intended as a caricature. I am sure he did not mean to document the enormities we invite when we empower untested and unqualified officials to spew wholesale sentences of "10, 15, 20 years or life for armed robberies involving a few dollars...." He was not applying for the analyst's couch when he tendered up his generations of patriotism, his cruelty, and his confident ownership of ultimate truths. He was not — I assume, regretfully, he still is not — slowed for a second by any shibboleth about "individualized treatment" when he offered advice on sentencing to a fellow judge based upon newspaper intelligence, without even seeing the defendant or reading a presentence report.

What that Florida colleague did was merely to dramatize the macabre point that sweeping penalty statutes allow sentences to be "individualized" not so much in terms of defendants but mainly in terms of the wide spectrums of character, bias, neurosis, and daily vagary encountered among occupants of the trial bench. It is no wonder that wherever supposed professionals in the field — criminologists, penologists, probation officers, and yes, lawyers and judges — discuss sentencing, the talk inevitably dwells upon the problem of "disparity." Some writers have quibbled about the definitiveness of the evidence showing disparity. It is among the least substantial of quibbles. The evidence is conclusive that judges of widely varying attitudes on sentencing, administering statues that confer huge measures of discretion, mete out widely divergent sentences where the divergences are explainable only by the variations among the judges, not by material differences in the defendants or their crimes. Even in our age of science and skepticism, the conclusion would seem to be among those still acceptable as self-evident. What would require proof of a weighty kind, and something astonishing in the way of theoretical explanation, would be the suggestion that assorted judges, subject to little more than their own unfettered wills, could be expected to impose consistent sentences. In any event, if proof were needed that sentences vary simply because judges vary, there is plenty of it. The evidence grows every time judges gather to discuss specific cases and compare notes on the sentences they would impose upon given defendants. The disparities, if they are no longer astonishing, remain horrible.

The broad experience of former Prison Director Bennett merits another quotation here from the 1964 Senate Document mentioned earlier:

> Take, for instance, the cases of two men we received last spring. The first man had been convicted of cashing a check for $58.40. He was out of work at the time of his offense, and when his wife became ill and he needed money for rent, food, and doctor bills, he became the victim of temptation. He had no prior criminal record. The other man cashed a check for $35.20. He was also out of work and his wife had left him for another man. His prior record consisted of a drunk charge and a non-support charge. Our examination of these two cases indicated no significant differences for sentencing purposes. But they appeared before different judges and the first man received 15 years in prison and the second man 30 days.
>
> These are not cases picked out of thin air. In January the President of the United States commuted to time served the sentence of a first offender, a former Army lieutenant, and a veteran of over 500 days in combat, who had been given 18 years for forging six small checks.
>
> In one of our institutions a middle-aged credit union treasurer is serving 117 days for embezzling $24,000 in order to cover his gambling debts. On the other hand, another middle-aged embezzler with a fine past record and a fine family is serving 20 years with 5 years probation to follow. At the same institution is a war veteran, a 39-year-old attorney who has never been in trouble before, serving 11 years for illegally importing parrots into this country. Another who is destined for the same institution is a middle-aged tax accountant who on tax fraud charges received 31 years and 31 days in consecutive sentences. In stark contrast, at the same institution last year an unstable young man served out his 98-day sentence for armed bank robbery.[7]

Protesting more than enough, let me say again that the tragic state of disorder in our sentencing practices is not attributable to any unique endowments of sadism or bestiality among judges as a species. Without claiming absolute detachment, I am prepared to hypothesize that judges in general, if only because of occupational conditioning, may be somewhat calmer, more dispassionate, and more humane than the average of people across the board. But nobody has the experience of being sentenced by "judges in general." The particular defendant on some existential day confronts a specific judge. The occupant of the bench on that day may be punitive, patriotic, self-righteous, guilt-ridden, and more than customarily dyspeptic. The vice in our system is that all such qualities have free rein as well as potentially fatal impact upon the defendant's finite life.

Such individual, personal powers are not evil only, or mainly, because evil people may come to hold positions of authority. The more pervasive wrong is that a regime of substantially limitless discretion is by definition arbitrary, capricious, and antithetical to the rule of law. Some judges I know believe (and act on the belief) that all draft resisters should receive the maximum sentence, five years; this iron view rests variously upon calculations concerning time off for good behavior, how long those in uniform serve, how contemptible it is to refuse military service, etc. Other judges I know have thought, at least lately, that persons opposing service on grounds of moral or other principle, even if technically guilty of a felony, should be subjected to token terms in prison, or none at all. It is not directly pertinent here whether either category of judge is right, or whether both have failed to exercise, case by case, the discretion with which the law entrusts them. The simple point at the moment is the contrast between such individual, personal, conflicting criterian and the ideal of the rule of law.

Beyond the random spreads of judicial attitudes, there is broad latitude in our sentencing laws for kinds of class bias that are commonly known, never explicitly acknowledged, and at war with the superficial neutrality of the statute as literally written. Judges are on the whole more likely to have known personally tax evaders, or people just like tax evaders, than car thieves or dope pushers. Dichotomies of a similar kind are obvious beyond the need to multiply examples. Can such items of personal experience fail to have effects upon sentencing? I do not stop at simpleminded observations about the substantial numbers of judges who simply do not impose prison sentences for tax evasion though the federal law, for example, provides a maximum of five years per count (and tax-evasion prosecutions frequently involve several tax years, with each a separate count). There are more things at stake than judicial "bias" when tax evaders average relatively rare and brief prison terms, while more frequent and much longer average terms (under a statute carrying the same five year maximum) are imposed for interstate transport of stolen motor vehicles.[8] Whatever other factors may be operating, however, it is not possible to avoid the impression that the judges' private senses of good and evil are playing significant parts no matter what the law on the books may define as the relative gravity of the several crimes. And, although it anticipates a later subject, this is certainly the focus of the familiar jailhouse complaint that "the more you steal, the less of a sentence you get." I believe the complaint has a basis in the fundamental realities and in the way justice is seen to be dispensed. The latter aspect is important in itself; among our sounder aphorisms is the one teaching that justice must not only be done, but must appear to be done.

Both objectives are missed by a system leaving to individual preferences and value judgments the kind of discretion our judges have over sentencing.

I have touched upon individual traits of temperament and variations of an ideological, political, or social character. The sentencing power is so far unregulated that even matters of a relatively technical, seemingly "legal" nature are left for the individual judge, and thus for whimsical handling, at least in the sense that no two judges need be the same. Should a defendant be deemed to deserve some leniency if he has pled guilty rather than going to trial? Many judges say yes; many, perhaps a minority, say no; all do as they please. Should a prior criminal record enhance punishment? Most judges seem to think so. Some take the view that having "paid the price" for prior offenses, the defendant should not pay again now. Again, dealer's choice. Many judges believe it a mitigating factor if defendant yields to the pressure, moral or other, to pay back what he has taken. Others condemn this view as an illicit use of criminal sanctions for private redress. Once more, no rule of law enforces either of these contradictory judgments. There are other illustrations — relating, for example, to family conditions, defendant's behavior at trial, the consideration, if any, for turning state's evidence — all subject to the varying and unregulated views of judges. The point is, I hope, sufficiently made that our sentencing judgments splay wildly as results of unpredicatable and numerous variables embodied in the numerous and variegated inhabitants of our trial benches.

Among the articles of wisdom for which we honor those who wrote the American Constitution was the keen concern to test all powers by the possiblity of having wicked or otherwise unsound men in office. In this realistic light, it was deemed vital to confine power as much as possible and to hedge it about with checking and balancing powers. Like everything, such precautions can be overdone. But we have lost sight of them almost entirely, and without justification, in our sweeping grants of sentencing authority.

Notes

[1]Everything in law, as in life, has exceptions. So I should acknowledge that there are here and there in the law schools some meaningful offerings on the subject. Professor Leonard Orland of the University of Connecticut Law School has lately been giving a well-stocked course on post-conviction matters, including significant and provocative ideas about sentencing. My thoughtful and energetic colleagues on the Federal District Court for the Southern District of New York, Judge Harold R. Tyler, Jr., has been finding time in recent years to offer enlightenment on similar subjects at the New York University School of Law. I am certain there are other things of the sort in progress elsewhere. The general point I have made remains basically accurate even today and was sound without noticeable qualification when people now judging went to law school.

[2]I am not myself in a position for exuberant stone-throwing. Before I became a trial judge in 1965, I had spent many years working mainly as an appellate lawyer. I had tried some cases and done a fair amount of trial lawyer's work, but had managed somehow never to face a jury. I had argued criminal appeals, but had never been on either side of a criminal trial. In defense of myself and the bar-association committees that found me acceptable, if not the answer to their prayers, I think it fair to add that the mechanics and economics of big-city law practice lead the members of large, respectable law firms to settle most of their clients' disputes short of actual trial.

[3]Judicail Conference of Senior Circuit Judges, *Report of the Committee on Punishment for Crime,* pp. 26, 27 (1942).

[4]"The Sentence—Its Relation to Crime and Rehabilitation," in *Of Prisons and Justice.* S. Doc. No. 70, 88th Cong., 2d sess., p. 311 (1964).

[5]Only the prissiness of a lawyer's training would require a footnote here to acknowledge that I have neglected the calculation of probable time off for good behavior.

[6]Dr. Willard Gaylin, in his work *In the Service of their Country — War Resisters in Prison* (New York, Viking Press, 1970), p. 283, reports an episode identical with mine about Judge X. There is other evidence—including, I fear, some results of my own introspection—that the defendant's rare outburst may carry a monstrous price.

[7]"Countdown for Judicial Sentencing" in *Of Prisons and Justice.* S. Doc. No. 70, 88th Cong., 2d sess., p. 331 (1964).

[8]It may serve only to confirm a priori hunches, but consider these illustrative figures for federal sentences in the fiscal year 1969. Of 502 defendants convicted for income tax fraud, 95, or 19 percent, received prison terms, the average term being three months. Of 3,791 defendants sentenced for auto theft, 2,373, or 63 percent, went to prison, the average term being 7.6 months. From the Administrative Office of the U.S. Courts' publication, *Federal Offenders in the United States District Courts,* 1969, pp. 146-7 (1971).

10

The Practice of Law as a Con Game

Abraham S. Blumberg

A recurring theme in the growing dialogue between sociology and law has been the great need for a joint effort of the two disciplines to illuminate urgent social and legal issues. Having uttered fervent public pronouncements in this vein, however, the respective practitioners often go their separate ways. Academic spokesmen for the legal profession are somewhat critical of sociologists of law because of what they perceive as the sociologist's preoccupation with the application of theory and methodology to the examination of legal phenomena, without regard to the solution of legal problems. Further, it is felt that "contemporary writing in the sociology of law...betrays the existence of painfully unsophisticated notions about the day-to-day operations of courts, legislatures and law offices."[1] Regardless of the merit of such criticism, scant attention—apart from explorations of the legal profession itself—has been given to the sociological examination of legal institutions, or their supporting ideological assumptions. Thus, for example, very little sociological effort is expended to ascertain the validity and viability of important court decisions, which may rest on wholly erroneous assumptions about the contextual realities of social structure. A particular decision may rest upon a legally impeccable rationale; at the same time it may be rendered nugatory

Blumberg, Abraham, "The Practice of Law as a Confidence Game," *Law and Society Review.* (June, 1967), pp. 15-39.

or self-defeating by contingencies imposed by aspects of social reality of which the lawmakers are themselves unaware.

Within this context, I wish to question the impact of three recent landmark decisions of the United States Supreme Court; each hailed as destined to effect profound changes in the future of criminal law administration and enforcement in America. The first of these, *Gideon vs. Wainwright,* 372 U.S. 335 (1963) required states and localities henceforth to furnish counsel in the case of indigent persons charged with a felony.[2] The Gideon ruling left several major issues unsettled, among them the vital question: What is the precise point in time at which a suspect is entitled to counsel?[3] The answer came relatively quickly in *Escobedo v. Illinois,* 378 U.S. 478 (1964), which has aroused a storm of controversy. Danny Escobedo confessed to the murder of his brother-in-law after the police had refused to permit retained counsel to see him, although his lawyer was present in the station house and asked to confer with his client. In a 5-4 decision, the court asserted that counsel must be permitted when the process of police investigative effort shifts from merely investigatory to that of accusatory: "when its focus is on the accused and its purpose is to elicit a confession—our adversary system begins to operate, and, under the circumstances here, the accused must be permitted to consult with his lawyer."

As a consequence, Escobedo's confession was rendered inadmissible. The decision triggered a national debate among police, district attorneys, judges, lawyers, and other law enforcement officials, which continues unabated, as to the value and propriety of confessions in criminal cases.[4] On June 13, 1966, the Supreme Court in a 5-4 decision underscored the principle enunciated in *Escobedo* in the case of *Miranda v. Arizona.*[5] Police interrogation of any suspect in custody, without his consent, unless a defense attorney is present, is prohibited by the self-incrimination provision of the Fifth Amendment. Regardless of the relative merit of the various shades of opinion about the role of counsel in criminal cases, the issues generated thereby will be in part resolved as additional cases move toward decision in the Supreme Court in the near future. They are of peripheral interest and not of immediate concern in this paper. However, the *Gideon, Escobedo,* and *Miranda* cases pose interesting questions. In all three decisions, the Supreme Court reiterates the traditional legal conception of a defense lawyer based on the ideological perception of a criminal case as an *adversary, combative* proceeding, in which counsel for the defense assiduously musters all the admittedly limited resources at his command to *defend* the accused.[6] The fundamental question remains to be answered: Does the Supreme Court's conception of the role of counsel in a criminal case square with social reality?

The task of this paper is to furnish some preliminary evidence toward the illumination of that question. Little empirical understanding of the function of defense counsel exists; only some ideologically oriented generalizations and commitments. This paper is based upon observations made by the writer during many years of legal practice in the criminal courts of a large metropolitan area. No claim is made as to its methodological rigor, although it does reflect a conscious and sustained effort for participant observations.

Court Structure Defines Role of Defense Lawyer

The overwhelming majority of convictions in criminal cases (usually over 90 per cent) are not the product of a combative, trial-by-jury process at all, but instead merely involve the sentencing of the individual after a nego-tiated, bargained-for plea of guilty has been entered.[7] Although more recently the overzealous role of police and prosecutors in producing pretrial confessions and admissions has achieved a good deal of notoriety, scant attention has been paid to the organizational structure and personnel of the criminal court itself. Indeed, the extremely high conviction rate produced without the features of an adversary trial in our courts would tend to suggest that the "trial" becomes a perfunctory reiteration and validation of the pretrial interrogation and investigation.[8]

The institutional setting of the court defines a role for the defense counsel in a criminal case radically different from the one traditionally depicted.[9] Sociologists and others have focused their attention on the deprivations and social disabilities of such variables as race, ethnicity, and social class as being the source of an accused person's defeat in a criminal court. Largely overlooked is the variable of the court organization itself, which possesses a thrust, purpose, and direction of its own. It is grounded in pragmatic values, bureaucratic priorities, and administrative instruments. These exalt maximum production and the particularistic career designs of organizational incumbents, whose ocupational and career commitments tend to generate a set of priorities. These priorities exert a higher claim than the stated ideological goals of "due process of law," and are often inconsistent with them.

Organizational goals and discipline impose a set of demands and conditions of practice on the respective professions in the criminal court, to which they respond by abandoning their ideological and professional commitments to the accused client, in the service of these higher claims of the court organization. All court personnel, including the accused's own lawyer, tend to be coopted to become agent-mediators[10] who help the accused redefine his situation and restructure his perceptions concomitant with a plea of guilty.

Of all the occupational roles in the court the only private individual who is officially recognized as having a special status and concomitant obligations is the lawyer. His legal status is that of "an officer of the court" and he is held to a standard of ethical performance and duty to his client as well as to the court. This obligation is thought to be far higher than that expected of ordinary individuals occupying the various occupational statuses in the court community. However, lawyers, whether privately retained or of the legal-aid, public defender variety, have close and continuing relations with the prosecuting office and the court itself through discreet relations with the judges via their law secretaries of "confidential" assistants. Indeed, lines of communication, influence and contact with those offices, as well as with the Office of the Clerk of the court, Probation Division, and with the press, are essential to present and prospective requirements of criminal law practice. Similarly, the subtle involvement of the press and other mass media in the court's organizational network is not readily discernible to the casual observer. Accused persons come and go in the court system schema, but the structure and its occupational incumbents remain to carry on their respective career, occupational and organizational enterprises. The individual stridencies, tensions, and conflicts a given accused person's case may present to all the participants are overcome, because the formal and informal relations of all the groups in the court setting require it. The probability of continued future relations and interactions must be preserved at all costs.

This is particularly true of the "lawyer regulars" i.e., those defense lawyers, who by virtue of their continuous appearances in behalf of defendants, tend to represent the bulk of a criminal court's non-indigént case workload, and those lawyers who are not "regulars," who appear almost casually in behalf of an occasional client. Some of the "lawyer regulars" are highly visible as one moves about the major urban centers of the nation, their offices line the back streets of the courthouses, at times sharing space with bondsmen. Their political "visibility" in terms of local club house ties, reaching into the judge's chambers and prosecutor's office, are also deemed essential to successful practitioners. Previous research has indicated that the "lawyer regulars" make no effort to conceal their dependence upon police, bondsmen, jail personnel. Nor do they conceal the necessity for maintaining intimate relations with all levels of personnel in the court setting as a means of obtaining, maintaining, and building their practice. These informal relations are the *sine qua non* not only of retaining a practice, but also in the negotiation of pleas and sentences.[11]

The client, then, is a secondary figure in the court system as in certain other bureaucratic settings.[12] He becomes a means to other ends of the organization's incumbents. He may present doubts, contingencies, and pressures which challenge existing informal arrangements or disrupt them; but these tend to be resolved in favor of the continuance of the organization and its relations as before. There is a greater community of interest among all the principal organizational structures and their incumbents than exists elsewhere in other settings. The accused's lawyer has far greater professional, economic, intellectual and other ties to the various elements of the court system than he does to his own client. In short, the court is a closed community.

This is more than just the case of the usual "secrets" of bureaucracy which are fanatically defended from an outside view. Even all elements of the press are zealously determined to report on that which will not offend the board of judges, the prosecutor, probation, legal-aid, or other officials, in return for privileges and courtesies granted in the past and to be granted in the future. Rather than any view of the matter in terms of some variation of a "conspiracy" hypothesis, the simple explanation is one of an ongoing system handling delicate tensions, managing the trauma produced by law enforcement and administration, and requiring almost pathological distrust of "outsiders" bordering on group paranoia.

The hostile attitude toward "outsiders" is in large measure engendered by a defensiveness itself produced by the inherent deficiencies of assembly line justice, so characteristic of our major criminal courts. Intolerably large caseloads of defendants which must be disposed of in an organizational context of limited resources and personnel, potentially subject the participants in the court community to harsh scrutiny from appellate courts, and other public and private sources of condemnation. As a consequence, an almost irreconcilable conflict is posed in terms of intense pressures to process large numbers of cases on the one hand, and the stringent ideological and legal requirements of "due process of law," on he other hand. A rather tenuous resolution of the dilemma has emerged in the shape of a large variety of bureaucratically ordained and controlled "work crimes," short cuts, deviations, and outright rule violations adopted as court practice in order to meet production norms. Fearfully anticipating criticism on ethical as well as legal grounds, all the significant participants in the court's social structure are bound into an organized system of complicity. This consists of a work arrangement in which the patterned, covert, informal breaches, and evasions of "due process" are institutionalized, but are nevertheless denied to exist.

These institutionalized evasions will be found to occur to some degree, in all criminal courts. Their nature, scope and complexity are largely determined by the size of the court, and the character of the community in which it is located, e.g., whether it is a large, urban institution, or a relatively small rural county court. In addition, idiosyncratic, local conditions may contribute to a unique flavor in the character and quality of the criminal law's administration in a particular community. However, in most instances a variety of strategems are employed—some subtle, some crude, in effectively disposing of what are often too large caseloads. A wide variety of coercive devices are employed against an accused-client, couched in a depersonalized, instrumental, bureaucratic version of due process of law, and which are in reality a perfunctory obeisance to the ideology of due process. These include some very explicit pressures which are exerted in some measure by all court personnel, including judges, to plead guilty and avoid trial. In many instances the sanction of a potentially harsh sentence is utilized as the visible alternative to pleading guilty, in the case of recalcitrants. Probation and psychiatric reports are "tailored" to organizational needs, or are at least responsive to the court organization's requirements for the refurbishment of a defendant's social biography, consonant with his new status. A resourceful judge can, through his subtle domination of the proceedings, impose his will on the final outcome of a trial. Stenographers and clerks, in their function as record keepers, are on occasion pressed into service in support of a judicial need to "rewrite" the record of a courtroom event. Bail practices are usually employed for purposes other than simply assuring a defendant's presence on the date of a hearing in connection with his case. Too often, the discretionary power as to bail is part of the arsenal of weapons available to collapse the resistance of an accused person. The foregoing is a most cursory examination of some of the more prominent "short cuts" available to any court organization. There are numerous other procedural strategies constituting due process deviations, which tend to become the work style artifacts of a court's personnel. Thus, only court "regulars" who are "bound in" are really accepted; others are treated routinely and in almost a coldly correct manner.

The defense attorneys, therefore, whether of the legal-aid, public defender variety, or privately retained, although operating in terms of pressures specific to their respective role and organizational obligations, ultimately are concerned with strategies which tend to lead to a plea. It is the rational, impersonal elements involving economies of time, labor, expense and a superior commitment of the defense counsel to these rationalistic values of maximum production[13] of court organization that prevail, in his relationship with a client. The lawyer "regulars" are frequently former staff members of the prosecutor's office and utilize the prestige, know-how and contacts of their former affiliation as part of their stock in trade. Close and continuing relations between the lawyer "regular" and his former colleagues in the prosecutor's office generally overshadow the relationship between the regular and his client. The continuing colleagueship of supposedly adversary counsel rests on real professional and organizational needs of a *quid pro quo*, which goes behond the limits of an accommodation or *modus vivendi* one might ordinarily expect under the circumstances of an otherwise seemingly adversary relationship. Indeed, the adversary

features which are manifest are for the most part muted and exist even in
their attenuated form largely for external consumption. The principals,
lawyer and assistant district attorney, rely upon one another's cooperation
for their continued professional existence, and so the bargaining between
them tends usually to be "reasonable" rather than fierce.

Fee Collection and Fixing

The real key to understanding the role of defense counsel in a criminal
case is to be found in the area of the fixing of the fee to be charged and its
collection. The problem of fixing and collecting the fee tends to influence to
a significant degree the criminal court process itself, and not just the
relationship of the lawyer and his client. In essence, a lawyer-client "confidence game" is played. A true confidence game is unlike the case of the
emperor's new clothes wherein that monarch's nakedness was a result of
inordinate gullibility and credulity. In a genuine confidence game, the perpetrator manipulates the basic dishonesty of his partner, the victim or
mark, toward his own (the confidence operator's) ends. Thus, "the victim
of a con scheme must have some larceny in his heart."[14]

Legal service lends itself particularly well to confidence games. Usually, a
plumber will be able to demonstrate empirically that he has performed a
service by clearing up the stuffed drain, repairing the leaky faucet or
pipe—and therefore merits his fee. He has rendered, when summoned, a
visible, tangible boon for his client in return for the requested fee. A
physician, who has not performed some visible surgery or otherwise
engaged in some readily discernible procedure in connection with a patient,
may be deemed by the patient to have "done nothing" for him. As a consequence, medical practitioners may simply prescribe or administer by
injection a placebo to overcome a patient's potential reluctance or dissatisfaction in paying a requested fee, "for nothing."

In the practice of law there is a special problem in this regard, no matter
what the level of the practitioner or his place in the hierarchy of prestige.
Much legal work is intangible either because it is simply a few words of
advice, some preventive action, a telephone call, negotiation of some kind,
a form filled out and filed, a hurried conference with another attorney or an
official of a government agency, a letter or opinion written, or a countless
variety of seemingly innocuous, and even prosaic procedures and actions.
These are the basic activities, apart from any possible court appearance, of
almost all lawyers, at all levels of practice. Much of the activity is not in the
nature of the exercise of the traditional, precise professional skills of
attorney such as library research and oral argument in connection with
appellate briefs, court motions, trial work, drafting of opinions,

memoranda, contracts, and other complex documents and agreements. Instead, much legal activity, whether it is at the lowest or highest "white shoe" law firm levels, is of the brokerage, agent, sales representative, lobbyist type of activity, in which the lawyer acts for someone else in pursuing the latter's interests and designs. The service is intangible.[15]

The large scale law firm may not speak as openly of the "contacts," their "fixing' abilities, as does the lower level lawyer. They trade instead upon a facade of thick carpeting, walnut panelling, genteel low pressure, and superficialities of traditional legal professionalism. There are occasions when even the large firm is on the defensive in connection with the fees they charge because the services rendered or results obtained do not appear to merit the fee asked.[16] Therefore, there is a recurrent problem in the legal profession in fixing the amount of fee, and in justifying the basis for the requested fee.

Although the fee at times amounts to what the traffic and the conscience of the lawyer will bear, one further observation must be made with regard to the size of the fee and its collection. The defendant in a criminal case and the material gain he may have acquired during the course of his illicit activities are soon parted. Not infrequently the ill gotten fruits of the various modes of larceny are sequestered by a defense lawyer in payment of his fee. Inexorably, the amount of the fee is a function of the dollar value of the crime committed, and is frequently set with meticulous precision at a sum which bears an uncanny relationship to that of the net proceeds of the particular offense involved. On occasion, defendants have been known to commit additional offenses while at liberty on bail, in order to secure the requisite funds with which to meet their obligations for payment of legal fees. Defense lawyers condition even the most obtuse clients to recognize that there is a firm interconnection between fee payment and the zealous exercise of professional expertise, secret knowledge, and organizational "connections" in their behalf. Lawyers, therefore, seek to keep their clients in a proper state of tension, and to arouse in them the precise edge of anxiety which is calculated to encourage prompt fee payment. Consequently, the client attitude in the relationship between defense counsel and an accused is in many instances a precarious admixture of hostility, mistrust, dependence, and sycophancy. By keeping his client's anxieties aroused to the proper pitch, and establishing a seemingly causal relationship between a requested fee and the accused's ultimate extrication from his onerous difficulties, the lawyer will have established the necessary preliminary groundwork to assure a minimum of haggling over the fee and its eventual payment.

In varying degrees, as a consequence, all law practice involves a manipulation of the client and a stage management of the lawyer-client relationship so that at least an *appearance* of help and service will be forthcoming. This is accomplished in a variety of ways, often exercised in combination with each other. At the outset, the lawyer-professional employs with suitable varition a measure of sales-puff which may range from an air of unbounding self-confidence, adequacy, and dominion over events, to that of complete arrogance. This will be supplemented by the affectation of a studied, faultless mode of personal attire. In the larger firms, the furnishings and office trappings will serve as the backdrop to help in impression management and client intimidation. In all firms, solo or large scale, an access to secret knowledge, and to the seats of power and influence is inferred, or presumed to a varying degree as the basic vendible commodity of the practicitioners.

The lack of visible end product offers a special complication in the course of the professional life of the criminal court lawyer with respect to his fee and in his relations with his client. The plain fact is that an accused in a criminal case always "loses" even when he has been exonerated by an acquittal, discharge, or dismissal of his case. The hostility of an accused which follows as a consequence of his arrest, incarceration, possible loss of job, expense and other traumas connected with his case is directed, by means of displacement, toward his lawyer. It is in this sense that it may be said that a criminal lawyer never really "wins" a case. The really satisfied client is rare, since in the very nature of the situation even an accused's vindication leaves him with some degree of dissatisfaction and hostility. It is this state of affairs that makes for a lawyer-client relationship in the criminal court which tends to be a somewhat exaggerated version of the usual lawyer-client confidence game.

At the outset, because there are great risks of nonpayment of the fee, due to the impecuniousness of his clients, and the fact that a man who is sentenced to jail may be a singularly unappreciative client, the criminal lawyer collects his fee *in advance*. Often, because the lawyer and the accused both have questionable designs of their own upon each other, the confidence game can be played. The criminal lawyer must serve three major functions, or stated another way, he must solve three problems. First, he must arrange for his fee; second, he must prepare and then, if necessary, "cool out" his client in case of defeat[17] (a highly likely contingency); third, he must satisfy the court organization that he has performed adequately in the process of negotiating the plea, so as to preclude the possibility of any sort of embarrassing incident which may serve to invite "outside" scrutiny.

In assuring the attainment of one of his primary objectives, his fee, the criminal lawyer will very often enter into negotiations with the accused's kin, including collateral relatives. In many instances, the accused himself is unable to pay any sort of fee or anything more than a token fee. It then becomes important to involve as many of the accused's kin as possible in the situation. This is especially so if the attorney hopes to collect a significant

part of a proposed substantial fee. It is not uncommon for several relatives
to contribute toward the fee. The larger the group, the greater the
possibility that the lawyer will collect a sizable fee by getting contributions
from each.

A fee for a felony case which ultimately results in a plea, rather than a
trail, may ordinarily range anywhere from $500 to $1,500. Should the case
go to trial, the fee will be proportionately larger, depending upon the length
of the trial. But the larger the fee the lawyer wishes to exact, the more
impressive his performance must be, in terms of his stage managed image as
a personage of great influence and power in the court organization. Court
personnel are keenly aware of the extent to which a lawyer's stock in trade
involves the precarious stage management of an image which goes beyond
the usual professional flamboyance, and for this reason alone the lawyer is
"bound in" to the authority system of the court's organizational discipline.
Therefore, to some extent, court personnel will aid the lawyer in the
creation and maintenance of.that impression. There is a tacit commitment
to the lawyer by the court organization, apart from formal etiquette, to aid
him in this. Such augmentation of the lawyer's stage managed image as this
affords, is the partial basis for the *quid pro quo* which exists between the
lawyer and the court organization. It tends to serve as the continuing basis
for the higher loyalty of the lawyer to the organization; his relationship with
his client, in contrast is transient, ephemeral and often superficial.

Defense Lawyer as Double Agent

The lawyer has often been accused of stirring up unnecessary litigation,
especially in the field of negligence. He is said to acquire a vested interest in
a cause of action or claim which was initially his client's. The strong
incentive of possible fee motivates the lawyer to promote litigation which
would otherwise never have developed. However, the criminal lawyer
develops a vested interest of an entirely different nature in his client's case:
to limit its scope and duration rather than do battle. Only in this way can a
case be "profitable." Thus, he enlists the aid of relatives not only to assure
payment of his fee, but he will also rely on these persons to help him in his
agent-mediator role of convincing the accused to plead guilty, and
ultimately to help in "cooling out" the accused if necessary.

It is at this point that an accused-defendant may experience his first sense
of "betrayal." While he had perhaps perceived the police and prosecutor to
be adversaries, or possibly even the judge, the accused is wholly unprepared
for his counsel's role performance as an agent-mediator. In the same vein, it
is even less likely to occur to an accused that members of his own family or
other kin may become agents, albeit at the behest and urging of other agents

or mediators, acting on the principle that they are in reality helping an accused negotiate the best possible plea arrangement under the circumstances. Usually, it will be the lawyer who will activate next of kin in this role, his ostensible motive being to arrange for his fee. But soon latent and unstated motives will assert themselves, with entreaties by counsel to the accused's next of kin, to appeal to the accused to "help himself" by pleading. *Gemeinschaft* sentiments are to this extent exploited by a defense lawyer (or even at times by a district attorney) to achieve specific secular ends, that is, of concluding a particular matter with all possible dispatch.

The fee is often collected in stages, each installment usually payable prior to a necessary court appearance required during the course of an accused's career journey. At each stage, in his interviews and communications with the accused, or in addition, with members of his family, if they are helping with the fee payment, the lawyer employs an air of professional confidence and "inside-dopesterism" in order to assuage anxieties on all sides. He makes the necessary bland assurances, and in effect manipulates his client, who is usually willing to do and say the things, true or not, which will help his attorney extricate him. Since the dimensions of what he is essentially selling, organizational influence and expertise, are not technically and precisely measurable, the lawyer can make extravagant claims of influence and secret knowledge with impunity. Thus, lawyers frequently claim to have inside knowledge in connection with information in the hands of the D.A., police, probation officials or to have access to these functionaries. Factually, they often do, and need only to exaggerate the nature of their relationships with them to obtain the desired effective impression upon the client. But, as in the genuine confidence game, the victim who has participated is loath to do anything which will upset the lesser plea which his lawyer has "conned" him into accepting.[18]

In effect, in his role as double agent, the criminal lawyer performs an extremely vital and delicate mission for the court organization and the accused. Both principals are anxious to terminate the litigation with a minimum of expense and damage to each other. There is no other personage or role incumbent in the total court structure more strategically located, who by training and in terms of his own requirements, is more ideally suited to do so than the lawyer. In recognition of this, judges will cooperate with attorneys in many important ways. For example, they will adjourn the case of an accused in jail awaiting plea or sentence if the attorney requests such action. While explicitly this may be done for some innocuous and seemingly valid reason, the tacit purpose is that pressure is being applied by the attorney for the collection of his fee, which he knows will probably not be forthcoming if the case is concluded. Judges are aware of this tactic on the part of lawyers, who, by requesting an adjournment, keep an accused incarcerated awhile longer as a not too subtle method of dunning a client for payment. However, the judges will go along with this, on the ground that important ends are being served. Often, the only end served is to protect a lawyer's fee.

The judge will help an accused's lawyer in still another way. He will lend the official aura of his office and courtroom so that a lawyer can stage manage an impression of an "all out" performance for the accused in justification of his fee. The judge and other court personnel will serve as a backdrop for a scene charged with dramatic fire, in which the accused's lawyer makes a stirring appeal in his behalf. With a show of restrained passion, the lawyer will intone the virtues of the accused and recite the social deprivations which have reduced him to his present state. The speech varies somewhat, depending on whether the accused has been convicted after trial or has pleaded guilty. In the main, however, the incongruity, superficiality, and ritualistic character of the total performance is underscored by a visibly impassive, almost bored reaction on the part of the judge and other members of the court retinue.

Afterward, there is a hearty exchange of pleasantries between the lawyer and district attorney, wholly out of context in terms of the supposed adversary nature of the preceding events. The fiery passion in defense of his client is gone, and the lawyers for both sides resume their offstage relations, chatting amiably and perhaps including the judge in their restrained banter. No other aspect of their visible conduct so effectively serves to put even a casual observer on notice, that these individuals have claims upon each other. These seemingly innocuous actions are indicative of continuing organizational and informal relations, which, in their intricacy and depth, range far beyond any priorities or claims a particular defendant my have.[19]

Criminal law practice is a unique form of private law practice since it really only appears to be private practice.[20] Actually it is bureaucratic practice, because of the legal practitioner's enmeshment in the authority, discipline, and perspectives of the court organization. Private practice, supposedly, in a professional sense, involves the maintenance of an organized, disciplined body of knowledge and learning; the individual practitioners are imbued with a spirit of autonomy and service, the earning of a livelihood being incidental. In the sense that the lawyer in the criminal court serves as a double agent, serving higher organizational rather than professional ends, he may be deemed to be engaged in bureaucratic rather than private practice. To some extent the lawyer-client "confidence game," in addition to its other functions, serves to conceal this fact.

The Client's Perception

The "cop-out" ceremony, in which the court process culminates, is not only invaluable for redefining the accused's perspectives of himself, but also in reiterating publicly in a formally structured ritual the accused person's guilt for the benefit of significant "others" who are observing. The accused not only is made to assert publicly his guilt of a specific crime, but also a complete recital of its details. He is further made to indicate that he is entering his plea of guilty freely, willingly, and voluntarily, and that he is not doing so because of any promises or in consideration of any commitments that may have been made to him by anyone. This last is intended as a blanket statement to shield the participants from any possible charges of "coercion" or undue influence that may have been exerted in violation of due process requirements. Its function is to preclude any later review by an appellate court on these grounds, and also to obviate any second thoughts an accused may develop in connection with his plea.

However, for the accused, the conception of self as a guilty person is in large measure a temporary role adaptation. His career socialization as an accused, if it is successful, eventuates in his acceptance and redefinition of himself as a guilty person.[21] However, the transformation is ephemeral, in that he will, in private, quickly reassert his innocence. Of importance is that he accept his defeat, publicly proclaim it, and find some measure of pacification in it.[22] Almost immediately after his plea, a defendant will generally be interviewed by a representative of the probation division in connection with a presentence report which is to be prepared. The very first question to be asked of him by the probation officer is: "Are you guilty of the crime to which you pleaded?" This is by way of double affirmation of the defendant's guilt. Should the defendant now begin to make bold assertions of his innocence, despite his plea of guilty, he will be asked to withdraw his plea and stand trial on the original charges. Such a threatened possibility is, in most instances, sufficient to cause an accused to let the plea stand and to request the probation officer to overlook his exclamations of innocence. Table I that follows is a breakdown of the categorized responses of a random sample of male defendants in Metropolitan Court[23] during 1962, 1963, and 1964 in connection with their statements during presentence probation interviews following their plea of guilty.

It would be well to observe at the outset, that of the 724 defendants who pleaded guilty before trial, only 43 (5.94 per cent) of the total group had confessed prior to their indictment. Thus, the ultimate judicial process was predicated upon evidence independent of any confession of the accused.[24]

As the data indicate, only a relatively small number (95) out of the total number of defendants actually will even admit their guilt, following the "cop-out" ceremony. However, even though they have affirmed their guilt, many of these defendants felt that they should have been able to negotiate a more favorable plea. The largest aggregate of defendants (373) were those who reasserted their "innocence" following their public profession of guilt during the "cop-out" ceremony. These defendants employed differential degrees of fervor, solemnity and credibility, ranging from really mild, wavering assertions of innocence which were embroidered with a variety of stock explanations and rationalizations, to those of an adamant, "framed" nature. Thus, the "Innocent" group, for the most part, were largely concerned with underscoring for their probation interviewer their essential "goodness" and "worthiness," despite their formal plea of guilty. Assertion of his innocence at the post-plea stage, resurrects a more respectable and acceptable self concept for the accused defendant who has pleaded guilty. A recital of the structural exigencies which precipitated his plea of guilt, serves to embellish a newly proffered claim of innocence, which many

Table I

Defendant Responses as to Guilt or Innocence after Pleading Guilty

N = 724   Years — 1962, 1963, 1964

Nature of Response		N of Defendants
Innocent (Manipulated)	"The lawyer or judge, police or D.A. 'conned me'"	86
Innocent (Pragmatic)	"Wanted to get it over with" "You can't beat the system" "They have you over a barrel when you have a record"	147
Innocent (Advice of counsel)	"Followed my lawyer's advice"	92
Innocent (Defiant)	"Framed" — "Betrayed by 'Complainant,' 'Police,' 'Squealers,' 'Lawyer,' 'Friends,' 'Wife,' 'Girlfriend'"	33
Innocent (Adverse social data)	Blames probation officer or psychiatrist for "Bad Report," in cases where there was pre-pleading investigation	15
Guilty	"But I should have gotten a better deal" Blames Lawyer, D.A., Police, Judge	74
Guilty	Won't say anything further	21
Fatalistic (Doesn't press his "Innocence," won't admit "Guilt")	"I did it for convenience" "My lawyer told me it was only thing I could do" "I did it because it was the best way out"	248
No Response		8
Total		724

defendants mistakenly feel will stand them in good stead at the time of sentence, or ultimately with probation or parole authorities.

Relatively few (33) maintained their innocence in terms of having been "framed" by some person or agent-mediator, although a larger number (86) indicated that they had been manipulated or "conned" by an agent-mediator to plead guilty, but as indicated, their assertions of innocence were relatively mild.

A rather substantial group (147) preferred to stress the pragmatic aspects of their plea of guilty. They would only perfunctorily assert their innocence and would in general refer to some adverse aspect of their situation which they believed tended to negatively affect their bargaining leverage, including in some instances a prior criminal record.

One group of defendants (92), while maintaining their innocence, simply employed some variation of a theme of following "the advice of counsel" as a covering response, to explain their guilty plea in the light of their new affirmation of innocence.

The largest single group of defendants (248) were basically fatalistic. They often verbalized weak suggestions of their innocence in rather halting terms, wholly without conviction. By the same token, they would not admit guilt readily and were generally evasive as to guilt or innocence, preferring to stress aspects of their stoic submission in their decision to plead. This sizable group of defendants appeared to perceive the total court process as being caught up in a monstrous organizational apparatus, in which the defendant role expectancies were not clearly defined. Reluctant to offend anyone in authority, fearful that clear-cut statements on their part as to their guilt or innocence would be negatively construed, they adopted a stance of passivity, resignation and acceptance. Interestingly, they would in most instances invoke their lawyer as being the one who crystallized the available alternatives for them, and who was therefore the critical element in their decision-making process.

In order to determine which agent-mediator was most influential in altering the accused's perspectives as to his decision of plead or go to trial (regardless of the proposed basis of the plea), the same sample of defendants were asked to indicate the person who first suggested to them that they plead guilty. They were also asked to indicate which of the persons or officials who made such suggestion, was most influential in affecting their final decision to plead.

The following table indicates the breakdown of the responses to the two questions:

It is popularly assumed that the police, through forced confessions, and the district attorney, employing still other pressures, are most instrumental in the inducement of an accused to plead guilty.[25] As Table II indicates, it is actually the defendant's own counsel who is most effective in this role.

Further, this phenomenon tends to reinforce the extremely rational nature of criminal law administration, for an organization could not rely upon the sort of idosyncratic measures employed by the police to induce confessions and maintain its efficiency, high production and overall rational-legal character. The defense counsel becomes the ideal agent-mediator since, as "officer of the court" and confidant of the accused and his kin, he lives astride both worlds and can serve the ends of the two as well as his own.[26]

Table II
Role of Agent-mediators in Defendant's Guilty Plea

Person or Official	First Suggested Plea of Guilty	Influenced the Accused Most in His Final Decision to Plead
Judge	4	26
District attorney	67	116
Defense counsel	407	411
Probation officer	14	3
Psychiatrist	8	1
Wife	34	120
Friends and kin	21	14
Police	14	4
Fellow inmates	119	14
Others	28	5
No response	8	10
Total	724	724

While an accused's wife, for example, may be influential in making him more amenable to a plea, her agent-mediator role has, nevertheless, usually been sparked and initiated by defense counsel. Further, although a number of first suggestions of a plea came from an accused's fellow jail inmates, he tended to rely largely on his counsel as an ultimate source of influence in his final decision. The defense counsel, being a crucial figure in the total organizational scheme in constituting a new set of perspectives for the accused, the same sample of defendants were asked to indicate at which stage of their contact with counsel was the suggestion of a plea made. There are three basic kinds of defense counsel available in Metropolitan Court: Legal-aid, privately retained counsel, and counsel assigned by the court (but may eventually be privately retained by the accused).

The overwhelming majority of accused persons, regardless of type of counsel, related a specific incident which indicated an urging or suggestion, either during the course of the first or second contact, that they plead guilty to a lesser charge if this could be arranged. Of all the agent-mediators, it is the lawyer who is most effective in manipulating an accused's perspectives, notwithstanding pressures that may have been previously applied by police, district attorney, judge or any of the agent-mediators that may have been activated by them. Legal-aid and assigned counsel would apparently be more likely to suggest a possible plea at the point of initial interview as response to pressures of time. In the case of the assigned counsel, the strong possibility that there is no fee involved, may be an added impetus to such a suggestion at the first contact.

In addition, there is some further evidence in Table III of the perfunctory, ministerial character of the system in Metropolitan Court and similar criminal courts. There is little real effort to individualize, and the lawyer's role as agent-mediator may be seen as unique in that he is in effect a double agent. Although, as "officer of the court" he mediates between the court organization and the defendant, his roles with respect to each are rent by conflicts of interest. Too often these must be resolved in favor of the organization which provides him with the means for his professional existence. Consequently, in order to reduce the strains and conflicts imposed in what is ultimately an overdemanding role obligation for him, the lawyer engages in the lawyer-client "confidence game" so as to structure more favorably an otherwise onerous role system.[27]

Table III
Stage at Which Counsel Suggested Accused to Plead

N = 724

| | Counsel Type | | | | | | | |
| | Privately Retained | | Legal-aid | | Assigned | | Total | |
Contact	N	%	N	%	N	%	N	%
First	66	35	237	49	28	60	331	46
Second	83	44	142	29	8	17	233	32
Third	29	15	63	13	4	9	96	13
Fourth or more	12	6	31	7	5	11	48	7
No response	0	0	14	3	2	4	16	2
Total	190	100	487	101*	47	101*	724	100

Conclusion

Recent decisions of the Supreme Court, in the area of criminal law administration and defendant's rights, fail to take into account three crucial aspects of social structure which may tend to render the more libertarian rules as nugatory. The decisions overlook (1) the nature of courts as formal organization; (2) the relationship that the lawyer-regular *actually* has with the court organization; and (3) the character of the lawyer-client relationship in the criminal court (the routine relationships, not those unusual ones that are described in "heroic" terms in novels, movies, and TV).

Courts, like many other modern large-scale organizations possess a monstrous appetite for the cooptation of entire professional groups as well as individuals.[28] Almost all those who come within the ambit of organizational authority, find that their definitions, perceptions and values have been refurbished, largely in terms favorable to the particular organization and its goals. As a result, recent Supreme Court decisions may have a long range effect which is radically different from that intended or anticipated. The more libertarian rules will tend to produce the rather ironic end result of augmenting the *existing* organizational arrangements, enriching court organizations with more personnel and elaborate structure, which in turn will maximize organizational goals of "efficiency" and production. Thus, many defendants will find that courts will possess an even more sophisticated apparatus for processing them toward a guilty plea!

Notes

[1]H.W. Jones, *A View From the Bridge,* Law and Society: Supplement to Summer, 1965 Issue of Social Problems 42 (1965). See G. Geis, *Sociology, Criminology, and Criminal Law,* 7 Social Problems 40-47 (1959); N.S. Timasheff, *Growth and Scope of Sociology of Law,* in *Modern Sociological Theory in Continuity and Change* 424-49 (H. Becker & A. Boskoff, eds. 1957), for further evaluation of the strained relations between sociology and law.

[2]This decision represented the climax of a line of cases which had begun to chip away at the notion that the Sixth Amendment of the Constitution (right to assistance of counsel) applied only to the federal government, and could not be held to run against the states through the Fourteenth Amendment. An exhaustive historical analysis of the Fourteenth Amendment and the Bill of Rights will be found in C. Fairman, *Does the Fourteenth Amendment Incorporate the Bill of Rights? The Original Understanding,* 2 Stan. L. Rev. 5-139 (1949). Since the Gideon decision, there is already evidence that its effect will ultimately extend to indigent persons charged with misdemeanors — and perhaps ultimately even traffic cases and other minor offenses. For a popular account of this important development in connection with the right to assistance of counsel, see A. Lewis, *Gideon's Trumpet* (1964). For a scholarly histor-

ical analysis of the right to counsel see W.M. Beaney, *The Right to Counsel in American Courts* (1955). For a more recent comprehensive review and discussion of the right to counsel and its development, see Note, *Counsel at Interrogation*, 73 Yale L.J. 1000-57 (1964).

With the passage of the Criminal Justice Act of 1964, indigent accused persons in the federal courts will be defended by federally paid legal counsel. For a general discussion of the nature and extent of public and private legal aid in the United States prior to the Gideon case, see E.A. Brownell, *Legal Aid in the United States* (1961); also R.B. von Mehren, et al., *Equal Justice for the Accused* (1959).

[3]In the case of federal defendants the issue is clear. In *Mallory v. United States,* 354 U.S. 449 (1957), the Supreme Court unequivocally indicated that a person under federal arrest must be taken "without any unnecessary delay "before a U.S. commissioner where he will receive information as to his rights to remain silent and to assistance of counsel which will be furnished, in the event he is indigent, under the Criminal Justice Act of 1964. For a most interesting and richly documented work in connection with the general area of the Bill of Rights, see C.R. Sowle, *Police Power and Individual Freedom* (1962).

[4]See N.Y. Times, No.v 20, 1965, p. 1, for Justice Nathan R. Sobel's statement to the effect that based on his study of 1,000 indictments in Brooklyn, N.Y. from February-April, 1965, fewer than 10% involved confessions. Sobel's detailed analysis will be found in six articles which appeared in the New York Law Journal, beginning November 15, 1965, through November 21, 1965, titled *The Exclusionary Rules in the Law of Confessions: A Legal Perspective — A Practical Perspective.* Most law enforcement officials believe that the majority of convictions in criminal cases are based upon confessions obtained by police. For example, the District Attorney of New York County (a jurisdiction which has the largest volume of cases in the United States), Frank S. Hogan, reports that confessions are crucial and indicates "if a suspect is entitled to have a lawyer during preliminary questioning... any lawyer worth his fee will tell him to keep his mouth shut," N.Y. Times, Dec. 2, 1965, p. 1. Concise discussions of the issue are to be found in D. Robinson, Jr. *Massiah, Escobedo and Rationales for the Exclusion of Confessions,* 56 J. Crim. L.C. & P.S. 412-31 (1965); D.C. Dowling, *Escobedo and Beyond: The Need for a Fourteenth Amendment Code of Criminal Procedure,* 56 J. Crim. L.C. & P.S. 143-57 (1965).

[5]*Miranda v. Arizona,* 384 U.S. 436 (1966).

[6]Even under optimal circumstances a criminal case is a very much one-sided affair, the parties to the "contest" being decidedly unequal in strength and resources. See A.S. Goldstein, *The State and the Accused: Balance of Advantage in Criminal Procedure,* 69 Yale L.J. 1149-99 (1960).

[7]F.J. Davis et al., *Society and the Law: New Meanings for an Old Profession* 301 (1962); L. Orfield, *Criminal Procedure from Arrest to Appeal* 297 (1947).

D.J. Newman, *Pleading Guilty for Considerations: A Study of Bargain Justice,* 46 J. Crim. L.C. & P.S. 780-90 (1954). Newman's data covered only one year, 1954, in a midwestern community, however, it is in general confirmed by my own data drawn from a far more populous area, and from what is one of the major criminal courts in the country, for a period of fifteen years from 1950 to 1964 inclusive. The English experience tends also to confirm American data, see N.Walker, *Crime and Punishment in Britain: An Analysis of the Penal System* (1965). See also D.J. Newman, *Conviction: The Determination of Guilt or Innocence Without Trial* (1966), for a comprehensive legalistic study of the guilty plea sponsored by the American Bar Foundation. The criminal court as a social system, an analysis of "bargaining" and its functions in the criminal court's organizational structure, are examined in my forthcoming book, *The Criminal Court: A Sociological Perspective,* to be published by Quadrangle Books, Chicago.

[8]G. Feifer, *Justice in Moscow* (1965). The Soviet trial has been termed "an appeal from the pretrial investigation" and Feifer notes that the Soviet "trial" is simply a recapitulation of

the data collected by the pretrial investigator. The notions of a trial being a "tabula rasa" and presumptions of innocence are wholly alien to Soviet notions of justice. "...the closer the investigation resembels the finished script, the better...." *Id.* at 86.

⁹For a concise statement of the constitutional and economic aspects of the right to legal assistance, see M.G. Paulsen, *Equal Justice for the Poor Man* (1964); for a brief traditional description of the legal profession see P.A. Freund, *The Legal Profession,* Daedalus 689-700 (1963).

¹⁰I use the concept in the general sense that Erving Goffman employed it in his *Asylums: Essays on the Social Situation of Mental Patients and Other Inmates* (1961).

¹¹A.L. Wood, *Informal Relations in the Practice of Criminal Law,* 62 Am. J. Soc. 48-55 (1956); J.E. Carlin, *Lawyers on Their Own* 105-109 (1962); R. Goldfarb, *Ransom—A Critique of the American Bail System* 114-15 (1965). Relatively recent data as to recruitment to the legal profession, and variables involved in the type of practice engaged in, will be found in J. Ladinsky, *Careers of Lawyers, Law Practice, and Legal Institutions,* 28 Am. Soc. Rev. 47-54 (1963). See also S. Warkov & J. Zelan, *Lawyers in the Making* (1965).

¹²There is a real question to be raised as to whether in certain organizational settings, a complete reversal of the bureaucratic-ideal has not occurred. That is, it would seem, in some instances the organization appears to exist to serve the needs of its various occupational incumbents, rather than its clients. A. Etzioni, *Modern Organizations* 94-104 (1964).

¹³Three relatively recent items reported in the New York Times, tend to underscore this point as it has manifested itself in one of the major criminal courts. In one instance the Bronx County Bar Association condemned "mass assembly-line justice," which "was rushing defendants into pleas of guilty and into convictions, in violation of their legal rights." N.Y. Times, March 10, 1965, p. 51. Another item, appearing somewhat later that year reports a judge criticizing his own court system (the New York Criminal Court), that "pressure to set statistical records in disposing of cases had hurt the administration of justice." N.Y. Times, Nov. 4, 1965, p. 49. A third, and most unusual recent public discussion in the press was a statement by a leading New York appellate judge decrying "instant justice" which is employed to reduce court calendar congestion "converting our courthouses into counting houses..., as in most big cities where the volume of business tends to overpower court facilities." N.Y. Times, Feb. 5, 1966, p. 58.

¹⁴R.L. Gasser, *The Confidence Game,* 27 Fed. Prob. 47 (1963).

¹⁵C.W. Mills, *White Collar* 121-29 (1951); J.E. Carlin, *supra,* note 11.

¹⁶E.O. Smigel, *The Wall Street Lawyer* (New York: The Free Press of Glencoe, 1964), p. 309.

¹⁷Talcott Parsons indicates that the social role and function of the lawyer can be therapeutic, helping his client psychologically in giving him necessary emotional support at critical times. The lawyer is also said to be acting as an agent of social control in the counseling of his client and in the influencing of his course of conduct. See T. Parsons, *Essays in Sociological Theory,* 382 et seq. (1954); E. Goffman, *On Cooling the Mark Out; Some Aspects of Adaptations to Failure,* in *Human Behavior and Social Processes* 482-505 (A. Rose ed., 1962). Goffman's "cooling out" analysis is especially relevant in the lawyer-accused client relationship.

¹⁸The question has never been raised as to whether "bargain justice," "copping a plea," or justice by negotiations is a constitutional process. Although it has become the most central aspect of the process of criminal law administration, it has received virtually no close scrutiny by the appellate courts. As a consequence, it is relatively free of legal control and supervision. But, apart from any questions of the legality of bargaining, in terms of the pressures and devices that are employed which tend to violate due process of law, there remain ethical and practical questions. The system of bargain-counter justice is like the proverbial iceberg, much of its danger is concealed in secret negotiations and its least alarming feature, the final plea, being the one presented to public view. See A.S. Trebach, *The Rationing of Justice* 74-

94 (1964); Note, *Guilty Plea Bargaining: Compromises by Prosecutors to Secure Guilty Pleas,* 112 U. Pa. L. Rev. 865-95 (1964).

[19]For a conventional summary statement of some of the inevitable conflicting loyalties encountered in the practice of law, see E.E. Cheatham, *Cases and Materials on the Legal Profession* 70-79 (2d ed., 1955).

[20]Some lawyers at either end of the continuum of law practice appear to have grave doubts as to whether it is indeed a profession at all. J.E. Carlin, *op. cit., supra,* note 11, at 192; E.O. Smigel, *supra,* note 16 at 304-305. Increasingly, it is perceived as a business with widespread evasion of the Canons of Ethics, duplicity and chicanery being practiced in an effort to get and keep business. The poet, Carl Sandburg, epitomized this notion in the following vignette: "Have you a criminal lawyer in this burg?" "We think so but we haven't been able to prove it on him." C. Sandburg, *The People, Yes* 154 (1936).

Thus, while there is considerable amount of dishonesty present in law practice involving fee splitting, thefts from clients, influence peddling, fixing, questionable use of favors and gifts to obtain business or influence others, this sort of activity is most often attributed to the "solo," private practice lawyer. See A.L. Wood, *Professional Ethics Among Criminal Lawyers,* Social Problems (1959). However, to some degree, large scale "downtown" elite firms also engage in these dubious activities. The difference is that the latter firms enjoy a good deal of immunity from these harsh charges because of their institutional and organizational advantages, in terms of near monopoly over more desirable types of practice, as well as exerting great influence in the political, economic and professional realms of power.

[21]This does not mean that most of those who plead guilty are innocent of any crime. Indeed, in many instances those who have been able to negotiate a lesser plea, have done so willingly and eagerly. The system of justice-by-negotiation, without trial, probably tends to better serve the interests and requirements of guilty persons, who are thereby presented with formal alternatives of "half a loaf," in terms of, at worst, possibilities of a lesser plea and a concomitant shorter sentence as compensation for their acquiescence and participation. Having observed the prescriptive etiquette in compliance with the defendant role expectancies in this setting, he is rewarded. An innocent person, on the other hand, is confronted with the same set of role prescriptions, structures and legal alternatives, and in any event, for him this mode of justice is often an ineluctable bind.

[22]Any communicative network between persons whereby the public identity of an actor is transformed into something looked on as lower in the local scheme of social types will be called a 'status degradation ceremony.'" H. Garfinkel, *Conditions of Successful Degradation Ceremonies,* 61 Am. J. Soc. 420-24 (1956). But contrary to the conception of the "cop out" as a "status degradation ceremony," is the fact that it is in reality a charade, during the course of which an accused must project an appropriate and acceptable amount of guilt, penitence and remorse. Having adequately feigned the role of the "guilty person," his hearers will engage in the fantasy that he is contrite, and thereby merits a lesser plea. It is one of the essential functions of the criminal lawyer that he coach and direct his accused-client in that role performance. Thus, what is actually involved is not a "degradation" process at all, but is instead, a highly structured system of exchange cloaked in the rituals of legalism and public professions of guilt and repentance.

[23]The name is of course fictitious. However, the actual court which served as the universe from which the data were drawn, is one of the largest criminal courts in the United States, dealing with felonies only. Female defendants in the years 1950 through 1964 constituted from 7-10% of the totals for each year.

[24]My own data in this connection would appear to support Sobel's conclusion (see note 4 *supra*), and appears to be at variance with the prevalent view, which stresses the importance of confessions in law enforcement and prosecution. All the persons in my sample were originally charged with felonies ranging from homicide to forgery; in most instances the

original felony charges were reduced to misdemeanors by way of a negotiated lesser plea. The vast range of crime categories which are available, facilitates the patterned court process of plea reduction to a lesser offense, which is also usually a socially less opprobrious crime. For an illustration of this feature of the bargaining process in a court utilizing a public defender office, see D. Sudnow, *Normal Crimes: Sociological Features of the Penal Code in a Public Defender Office,* 12 Social Problems 255-76 (1964).

[25] Failures, shortcomings and oppressive features of our system of criminal justice have been attributed to a variety of sources including "lawless" police, overzealous district attorneys, "hanging" juries, corruption and political connivance, incompetent judges, inadequacy or lack of counsel, and poverty or other social disabilties of the defendant. See A. Barth, *Law Enforcement versus the Law* (1963), for a journalist's account embodying this point of view; J.H. Skolnick, *Justice without Trial: Law Enforcement in Democratic Society* (1966), for a sociologist's study of the role of the police in criminal law administration. For a somewhat more detailed, albeit legalistic and somewhat technical discussion of American police procedures, see W.R. LaFave, *Arrest: The Decision to Take a Suspect into Custody* (1965).

[26] Aspects of the lawyer's ambivalences with regard to the expectancies of the various groups who have claims upon him, are discussed in H.J. O'Gorman, *The Ambivalence of Lawyers,* paper presented at the Eastern Sociological Association meetings, April 10, 1965.

[27] W.J. Goode, *A Theory of Role Strain,* 25 Am. Soc. Rev. 483-96 (1960); J.D. Snok, *Role Strain in Diversified Role Sets,* 71 Am. J. Soc. 363-72 (1966).

[28] Some of the resources which have become an integral part of our courts, e.g., psychiatry, social work and probation, were originally intended as part of an ameliorative, therapeutic effort to individualize offenders. However, there is some evidence that a quite different result obtains, than the one originally intended. The ameliorative instruments have been coopted by the court in order to more "efficiently" deal with a court's caseload, often to the legal disadvantage of an accused person. See F.A. Allen, *The Borderland of Criminal Justice* (1964); T.S. Szasz, *Law, Liberty and Psychiatry* (1963) and also Szasz's most recent, *Psychiatric Justice* (1965); L. Diana, "The Rights of Juvenile Delinquents: An Appraisal of Juvenile Court Procedures," 47 *J. Crim. L. C. & P.S.* 561-69 (1957).

11

Plea Bargaining

Donald J. Newman

By far the majority of American criminals are convicted by their own guilty pleas. Various estimates of the number of guilty pleas put the national proportion close to 90% of all those charged with serious crimes.[1] If minor offenses—misdemeanors—are included, the frequency of convictions by plea approaches 98% of all those charged. And in many, if not most jurisdictions, a high percentage of such pleas are the result of bargaining between state and accused.

Interestingly, the proportion of pleas remains about the same whether the court district is metropolitan and crowded or rural and less overburdened. The percentage of people pleading guilty to crimes in Vermont is about the same as the percentage of "cop outs" in New York City.

Most defendants who are so "probably guilty" as to be indicted, waive their chances—remote perhaps—for acquittal, and plead guilty hoping for some sentencing mercy from the court. In fact a high proportion of them seek to negotiate this leniency prior to entering their pleas. In brief, not only is the guilty plea characteristic of American criminal justice, but "plea bargaining" is common, even normative, in many jurisdictions.

A person accused of a crime, who in fact is guilty of *some* criminal conduct, understandably has two major concerns: whether the state can

Reprinted by permission from *Trial* magazine, March/April, 1973, The Association of Trial Lawyers of America.

prove the case against him and if so what will happen to him at sentencing. He also may be worried about other corollary matters such as possible reputational damage flowing from the publicity of a trial even if he is later acquitted, or he may wish to modify the charge by which he is labeled after conviction.

Conviction of a misdemeanor is almost always better than a felony conviction—the negative consequences of the record itself are much less severe and the sentence is usually shorter—and conviction for assault generally provides a label more vague and less implicitly depraved than conviction of rape.

There is in every guilty plea an "implicit bargain" with the state, for defendants usually expect and in fact receive greater leniency if they plead guilty than if they put the state through the time, expense and uncertainty of a trial.

This poses an important and controversial question for sentencing judges. The majority position of polled judges was that it was perfectly proper for the court to show some sentence leniency to the pleading defendant but not, however, to give the defendant who went to trial a *longer* sentence. Instead, the reasoning went, it was all right to shorten terms of "repentant" offenders who admitted guilt and save the state the expense and time of trials.[2]

In 1968, a committee of the American Bar Association, charged to develop "minimum standards" for criminal justice administration, formally took the position that it was a proper exercise of discretion for the judge to reflect in his sentencing determination the fact that the defendant pleaded guilty.[3]

The Negotiated Plea

Throwing oneself on the mercy of the court is one thing; arranging for charge and sentencing concession ahead of time is, or may be, a more complex and even more controversial issue. When the term "plea bargaining" is used, it rarely refers to simple mercy-of-the-court situations. What is generally meant is a prearraignment "deal" between the prosecution and the defense in which charges are dropped (in spite of sufficient evidence) or where specific sentence promises are made in exchange for the defendant's willingness to plead guilty. There is ample research today to indicate that plea negotiations are common, even routine, in many—perhaps all—jurisdictions in the country.

At present there is a good deal of interest in this topic, not only on the part of lawyers and judges but among the general public as well, and it is interesting to speculate as to why plea bargaining has become an issue of controversy and concern at this time.

Plea agreements are not new; in all probability such bargaining has gone on as long as there have been criminal courts. While it wouldn't surprise many knowledgeable court observers to learn that Cain had pleaded to a lesser charge after having murdered Abel, until recently the various practies of plea bargaining were discussed only by habitues of the criminal courts.

One reason why practices of plea bargaining have not been accorded more public attention is that the whole process in the past was essentially a private, out-of-court, virtually invisible matter. In many places the actual open-court process of pleading guilty takes perhaps five minutes even in cases involving the most complex or heinous crimes. At a typical arraignment, the defendant is brought before the court, warned of his rights, hears the charge read and asked to plead to it. If he pleads guilty and the judge is satisfied that the plea is "voluntary," he stands convicted as surely as if he had had a three-month jury trial.

Out-of-court negotiations and arrangements have customarily been made off-the-record, sub rosa, in the prosecutor's office or in the hallways of the courthouse. Not only is the process non-public but, as might be expected, successful plea bargaining rarely has reached the appellate court level where, after all, the great legal debates take place and controversial issues are resolved. If a defendant charged with murder offers to plead guilty to assault and is convicted and sentenced accordingly. there is no injured party to bring an appeal.

The state has won a conviction, the defendant has benefited from the lesser charge and lower sentence, no major legal controversies have been raised, and the smooth, quick and relatively anonymous plea process has worked to the benefit of all—with the possible exception of the victim who is dead in any case, but even in nonhomicide cases has no standing to prosecute or to appeal in criminal matters. This means that the practice of plea bargaining has been largely confined to the workings of trial courts, coming infrequently to appellate court attention.

Professional literature in law and social sciences made scattered references to negotiation practices but until recently it was of minimum interest to legal scholars and social scientists alike. In the 1950's the American Bar Association sponsored a research study of the *Criminal Lawyer*[4] out of which came a few prominent journal articles which detailed some of the bargaining practices in selected jurisdictions. These received scholarly attention but did little to modify or influence court decisions or practices.

About ten years later the American Bar Foundation began a comprehensive survey of criminal justice administration in the United States. As part of this, one area of research (and one of the five volumes of results) was devoted to the guilty plea generally and to practices of plea negotiation in detail.

This book (*Conviction: The Determination of Guilt or Innocence Without Trial*, Little Brown, 1966) in turn influenced the reports of the President's Crime Commission, became the basis of the American Bar Association's recommended guilty plea standards, influenced changes in federal rules of criminal procedure and provided general information about bargaining for citation in a number of appellate court decisions, including decisions of the United States Supreme Court. By the 1970's, plea bargaining was and is an open and hotly debated issue in courts, conferences and even in the press and other media.

Plea Negotiation Practices

While research has shown plea bargaining to be common in courts across the land, there are variations in types of plea-agreements and in the actual procedures followed by prosecutors and defense in different jurisdictions. Part of this variation is the result of differences in criminal codes, especially sentencing provisions, from one place to another. In states with statutorily mandated sentences for certain crimes (20-to-life for armed robbery, for example), the only way a defendant can achieve sentence leniency is to have the charges lowered. In other places, where indeterminate sentences are common and the judge has wide discretion to choose among types and lengths of sentences regardless of charge, reduction is less important than a pre-plea promise from the prosecutor to "recommend" probation or some other lenient penalty.

The way a typical bargaining session works is as follows: A defendant is apprehended and initially charged with armed robbery, an offense carrying a mandatory minimum prison term of 20 years. Either on his own or through counsel he indicates to the prosecutor a willingness to plead guilty to a lesser crime in order to avoid the mandatory sentence of the higher charge.

In some cases, though actually a settlement process, negotiation can be quite adversary in its own right. The defense counsel may indicate to the prosecutor that he thinks the state has no evidence against his client except possibly a charge of disorderly conduct. The prosecutor in turn may state that he is not only going to push the armed robbery charge but plans to level a special count of being a habitual offender unless the defendant cooperates. Defense counsel then offers to have his client plead guilty to petty larceny with the prosecutor countering by offering to reduce the charge to second degree robbery.

So it goes. Eventually an agreed upon lesser charge—burglary or grand larceny, for example—may result and the defendant will plead guilty, facing at most a substantially reduced prison sentence and at best perhaps probation.

If the defendant wishes to be placed on probation, he may push in negotiation for more than charge reduction. He may also ask the prosecuting attorney to promise that at sentencing the state will "recommend" probation if and when asked by the court. This is a customary (though not universal) practice.

A prosecutor's recommendation of probation is a strong factor in the defendant's favor although a weaker, and also a vigorously sought after promise, is for the prosecutor to make no recommendation at the time of sentencing or to agree "not to oppose" probation if requested by the defendant. After all, the offender knows that should the prosecutor arise at sentencing and recommend a long prison term (perhaps reading prior convictions into the record) it is highly likely that incarceration will result.

Therefore, in most jurisdictions, a preplea sentence promise by the prosecutor is a major concession, even though the district attorney has no official authority to actually impose sentence.

There are other considerations that occasionally arise in plea negotiation depending upon the particular defendant, the crime or crimes charged and the sentencing structure and practices of the jurisdiction in question.

For example, often a person arrested for one crime is subsequently charged with others. It is rare that a burglar is apprehended on his first attempt and, once nabbed, the police may "solve" 20 or 30 separate burglaries, all potential charges against the defendant. Theoretically he could be tried on each count and could receive consecutive sentences. If, for example, he were accused of ten burglaries, tried separately on each and convicted on only half yet got one to three on each (to be served consecutively) he would in effect face a five to fifteen-year sentence. Therefore he may seek to have charges joined into a single accusation, or have some of the counts dismissed if he is willing to plead to one or perhaps two.

Additionally, some offenders may be facing a habitual offender rap, which is normally filed as a separate indictment or information. In exchange for pleading to the crime as charged he may avoid such "supercharging" by the state. Then, too, some defendants are on parole or probation for prior convictions and may negotiate for revocation of the old sentence if the new charge is dismissed or sufficiently reduced.

There is even some "lateral" bargaining, primarily to modify the conviction label without affecting sentence at all. Some defendants are willing to plead guilty to serious crimes such as robbery to avoid conviction of certain sex crimes like rape or sodomy because, while the potential sentence may be longer, the label and its attendant consequences throughout the life of the defendant are considered to be a better deal.

Permutations and combinations of plea agreements are almost endless especially where multiple charges are involved, but the end result is always the same: The defendant is allowed to plead guilty to lesser offenses or receives a preadjudication sentence promise in exchange for his willingness to give up his right to trial.

Why Plea Bargain

Motivations of the guilty defendant in plea bargaining are readily discernible. He wishes to minimize both the sentence which follows conviction and the label which attaches to it. He also usually hopes to avoid publicity, not only for himself, but perhaps to protect his family and friends from likely notoriety if he demands trial. Occasionally he may wish to protect accomplices or confederates by taking the rap himself.

The bargaining motivations of the state are somewhat less readily discernible, though in every instance the bargained plea is much more efficient, cheaper and more certain than a contested case.

There are, however, other more subtle but no less important motivations on the part of the prosecutor and other state officials for engaging in plea negotiation and in fact encouraging it. Some of these are self-seeking, but others rest on a sincere attempt to individualize justice, to build equity into a system that otherwise would be too harsh in certain types of cases.

One of the self-seeking motivations on the part of the state is to avoid challenge not only of the amount of evidence but the ways it was obtained. In spite of all the current controversy about illegal searches, wiretaps, failure to give *Miranda* warnings and the like, such issues are really paramount only in cases where pretrial motions are denied and which go to trial.

A plea of guilty waives almost all defects in the state's case. The way evidence was obtained is never tested. Whether the *Miranda* warning was given or not is irrelevant in the case of the defendant who pleads guilty. The insanity defense, or entrapment, and other important procedural and substantive issues are mooted by the guilty plea.

In short, the guilty plea doesn't refine and hone the law, rather it avoids sticky questions of police practices, prosecutorial trial skills and even the adequacy of legislative sentencing provisions. Furthermore, in most cases the plea satisfies all interested parties. The defendant has his deal; the prosecutor has an assured conviction (for a trial, no matter how carefully prepared, is always an uncertainty given the vagaries of juries), the victim is theoretically satisfied by conviction of the perpetrator and correctional agencies receive an offender who has admitted his guilt. It is always a difficult task for correctional authorities who receive an offender who, though sentenced after a full jury trial, still protests his innocence. How does rehabilitation begin?

At any rate, given the absence of challenge to police methods at one end, and a confessed criminal received in prison at the other, there is more than simple overcrowding behind the state's willingness to accept the plea. It is not only a quick and efficient way of processing defendants, it is a safe way, for pleading defendants do not rock the boat.

There are, however, a number of other state considerations underlying plea negotiation that are less self-seeking, and perhaps more consistent with a general desire to build equity into our criminal justice system, particularly in regard to sentencing.

It is common practice in many state legislatures (and in Congress as well) for very severe laws to be passed in the heat of anger or at the height of public indignation over what appears to be a serious crime wave. A few years ago about half the states adopted very harsh "sex psychopath" laws. In recent years a number of states have adopted severe sale-of-narcotic laws, mandating life imprisonment or even death to "pushers."

In passing such laws the drafters typically have in mind the worst offenders — the organized criminal or the professional dope-fiend who sells heroin to school children or is otherwise the most vicious or professional violator. However, in the day-to-day operation of courts the types of sale-of-narcotics defendants who appear are rarely professional heroin pushers but are more likely to be young men or women who have sold a couple of pills or marijuana cigarettes to friends.

Technically they are guilty of sale of narcotics and in most cases there is little doubt that the evidence held by the state is sufficient to prove the charge. Yet confronted with these cases it is a rare prosecutor or trial judge who wishes to give a mandatory life sentence (sometimes non-paroleable) to an 18-year-old offender whose crime is selling a few reefers to a buddy. On the other hand the district attorney may be unwilling or reluctant to dismiss the case entirely so that the lesser charge of "possession" or some related crime may be offered as a desirable solution.

This motivation pattern for bargaining is an extension of traditional prosecutor's discretion but here instead of dismissing the case the prosecutor in effect sentences the defendant. The reason for this is the nature of criminal law itself. Legislation defining crimes and fixing penalties is necessarily general and broad and if the prosecutor and other court officials are confronted with individual cases which, while they technically fit the same statutory category, are readily distinguishable in terms of the actual harm they have done to victims of to the social order in general they can only achieve individualization of sentences by reducing charges. There are a number of such situations where charge reduction is used to individualize justice without really violating the legislative intent of proceeding against very serious criminals.

In addition to the avoidance of inappropriately excessive mandatory sentences, other motivations which have been identified are:

- reduction to avoid a criminal label which would imply in the public mind that the defendant was guilty of conduct which is really not consistent with the actions that form his criminal violation.

For example, in a case in which a number of college students were having a noisy party in an apartment near their campus, the police arrested and charged the student owner of the apartment with, of all things, "operating a disorderly house." Confronted with this charge, the trial judge explained to the prosecutor and the arresting police officer that the connotations of such a label were so negative that he would not accept the plea of guilty even though the offense was a misdemeanor. The charge was modified (not really reduced) to disorderly conduct.

This label of disorderly conduct against the male owner of an apartment was not felt to be particularly onerous or misleading. However, in another case where a girl was arrested for shoplifting and charged with disorderly conduct, a trial judge refused to accept the plea to this count, pointing out that a record of disorderly conduct in the case of a young girl could be wrongfully interpreted as involving sexual misbehavior, whereas the charge of petty larceny (again not really a lesser charge) would likely be less damaging to the defendant in the long run.

- where there is a crime involving codefendants of unequal culpability. This is simply a recognition of the prosecutor's discretion to distinguish what the legislatures cannot do; that is, to determine the degree of involvement in a single offense on the part of multiple persons involved in a crime.

An older, sophisticated armed robber who has as a look-out a young, inexperienced, clean-record accomplice may be convicted "on the nose" but his accomplice offered a lesser charge (perhaps attempted robbery or burglary) to balance culpability and consequences. The same thing occurs when there are other mitigating circumstances in the crime, such as the participation of the victim in the criminal activity itself as, for example, in certain forms of confidence games.

- where the therapeutic benefits of alternative sentences can best be achieved by charge reduction or by awarding probation when normally such would not be the case. This is indeed a mercy-of-the-court situation but one which ignores the other administrative advantages of negotiation.

This is an extension of sentencing discretion, with primary concern to place the defendant in the best correctional setting possible which might be precluded if he's convicted on the nose. A mandatory prison term for a good-risk young violator may be more damaging to the community in the long run than if he is given a break on his first sentence.

- reduction to support law enforcement efforts by rewarding informants, state witnesses and the like with lesser charges and sentences. This is sometimes called "trading the little ones for the big ones," but the fact remains that unless differential court leniency is shown major cases cannot be developed.

This is harder to justify on propriety grounds if one is initially unwilling to support an informant system. If, however, the relationship between the activities of the court and the activities of law enforcement is conceded, then a decision about the propriety of using charge reduction or sentencing leniency must be made.

In short, there are a number of circumstances that arise in daily operation of any court system where it seems not only more efficient but more fair to utilize charge reduction or other assured leniency in sentencing to achieve more equitable justice. This is a part of the whole process that is rarely understood and, for that matter, rarely considered when plea bargaining is discussed.

The prevailing attitude toward the process (until recently at least) on the part of many, including some appellate courts, is that there is something dirty about plea bargaining, something corruptive or potentially corruptive in negotiating with criminals for punishment less than could be levied if the full force of the law were used. While it is true that from one perspective plea negotiation does act to avoid legislative mandate, and, like the exercise of all administrative discretion, has the *potential* for corruption, another side of the coin is presented by equity decisions, by a conscientious attempt to introduce "justice" into individual cases.

When translating the law from the abstract of statutes and cases to individual persons, there is always room for discretion properly applied by appropriate officials. If such discretion were denied our criminal justice system would, in the words of Judge Charles Breitel, be "ordered but intolerable."[5]

Is 'Settling' Proper?

Increasing awareness of the widespread nature of plea negotiation in the trial courts has raised a continual storm of controversy. Some legal scholars and judges, though used to "settling" all kinds of civil legal matters from estates to disputed automobile accidents, see the settlement of criminal cases as different and somehow abhorrent to American criminal justice ideology.

A well-known case of a bargained plea coming before the U.S. Court of Appeals of the Fifth Circuit, elicited from one judge the flat statement that "liberty and justice are not subjects for bargaining and barter."[6]

An appellate judge in Michigan commented; "...the negotiated guilty plea is...fundamentally unsound. Besides the fact that it is inconsistent with established standards—those regarding the exercise of discretion by public officers and those surrounding the administration of justice generally—it is turning what used to be an accusatorial-adversary judicial system into an inquisitorial-administrative process. It encourages practices in which neither the profession nor the judiciary can take pride."[7]

These two statements are characteristic of a stance taken by what turns out to be a minority of judicial spokesmen who see the problem of plea negotiation as intrinsically contradictory to the American system of justice. More common is the position taken by judges and legal scholars who argue that such practices have always been with us, will continue to exist as long as there are defendants and courts, and that the proper thing to do is to recognize plea bargaining, to get with it, make it more visible and attempt to control it.

Somewhat surprisingly, given the long history of silence about plea bargaining in the past, in the last couple of years a number of prominent legal organizations, advisory councils and appellate judges have taken the position that plea bargaining *is not* intrinsically improper but is indeed necessary and perhaps even a desirable part of American court practices.

The American Bar Association adopted the following position in its recently published Minimum Standards for Criminal Justice: "In cases in which it appears that the interest of the public and the effective administration of criminal justice would thereby be saved, the prosecuting attorney may engage in plea discussions for the purposes of reaching a plea agreement."[8] The report further recommends that the judge *not* be directly involved in negotiations, that such plea agreement proceedings should occur only through counsel and that "similarly situated defendants should be afforded equal plea agreement opportunities."[9]

The committee empowered to revise the Rules of Federal Criminal Procedure has recently submitted to the Supreme Court for its approval a revision of the practices to be followed by federal judges in accepting pleas of guilty. After discussion and debate, this committee not only approved the practice of plea bargaining but spelled out methods for recording sentence promises and otherwise making negotiation into a veritable contract, binding on both the state and the defendant.[10]

Given the historical silence in regard to negotiation over the past two centuries, these are astounding developments.

Moreover, within the past two years the Supreme Court of California has not only approved plea bargaining but in an important opinion has spelled out ways to record plea agreements so that failure to follow through on them may be subject to appeal.[11] Likewise, the United States Supreme Court has recently considered two cases involving plea negotiation and in both, *Brady v. United States*[12] and *Santobello v. New York,*[13] have recognized the propriety of such bargaining. In *Santobello*, Mr. Justice Burger said:

The disposition of criminal charges by agreement between the prosecutor and the accused, sometimes loosely called "plea bargaining," is an essential component of the administration of justice. Properly administered, it is to be encouraged. If every criminal charged were subjected to a full-scale trial, the States and the Federal Government would need to multiply by many times the number of judges and court facilities.

Disposition of charges after plea discussions is not only an essential part of the process but a highly desirable part for many reasons. It leads to prompt and largely final disposition of most criminal cases; it avoids much of the corrosive impact of enforced idleness during pre-trial confinement for those accused persons who are prone to continue criminal conduct even while on pre-trial release; and by shortening the time between charge and disposition, it enhances whatever may be the rehabilitative prospects of the guilty when they are ultimately imprisoned."[14]

The propriety issue does not end here, however. In spite of the words of the Chief Justice, at a National Conference on Criminal Justice held in Washington in January of this year, a resolution was adopted to "abolish" plea bargaining "no later than 1978." The commission, however, does provide "interim" measures for improvement in plea negotiation" until such time as abolition comes about.[15]

Unresolved Issues

Dilemmas presented by negotiated justice are not fully met by the words of Mr. Justice Burger, the standards of the ABA, and other proposals to improve plea bargaining by requiring counsel to be present, judges to be absent and a record of negotiations to be kept. There are still a number of unresolved issues about plea bargaining which need to be addressed.[16] These include:

The Range of Plea Bargaining. Though the language of new rules and procedures indicate that there should be some limits to the range of downgrading or sentence promises, the details have yet to be worked out. It may be one thing, for example, for a person charged with murder to be allowed to plead guilty to manslaughter. It might well be another thing, however, if the charge were reduced to disorderly conduct or to third-degree assault.

In short, there is a question of whether it is possible to set a limit on the range of downgrading or to require that promises of probation may be offered only to those persons who are otherwise eligible for probation. If the latter were held to be the case, then a difficult question arises as to how the prosecutor would know this since normally a presentence investigation cannot be conducted until after the person is duly convicted.

Equal Opportunity to Bargain. At one time in Michigan the charge of breaking and entering in the nighttime carried a mandatory prison sentence of 15 years and was not a probationable offense. Daytime breaking, on the other hand, was probationable and carried a five-year maximum sentence with a minimum to be set as low as the judge wished. In a study of bargaining in Michigan, it was found that knowledgeable defendants arrested for nighttime burglary almost universally pleaded to daylight breaking to achieve a sentencing break.

Such reductions were common, even normative, but always informally arranged. No signs were posted explaining this; the formal words of Michigan law contained no hint of downgrading practices. A Michigan prosecutor said, "Looking at the official conviction records, you would think all our burglaries took place at high noon." How though would a stranger know this was the normal practice in most of the courts of the jurisdiction? Perhaps if he hired an attorney familiar with the practice, he too could deal.

This raises the question of whether common practice must be posted so that all may avail themselves of normative sentencing breaks. Should the prosecutor be required to explain "routine" bargaining? Must there be consistency from one case to another on the part of the prosecutor in offering sentencing promises or in reducing charges?

Is there, in short, an equal protection issue that can be realistically solved in the day-by-day administration of plea bargaining or, in fact, do most of the problems of sentence disparity actually originate in disparate practices of charging?

Quick Justice. At present there is considerable concern about delay in the courts. Judicial and legislative committees in most jurisdictions are looking into ways of speeding up court processing, particularly reducing the time defendants spend in jail awaiting trial.

There is another side to the coin of court delay, however, that has been called "quick justice," which occurs in some guilty-plea convictions. Cases have been noted where a defendant is taken at gunpoint in the morning, is charged with a crime, immediately brought before a judge where, waiving all rights, he enters a guilty plea, is sentenced on the spot and begins serving his term in prison in the afternoon.

The question raised by such processing is whether justice can be too swift as well as too slow. A number of state appellate courts have overturned swift justice convictions and the United States Supreme Court upset a guilty-plea conviction in a Michigan case in which a 17-year-old boy was arrested in the morning for the murder of a neighbor, pleaded guilty and was moved to the prison in the afternoon of the same day to begin his life sentence. His parents were never even notified of his arrest.[17]

The Public's 'Right to Know'. The relatively quick and anonymous guilty plea in most routine criminal cases is neither newsworthy nor of general public concern. However, guilty pleas in cases involving prominent or notorious defendants (whether to reduce charges or not) not only act to avoid the time and effort of trial but also prevent the details of the crime (including possible accomplices) from becoming public knowledge.

In prominent cases there is some public dissatisfaction with such sparse details. There have been a number of recent illustrations, including the Watergate Affair. Another involved Senator Edward Kennedy, who pleaded guilty to a traffic violation after the events at Chappaquiddick Island. Still another involved the bargained plea of James Earl Ray, the admitted assassin of the Reverend Martin Luther King.

Following guilty pleas in these latter two instances, there was widely expressed public disappointment with the processing of each case, dissatisfaction which rested on the general grounds that the full facts and details were not made public, though, given the prominence of the senator and of Dr. King, the public has a "right to know." Senator Kennedy felt enough of this pressure to appear on national television in an attempt to explain his position. However, the details of Dr. King's murder, though "solved" by Ray's plea, remain naggingly unclear and perhaps permanently unresolved.

The Corruption of Ideology. There is always a thin line between the proper exercise of discretion and discrimination or even corruption. Some critics of plea bargaining point out that extending such broad discretionary powers to the prosecutor and to trial courts not only usurps legislative prerogative, but offers the opportunity for concealing discriminatory or corrupt practices under the guise of administrative discretion. Further, the argument goes, even if the system is perfectly administered with the prosecutor being scrupulous in authorizing and following through on appropriate bargains with "deserving" offenders, there is nevertheless an aura of disrespect of the law emanating from a system in which crime and punishment are matters of dealing and settling.

Some observers say that a plea bargain is little different from a "fix," for though there is clearly no corrupt practice involved, the law has in fact been manipulated and, no matter how well meaning, such manipulation destroys faith in justice among the public at large, and breeds cynicism in those processed in this manner through our criminal justice system.[18]

Others, however, see bargaining, if properly administered and contained, as the *only* way we can bring the individualization of justice into our court system. The conscientious prosecutor and judge can do what the legislature and appellate courts cannot—and cannot even mandate—namely, tailor charges and sentences to specific guilty persons, distributing punishments and labels as accurately deserved among the tens of thousands of offenders processed through our courts.

There are, at present, no good answers to all of the unresolved bargaining issues. One thing, however, is abundantly clear: Plea bargaining is with us and is probably here to stay in most jurisdictions throughout the country. The issues and dilemmas posed by its practices will have to be met, as usual, in the best manner and in the best fashion we can develop. Today in contrast to even two years ago, plea bargaining is a much more visible practice and a more generally accepted procedure at the trial court level. Facts of negotiation are less often deliberately hidden; stories of bargaining appear more frequently in press, and negotiation sessions have even been dominant themes in recent episodes on some of the perennial lawyer series on television.

Whether we like it or not, all of us are increasingly compelled to admit that criminal justice in America is predominantly a system of negotiation and settlement — not unlike private lawsuits. The fact that it is becoming more visible, more public, can only be to the good for after all it is our system of justice and, where crime and punishment are involved, we may be forced to agree to public settlement but *not* to private dealings.

Notes

[1]See Donald J. Newman, *Conviction: The Determination of Guilt or Innocence Without Trial.* (Boston: Little, Brown, 1966).

[2]Pilot Institute on Sentencing, 26 F.R.D. 285 (1960).

[3]American Bar Association, *Standards Relating to Pleas of Guilty,* Approved Draft 1968, Sec. 1.8.

[4]Arthur L. Wood, *Criminal Lawyer* (New Haven: College and University Press, 1967). See also Newman, "Pleading Guilty For Considerations: A Study of Bargain Justice," 46 *J. Crim. L., C. & P.S.* 780 (1956).

[5]Breitel, "Controls in Criminal Law Enforcement," 27 *U. Chi. L. Rev.* 427, 428 (1960).

[6]*Shelton v. United States,* 242 F. 2d. 101, 113 (5th Cir. 1957).

[7]*People V. Byrd,* 12 Mich App 186, 162 N.W. 2d 777, 796 (1968).

[8]ABA, *Standards Relating to Pleas of Guilty,* op cit note 3, Sec. 3.1.

[9]*Ibid.*

[10]Federal Rules of Criminal Procedure, *Rule 11. Pleas,* (Preliminary Draft of Proposed Amendments, April 1971).

[11]*People v. West,* 3 Cal 3d 595, 91 Cal. Rptr. 385, 477 P. 2d. 409 (1970).

[12]397 U.S. 742 (1970).

[13]404 U.S. 257 (1971).

[14]*Ibid.,* 260.

[15]National Conference on Criminal Justice, *Preliminary Report,* Jan. 1973, Standard 3.1; Standard 3.2.

[16]See generally, Newman and NeMoyer, "Issues of Propriety in Negotiated Justice," 47 Denver L.J. 367 (1970).

[17]*DeMeerleer v. Michigan, 329 U.S. 663 (1947).*

[18]Dash, "Cracks in the Foundation of Criminal Justice," *46 Ill. L. Rev. Rev.* 385 (1951).

12

Making the Punishment Fit the Crime

Franklin E. Zimring

In its current crisis the American system of criminal justice has no friends. Overcrowded, unprincipled, and ill-coordinated, the institutions in our society that determine whether and to what extent a criminal defendant should be punished are detested in equal measure by prison wardens and prisoners, cab drivers and college professors. What is more surprising (and perhaps more dangerous), a consensus seems to be emerging on the shape of desirable reform — reducing discretion and the widespread disparity that is its shadow, abolishing parole decisions based on whether a prisoner can convince a parole board that he has been "reformed," and creating a system in which punishment depends much more importantly than at present on the seriousness of the particular offense.

A number of books and committee reports that have endorsed these goals and proposed various structural reforms to achieve them are the stimulus for this essay. While diverse in style, vocabulary, and emphasis, at least six books in the past two years have proposed eroding the arenas of discretion

Franklin E. Zimring, J.D., is professor of law and director of the Center for Studies in Criminal Justice at the University of Chicago. His published works include *Deterrence: The Legal Threat in Crime Control* (with Gordon Hawkins) and *Firearms and Violence in American Life* (with George D. Newton). This article copyright © Franklin E. Zimring.

From *Hastings Center Report* (December, 1976). Reprinted by permission of the author.

in the system.[1] Some authors, such as James Q. Wilson and Ernest van den Haag, see reform as a path to enhancing crime control. Others, such as Andrew von Hirsh, the Twentieth Century Fund Committee, and David Fogel, advocate reform for less utilitarian reasons, with titles or subtitles such as "Doing Justice," "A Justice Model of Corrections," and "Fair and Certain Punishment."

This essay cannot comprehensively review such a rich collection of literature, nor is it politic for me to oppose justice, fairness, or certainty. Rather, I propose to summarize the present allocation of sentencing power in the criminal justice system and discuss some of the implications of the "structural reforms" advocated in some current literature.

Multiple Discretion in Sentencing

The best single phrase to describe the allocation of sentencing power in state and federal criminal justice is "multiple discretion." Putting aside the enormous power of the police to decide whether to arrest, and to select initial charges, there are four separate institutions that have the power to determine criminal sentences—the legislature, the prosecutor, the judge, and the parole board or its equivalent.

The *legislature* sets the range of sentences legally authorized after conviction for a particular criminal charge. Criminal law in the United States is noted for extremely wide ranges of sentencing power, delegated by legislation to discretionary agents, with extremely high maximum penalties and very few limits on how much less than the maximum can be imposed. In practice, then, most legislatures delegate their sentencing powers to other institutions. For example, second-degree murder in Pennsylvania, prior to 1973, was punishable by "not more than 20 years" in the state penitentiary.[2] An sentence above twenty years could not be imposed; any sentence below twenty years—including probation—was within the power of the sentencing judge.

The *prosecutor* is not normally thought of as an official who has, or exercises, the power to determine punishment. In practice, however, the prosecutor is the most important institutional determinant of a criminal sentence. He has the legal authority to drop criminal charges, thus ending the possibility of punishment. He has the legal authority in most systems to determine the specific offense for which a person is to be prosecuted, and this ability to select a charge can also broaden or narrow the range of sentences that can be imposed upon conviction. In congested urban court systems (and elsewhere) he has the absolute power to reduce charges in exchange for guilty pleas and to recommend particular sentences to the court as part of a "plea bargain"; rarely will his recommendation for a lenient sentence be refused in an adversary system in which he is supposed to represents the punitive interests of the state.

The *judge* has the power to select a sentence from the wide range made available by the legislature for any charge that produces a conviction. His powers are discretionary—within this range of legally authorized sanctions his selection cannot be appealed, and is not reviewed. Thus, under the Pennsylvania system we studied, a defendant convicted of second-degree murder can be sentenced to probation, one year in the penitentiary, or twenty years. On occasion, the legislature will provide a mandatory minimum sentence, such as life imprisonment for first-degree murder, that reduces the judge's options once a defendant has been convicted of that particular offense. In such cases the prosecutor and judge retain the option to charge or convict a defendant for a lesser offense in order to retain their discretionary powr.[3] More often the judge has a wide range of sentencing choices and, influenced by the prosecutor's recommendation, will select either a single sentence (such as two years) or a minimum and maximum sentence (not less than two nor more than five years) for a particular offender.

The *parole* or *correctional authority* normally has the power to modify judicial sentences to a considerable degree. When the judge pronounces a single sentence, such as two years, usually legislation authorizes release from prison to parole after a specified proportion of the sentences has been served. When the judge has provided for a minimum and maximum sentence, such as two to five years, the relative power of the correctional or parole authority is increased, because it has the responsibility to determine at what point in a prison sentence the offender is to be released. The parole board's decision is a discretionary one, traditionally made without guidelines or principles of decision.

This outline of our present sentencing system necessarily misses the range of variation among jurisdictions in the fifty states and the federal system, and oversimplifies the complex interplay among institutions in each system. It is useful, however, as a context in which to consider specific proposed reforms; it also helps to explain why the labyrinthine status quo has few articulate defenders. With all our emphasis on due process in the determination of guilt, our machinery for setting punishment lacks any sanctioned principle except unguided discretion. Plea bargaining, disparity of treatment, and uncertainty are all symptoms of a larger malaise—the absence of rules or even guidelines in determining the distribution of punishments. Other societies, less committed to the rule of law, or less infested with crime, might suffer such a system. Powerful voices are beginning to tell us we cannot.

> *What emerges from our study is a conceptual model that differs considerably from the dominant thinking about punishment in this century.... We conclude that the severity of the sentence should depend on the seriousness of the defendant's crime or crimes—on what he did rather than on what the sentencer expects he will do if treated in a certain fashion.*
>
> Andrew von Hirsch
> *Doing Justice*

Parole Under Attack

Of all the institutions that comprise the present system, parole is the most vulnerable—a practice that appears to be based on a now-discredited theoretical foundation of rehabilitation and individual predictability. The theory was that penal facilities rehabilitate prisoners and that parole authorities could select which inmates were ready, and when they were ready, to reenter the community. The high-water mark of such thinking is the indeterminate sentence—a term of one-year-to-life at the discretion of the correctional authority for any adult imprisoned after conviction for a felony. Ironically, while this theory was under sustained (and ultimately successful) attack in California, New York was passing a set of drug laws that used the one-year-to-life sentence as its primary dispositive device. Yet we know (or think we know) that prison rehabilitation programs "don't work," and our capacities to make individual predictions of future behavior are minimal.

So why not abolish parole in favor of a system where the sentence pronounced by the judge is that which is served by the offender? The cost of post-imprisonment sentence adjustments are many: they turn our prisons into "acting schools," promote disparity, enrage inmates, and undermine both justice and certainty.[4]

There are, however, a number of functions performed by parole that have little to to with the theory of rehabilitation or individual predictability. A parole system allows us to advertise heavy criminal sanctions loudly at the time of sentencing and later reduce sentences quietly. This "discounting" function is evidently of some practical importance, because David Fogel's plan to substitute "flat time" sentences for parole is designed so that the advertised "determinate sentences" for each offense are twice as long as the time the offender will actually serve (since each prisoner gets a month off his sentence for every month he serves without a major disciplinary infraction). In a system that seems addicted to barking louder than it really wants to bite, parole (and "good time" as well) can help protect us from harsh sentences while allowing the legislature and judiciary the posture of law and order.

> *Now suppose we abandon entirely the rehabilitation theory of sentencing and corrections—not the effort to rehabilitate, just the theory that the governing purpose of the enterprise is to rehabilitate... Instead, we would view the correctional system as having a very different function—namely, to isolate and to punish. It is a measure of our confusion that such a statement will strike many enlightened readers today as cruel, even barbaric. It is not. It is merely a recognition that society at a minimum must be able to protect itself from dangerous offenders and to impose some costs (other than the stigma and inconvenience of an arrest and court appearance) on criminal acts; it is also a frank admission that society really does not know how to do much else.*
>
> James Q. Wilson
> *Thinking About Crime*

It is also useful to view the abolition of parole in terms of its impact on the distribution of sentencing power in the system. Reducing the power of the parole board increases the power of the legislature, prosecutor, and judge. If the abolition of parole is not coupled with more concrete legislative directions on sentencing, the amount of discretion in the system will not decrease; instead, discretionary power will be concentrated in two institutions (judge and prosecutor) rather than three. The impact of this reallocation is hard to predict. Yet parole is usually a statewide function, while judges and prosecutors are local officials in most states. One function of parole may be to even out disparities in sentencing behavior among different localities. Abolishing parole, by decentralizing discretion, may increase sentencing disparity, at least as to prison sentences, because the same crime is treated differently by different judges and prosecutors. Three discretions may be better than two!

There are two methods available to avoid these problems. Norval Morris argues for retaining a parole function but divorcing it from rehabilitation and individual prediction by providing that a release date be set in the early stages of an offender's prison career. This would continue the parole functions of "discounting" and disparity reduction, while reducing uncertainty and the incentive for prisoners to "act reformed." It is a modest, sensible proposal, but it is not meant to address the larger problems of discretion and disparity in the rest of the system.[5]

Legislative Sentencing

A more heroic reform is to reallocate most of the powers now held by judges and parole authorities back to the legislature. Crimes would be defined with precision and specific offenses would carry specific sentences, along with lists of aggravating and mitigating circumstances that could modify the penalty. The three books with "justice" or "fairness" in their titles advocate this "price list" approach, albeit for different reasons and with different degrees of sophistication. The Twentieth Century Fund study goes beyond advocating this approach and sets out sections of a sample penal code, although all members of the committee do not agree on the specific "presumptive sentences" provided in the draft.

There is much appeal in the simple notion that a democratically elected legislature should be ·capable of fixing sentences for crimes against the community. Yet this is precisely what American criminal justice has failed to do, and the barriers to a fair and just system of fixed sentences are imposing. The Twentieth Century Fund scheme of "presumptive sentences," because it is the most sophisticated attempt to date, will serve as an illustration of the formidable collection of problems that confront a system of "fair and certain" legislatively determined punishments. In brief, the proposal outlines a scale of punishments for those first convicted that ranges (excluding murder) from six years in prison (aggravated assault) to probation (shoplifting). Premeditated murder is punished with ten years' imprisonment. Burglary of an empty house by an unarmed offender has a presumptive sentence of six months; burglary of an abandoned dwelling yields a presumptive sentence of six months' probation. The sample code clearly aims at singling out violent crimes such as armed robbery for heavier penalties, while the scale for nonviolent offenders led two of the eleven Task Force members to argue that the "range...appears to be unrealistically low in terms of obtaining public or legislative support."[6] Repeat offenders receive higher presumptive sentences, under specific guidelines.

The Task Force proposal produces in me an unhappily schizophrenic response. I agree with the aims and priorities of the report, at the same time that I suspect the introduction of this (or many other) reform proposals into the legislative process might do more harm than good.

Roadblocks to Reform

Why so skeptical? Consider a few of the obstacles to making the punishment fit the crime:

1. *The incoherence of the criminal law.*[7] Any system of punishment that attaches a single sanction to a particular offense must define offenses with a

morally persuasive precision that present laws do not possess. In my home state of Illinois, burglary is defined so that an armed housebreaker is guilty of the same offense as an eighteen-year-old who opens the locked glove compartment of my unlocked station wagon. Obviously, no single punishment can be assigned to crimes defined in such sweeping terms. But can we be precise? The Task Force tried, providing illustrative definitions of five different kinds of nighttime housebreaking with presumptive sentences from two years (for armed burglary, where the defendant menaces an occupant) through six months' probation. The Task Force did not attempt to deal with daylight or non-residential burglary.

> *[Judges] must labor under laws, procedures, precedents, and appeals court decisions that so favor the defendants as to compel the courts to reduce charges of which defendants are, in many cases, clearly guilty. An overhaul of the whole criminal justice system is needed. Crime rates depend not on statutory prescriptions but on what is actually done to make crime costly to the criminal and to make the cost obvious. At present crime is costly mainly to the victim. Surely it is more beneficial—as well as easier—and more effective to modify the criminal justice system than to undertake the far-reaching social reforms so often proposed.*
>
> Ernest van den Haag
> *Punishing Criminals*

The problem is not simply that any such penal code will make our present statues look like Reader's Digest Condensed Books; we lack the capacity to define into formal law the nuances of situation, intent, and social harm that condition the seriousness of particular criminal acts. For example, the sample code provides six years in prison for "premeditated assault" in which harm was intended and two years for serious assaults where vital harm was not intended. While there may be some conceptual distinction between these two mental states, one cannot confidently divide hundreds of thousands of gun and knife attacks into these categories to determine whether a "fair and certain punishment" is six years or two.

Rape, an offense that encompasses a huge variety of behaviors, is graded into three punishments: six years (when accompanied by an assault that causes bodily injury); three years (when there is no additional bodily harm); and six months (when committed on a previous sex partner, with no additional bodily harm). Two further aggravating conditions are also specified.[8] Put aside for a moment the fact that prior consensual sex reduces the punishment by a factor of six and the problem that rape with bodily harm has a "presumptive sentence" one year longer than intentional killing. Have we really defined the offense into its penologically significant categories? Can we rigorously patrol the border between forcible rape without additional bodily harm and that with further harm—when that distinction can mean the difference between six months and six years in the penitentiary?

I am not suggesting that these are problems of sloppy drafting. Rather, we may simply lack the ability to comprehensively define in advance those elements of an offense that should be considered in fixing a criminal sentence.

2. *The paradox of prosecutorial power.* A system of determinate sentences reallocates the sentencing power shared by the judge and parole authorities to the legislature and the prosecutor. While the judge can no longer select from a wide variety of sanctions after conviction, the prosecutor's powers to select charges and to plea-bargain remain. Indeed, a criminal code like that proposed by the Twentieth Century Fund Task Force will enhance the relative power of the prosecutor by removing parole and restricting the power of judges. The long list of different offenses proposed in the report provides the basis for the exercise of prosecutorial discretion: the selection of initial charges and the offer to reduce charges (charge-bargaining) are more important in a fixed-price system precisely because the charge at conviction determines the sentence. The prosecutor files a charge of "premeditated" killing (ten years) and offers to reduce the charge to "intentional" killing (five years) in exchange for a guilty plea. In most of the major crimes defined by the Task Force—homicide, rape, burglary, larceny, and robbery—a factual nuance separates two grades of offense where the presumptive sentence for the higher grade is twice that of the lower grade.[9]

This means that the disparity between sentences following a guilty plea and those following jury trial are almost certain to remain. Similarly, disparity between different areas and different prosecutors will remain, because one man's "premeditation" can always be another's "intention." It is unclear whether total disparity will decrease, remain stable, or increase under a regime of determinate sentences. It is certain that disparities will remain.

The paradox of prosecutorial power under determinate sentencing is that exorcising discretion from two of the three discretionary agencies in criminal sentencing does not necessarily reduce either the role of discretion in sentence determination or the total amount of sentence disparity. Logically, three discretions may be better than one. The practical lesson is that no serious program to create a rule of law in determining punishment can ignore the pivotal role of the American prosecutor.

3. *The legislative law-and-order syndrome.* Two members of the Twentieth Century Fund Task Force express doubts that a legislature will endorse six-month sentences for burglary, even if it could be shown that six months is above or equal to the present sentence served. I share their skepticism. When the legislature determines sentencing ranges, it is operating at a level of abstraction far removed from individual case dispositions, or even the allocation of resources to courts and correctional agencies. At that level of abstraction the symbolic quality of the criminal sanction is of great importance. The penalty provisions in most of our criminal codes are symbolic denunciations of particular behavior patterns, rather than decisions about just sentences. This practice has been supported by the multiple ameliorating discretions in the present system.

It is the hope of most of the advocates of determinate sentencing that the responsibilities thrust on the legislature by their reforms will educate democratically elected officials to view their function with realism and responsibility—to recognize the need for priorities and moderation in fixing punishment. This is a hope, not firmly supported by the history of penal policy and not encouraged by a close look at the operation and personnel of the state legislatures.

Yet reallocating power to the legislature means gambling on our ability to make major changes in the way elected officials think, talk, and act about crime. Once a determinate sentencing bill is before a legislative body, it takes only an eraser and pencil to make a one-year "presumptive sentence" into a six-year sentence for the same offense. The delicate scheme of priorities in any well-conceived sentencing proposal can be torpedoed by amendment with ease and political appeal. In recent history, those who have followed the moral career of the sentencing scheme proposed by Governor Edmund Brown Sr.'s Commission on Law Reform through the Senate Subcommittee on Crime can testify to the enormous impact of apparently minor structural changes on the relative bite of the sentencing system.[10]

If the legislative response to determinate sentencing proposals is penal inflation, this will not necessarily lead to a reign of terror. The same powerful prosecutorial discretions that limit the legislature's ability to work reform also prevent the legislature from doing too much harm. High fixed sentences could be reduced; discretion and disparity could remain.

4. *The lack of consensus and principle.* But what if we could trade disparity for high mandatory sentences beyond those merited by utilitarian or retributive demands of justice? Would it be a fair trade? It could be argued that a system which treats some offenders unjustly is preferable to one in which all are treated unjustly. Equality is only one, not the exclusive, criterion for fairness.

> *It is clear that no democratic society would ever leave it to judges, administrators, or experts to decide which acts should constitute crimes. That decision is quintessentially legislative, involving, as it does, fundamental questions of policy. Likewise, it should not be left to judges, administrators, or experts to determine the bases on which criminal offenders in a democratic society should be deprived lawfully of their freedom.*
>
> *Fair and Certain Punishment*
> Report of the Twentieth Century Fund
> Task Force on Criminal Sentencing

This last point leads to a more fundamental concern about the link between structural reform and achieving justice. The Task Force asks the question with eloquent simplicity: "How long is too long? How short is too short?"[11] The question is never answered in absolute terms; indeed, it is unanswerable. We lack coherent principles on which to base judgments of relative social harm. Current titles of respectable books on this subject range from *Punishing Criminals* to *The End of Imprisonment,* and the reader can rest assured that the contents vary as much as the labels. Yet how can we mete out fair punishment without agreeing on what is fair? How can we do justice before we define it?

Determinate sentencing may do more good than harm; the same can be said for sharp curtailment of judicial and parole discretion. Such reforms will, however, be difficult to implement, measure, and judge. Predicting the impact of any of the current crop of reform proposals with any degree of certainty is a hazardous if not foolhardy occupation.

Not the least of the vices of our present lawless structures of criminal sentencing is that they mask a deeper moral and intellectual bankruptcy in the criminal law and the society it is supposed to serve. The paramount value of these books and reform proposals is not the "structural reforms" that each proposes or opposes. It is the challenge implicit in all current debate: no matter what the problems with particular reforms, the present system is intolerable. The problems are deeper than overcrowding or lack of coordination, more profound than the structure of the sentencing system. These problems are as closely tied to our culture as to our criminal law. They are problems of principle that have been obscured by the tactical inadequacies of the present system.

Notes

[1]Norval Morris, *The Future of Imprisonment* (Chicago: University of Chicago Press, 1974); James Q. Wilson, *Thinking About Crime* (New York: Basic Books, 1975); Ernest van den Haag, *Punishing Criminals* (New York: Basic Books, 1975); Andrew von Hirsch, *Doing Justice — The Choice of Punishments, the Report of the Committee for the Study of Incarceration* (New York: Hill and Wang, 1976); David Fogel, *We are the Living Proof: The Justice Model of Corrections* (Cincinnati: W.H. Anderson, 1975); Task Force on Criminal Sentencing, *Fair and Certain Punishment — Report of the Twentieth Century Task Force on Criminal Sentencing* (New York: McGraw-Hill, 1976).

The central concern of these books, the coercive control of convicted offenders, is very much an issue for bioethics. Imprisonment, while centuries old, is essentially a form of experimentation with human subjects. Various new treatment technologies available to the prison system have been widely discussed among those concerned about the impact of scientific knowledge on social institutions; but the basic problems posed by imprisonment itself have been less widely recognized.

[2]The old Pennsylvania statute is used as an example because we have recently studied the distribution of punishment in Philadelphia for those convicted of criminal homicides occurring during the first five months of 1970. See Franklin E. Zimring, Joel Eigen, and Sheila O'Malley, "Punishing Homicide in Philadelphia: Perspectives of the Death Penalty," *University of Chicago Law Review* 43 (1976), 227.

[3]*Ibid.,* pp. 229-41.

[4]Fogel, pp. 196-99.

[5]Morris, pp. 47-50.

[6]Task Force Report, pp. 55-56.

[7]The phrase is borrowed from my colleague, James White, who is preparing a book with this title.

[8]The aggravating factors are (1) "the victim was under 15 or over 70 years of age" and (2) the victim was held captive for over two hours. Task Force Report, p. 59.

[9]The presumptive sentence for rape doubles with an assault causing bodily injury. The penalty for armed robbery where the offender discharges a firearm is three years if the offender did not intend to injure and five years if intent can be established. The presumptive sentence is two years if the weapon is discharged but the prosecutor cannot or does not establish that "the likelihood of personal injury is high." The penalty for armed burglary doubles when the dwelling is occupied. An armed burglar who "brandishes a weapon" in an occupied dwelling receives twenty-four months while a nonbrandishing armed burglar receives eighteen. Assault is punished with six years when "premeditated" and committed with intent to cause harm. Without intent, the presumptive sentence is two years. See *Fair and Certain Punishment,* pp. 38-39, 56-59. Threat of force in larceny means the difference between six and twenty-four months. As I read the robbery statute, armed taking of property by threat to use force is punished with a presumptive sentence of six months on page 40 of the report, while the same behavior receives twenty-four months on pages 60-61.

[10]Compare the Final Report of the National Commission on Reforms of Federal Criminal Laws (Government Printing Office, 1971) with Senate Bill 1, 94th Cong., 1st Session (1975). Among other things, the Senate bill changes a presumption in favor of probation to a presumption against probation, increases the number of felonies in the proposed code and increases the length of authorized sentences by a considerable margin. See Louis Schwartz, "The Proposed Criminal Code," *Criminal Law Reporter,* 17 (1975), 3203.

[11]Task Force Report, p. 4.

Section IV

Change Without Progress: Corrections

Corrections is in need of reforms which are unlikely to occur. Many of the problems facing corrections can be attributed to philosophical and operational conflicts. There is a lack of consensus regarding the purpose of punishment. On the one hand, there are those who hold the retributive position and contend that we are right and proper in our desires to seek revenge for wrongs suffered and that those who commit those wrongs must be severely punished. On the other hand, there are those who support a utilitarian position and contend that the purpose of punishment is to prevent antisocial behavior. Punishment, according to this position, should be assessed with the goal of influencing the future behavior of the offender. Millions of dollars are annually invested in a large variety of rehabilitation and treatment programs. Many of these programs have proven to be of questionable value and some are not appreciated by the participating offenders.

Because there is little agreement regarding the purpose of punishment, individuals and groups argue and debate in the legislative process as a part of an effort to make certain that their particular perspective is reflected in criminal codes. As a result, we find corrections riding the pendulum movements of the political process and many aspects of corrections are perceived as confused and purposeless.

Public attitudes toward corrections are inconsistent. Many Americans believe that persons convicted of crimes should spend longer periods of time incarcerated in prison. At the same time the public is also likely to agree with the contention that prisons do not rehabilitate and that a person may be more dangerous *after* incarceration in one of our overpopulated, violent prisons. We seem to want a continued reliance on the kinds of punishment mechanisms we have used in the past even though we readily acknowledge they have not worked.

While there are a number of topics and issues in the field of corrections, this section focuses on incarceration, inmate subcultures, parole, and community based corrections. Incarceration in a maximum security prison is a terribly degrading experience. Overpopulated and understaffed, a number of prisons have become unmanageable as inmate gangs control major aspects of institutional life. Narcotics traffic flourishes in many prisons and homosexual rape is a common occurrence as the weak succomb to the strong in this human jungle. Few of us have any conception of the levels of violence that occur behind prison walls. While prison riots have called public attention to the degrading and dehumanizing experience of incarceration, there is an abundance of public apathy that overwhelms any short term concern. In the process of incarceration, we heap deprivation upon the inmate failing to realize that ninety-eight percent of those incarcerated will be released to society in the future, many after being incarcerated only two to five years. We cannot constantly and continually expose these persons to violent behavior without their internalizing violent attitudes and the predisposition for violence. Simply stated, violence begets violence.

In some respects conditions for incarcerated women are not terribly different than those for men in that both suffer the same deprivations and inhumane treatment. Some writers contend that the experience may be even more depriving for women than for men because of the increased humiliation they feel as a result of societal rejection. Study of the female offender has been pervaded by myth and it is only in recent years that we have come to develop sound research methodologies in this area.

Parole is one of the most controversial aspects of corrections. Decision-making by parole boards appears random and senseless. Many people feel that parole is evidence of the corrections system being "soft." At the same time, the parole process is one of the most frustrating and at times humiliating experiences for the inmate. Parole boards often have little time to give adequate attention to a case and some parole boards lack the needed training and expertise to make good decisions.

In "The Pains of Imprisonment," Gresham Sykes presents a classic analysis of the degrading aspects of incarceration for the individual offender. Anthony Guenther, in "Prison Rackets," provides the reader with a glimpse of inmate subcultures and the extent to which these subcultures are pervaded by violence and narcotics. Arthur Paddock and Robert Culbertson describe incarceration in women's prisons: problems in the area of female criminality are examined with a focus on institutional issues and argot rules in "Incarcerated Women."

"The Parole Board Hearing," by David Stanley, portrays the parole process in a manner that most would find objectionable if it were not so terribly true. The level of injustice in this area is also indicative of much deeper problems throughout the corrections system. It is important to note that a large number of community based corrections projects emerged as a result of a general consensus that incarceration is debilitating rather than rehabilitating. In this context, Paul Hahn's "Residential Alternatives to Incarceration" describes potential solutions to the current problems of prison overcrowding.

13

The Pains of Imprisonment

Gresham Sykes

The Deprivation of Liberty

Of all the painful conditions imposed on the inmates of the New Jersey State Prison, none is more immediately obvious than the loss of liberty. The prisoner must live in a world shrunk to thirteen and a half acres and within this restricted area his freedom of movement is further confined by a strict system of passes, the military formations in moving from one point within the institution to another, and the demand that he remain in his cell until given permission to do otherwise. In short, the prisoner's loss of liberty is a double one — first, by confinement to the institution and second, by confinement within the institution.

The mere fact that the individuals's movements are restricted, however, is far less serious than the fact that imprisonment means that the inmate is cut off from family, relatives, and friends, not in the self-isolation of the hermit or the misanthrope, but in the involuntary seclusion of the outlaw. It is true that visiting and mailing privileges partially relieve the prisoner's isolation — if he can find someone to visit him or write to him and who will be approved as a visitor or correspondent by the prison officials. Many inmates, however, have found their links with persons in the free

"The Pains of Imprisonment," in Gresham M. Sykes, *The Society of Captives: A Study of A Maximum Security Prison* (copyright © 1958 by Princeton University Press), pp. 65-78. Reprinted by permission of Princeton University Press.

community weakening as the months and years pass by. This may explain in part the fact that an examination of the visiting records of a random sample of the inmate population, covering approximately a one-year period, indicated that 41 percent of the prisoners in the New Jersey State Prison have received no visits from the outside world.

It is not difficult to see this isolation as painfully depriving or frustrating in terms of lost emotional relationships, of loneliness and boredom. But what makes this pain of imprisonment bite most deeply is the fact that the confinement of the criminal represents a deliberate, moral rejection of the criminal by the free community. Indeed, as Reckless has pointed out, it is the moral condemnation of the criminal—however it may be symbolized—that converts hurt into punishment, i.e. the just consequence of committing an offense, and it is this condemnation that confronts the inmate by the fact of his seclusion.

Now it is sometimes claimed that many criminals are so alienated from conforming society and so identified with a criminal subculture that the moral condemnation, rejection, or disapproval of legitimate society does not touch them; they are, it is said, indifferent to the penal sanctions of the free community, at least as far as the moral stigma of being defined as a criminal is concerned. Possibly this is true for a small number of offenders such as the professional thief described by Sutherland[1] or the psychopathic personality delineated by William and Joan McCord.[2] For the great majority of criminals in prison, however, the evidence suggests that neither alienation from the ranks of the law-abiding nor involvement in a system of criminal value is sufficient to eliminate the threat to the prisoner's ego posed by society's rejection.[3] The signs pointing to the prisoner's degradation are many—the anonymity of a uniform and a number rather than a name, the shaven head,[4] the insistence on gestures of respect and subordination when addressing officials, and so on. The prisoner is never allowed to forget that, by committing a crime, he has foregone his claim to the status of a full-fledged, *trusted* member of society. The status lost by the prisoner is, in fact, similar to what Marshall has called the status of citizenship—that basic acceptance of the individual as a functioning member of the society in which he lives.[5] It is true that in the past the imprisoned criminal literally suffered civil death and that although the doctrines of attainder and corruption of blood were largely abandoned in the 18th and 19th Centuries, the inmate is still stripped of many of his civil rights such as the right to vote, to hold office, to sue in court, and so on.[6] But as important as the loss of these civil rights may be, the loss of that more diffuse status which defines the individual as someone to be trusted or as morally acceptable is the loss which hurts most.

In short, the wall which seals off the criminal, the contaminated man, is a constant threat to the prisoner's self-conception and the threat is continually repeated in the many daily reminders that he must be kept apart from "decent" men. Somehow this rejection or degradation by the free community must be warded off, turned aside, rendered harmless. Somehow the imprisoned criminal must find a device for rejecting his rejectors, if he is to endure psychologically.[7]

The Deprivation of Goods and Services

There are admittedly many problems in attempting to compare the standard of living existing in the free community and the standard of living which is supposed to be the lot of the inmate in prison. How, for example, do we interpret the fact that a covering for the floor of a cell usually consists of a scrap from a discarded blanket and that even this possession is forbidden by the prison authorities? What meaning do we attach to the fact that no inmate owns a common piece of furniture, such as a chair, but only a home-made stool? What is the value of a suit of clothing which is also a convict's uniform with a stripe and a stencilled number? The answers are far from simple although there are a number of prison officials who will argue that some inmates are better off in prison, in strictly material terms, than they could ever hope to be in the rough-and-tumble economic life of the free community. Possibly this is so, but at least it has never been claimed by the inmates that the goods and services provided the prisoner are equal to or better than the goods and services which the prisoner could obtain if he were left to his own devices outside the walls. The average inmate finds himself in a harshly Spartan environment which he defines as painfully depriving.

Now it is true that the prisoner's basic material needs are met — in the sense that he does not go hungry, cold, or wet. He receives adequate medical care and he has the opportunity for exercise. But a standard of living constructed in terms of so many calories per day, so many hours of recreation, so many cubic yards of space per individual, and so on, misses the central point when we are discussing the individual's feeling of deprivation, however useful it may be in setting minimum levels of consumption for the maintenance of health. A standard of living can be hopelessly inadequate, from the individual's viewpoint, because it bores him to death or fails to provide those subtle symbolic overtones which we invest in the world of possessions. And this is the core of the prisoner's problem in the area of goods and services. He wants — or needs, if you will — not just the so-called necessities of life but also the amenities: cigarettes and liquor as well as calories, interesting foods as well as sheer bulk, individual clothing as well as adequate clothing, individual furnishings for his living quarters as well as shelter, privacy as well as space. The "rightfulness" of the prisoner's feeling of deprivation can be questioned. And the objective reality of the prisoner's deprivation—in the sense that he has actually suffered a fall from his economic position in the free community—can be viewed with skepticism, as we have indicated above. But these criticisms are irrelevant to the significant issue, namely that legitimately or illegitimately, rationally or irrationally, the inmate population defines its present material impoverishment as a painful loss.

Now in modern Western culture, material possessions are so large a part of the individual's conception of himself that to be stripped of them is to be attacked at the deepest layers of personality. This is particularly true when poverty cannot be excused as a blind stroke of fate or a universal calamity. Poverty due to one's own mistakes or misdeeds represents an indictment against one's basic value or personal worth and there are few men who can philosophically bear the want caused by their own actions. It is true some prisoners in the New Jersey State Prison attempt to interpret their low position in the scale of goods and services as an effort by the State to exploit them economically. Thus, in the eyes of some inmates, the prisoner is poor not because of an offense which he has committed in the past but because the State is a tyrant which uses its captive criminals as slave labor under the hypocritical guise of reformation. Penology, it is said, is a racket. Their poverty, then, is not punishment as we have used the word before, i.e., it is just consequence of criminal behavior; rather, it is an unjust hurt or pain inflicted without legitimate cause. This attitude, however, does not appear to be particularly widespread in the inmate population and the great majority of prisoners must face their privation without the aid of the wronged man's sense of injustice. Furthermore, more prisoners are unable to fortify themselves in their low level of material existence by seeing it as a means to some high or worthy end. They are unable to attach any significant meaning to their need to make it more bearable, such as present pleasures foregone for pleasures in the future, self-sacrifice in the interests of the community, or material asceticism for the purpose of spiritual salvation.

The inmate, then, sees himself as having been made poor by reason of his own acts and without the rationale of compensating benefits. The failure is *his* failure in a world where control and possession of the material environment are commonly taken as sure indicators of a man's worth. It is true that our society, as materialistic as it may be, does not rely exclusively on goods and services as a criterion of an individual's value; and, as we shall see shortly, the inmate population defends itself by stressing alternative or supplementary measures of merit. But impoverishment remains as one of the most bitter attacks on the individual's self-image that our society has to offer and the prisoner cannot ignore the implications of his straitened circumstances.[8] Whatever the discomforts and irritations of the prisoner's Spartan existence may be, he must carry the additional burden of social definitions which equate his material deprivation with personal inadequacy.

The Deprivation of Heterosexual Relationships

Unlike the prisoner in many Latin-American countries, the inmate of the maximum security prison in New Jersey does not enjoy the privilege of so-called conjugal visits. And in those brief times when the prisoner is allowed to see his wife, mistress, or "female friend," the woman must sit on one side of a plate glass window and the prisoner on the other, communicating by means of a phone under the scrutiny of a guard. If the inmate, then, is rejected and impoverished by the facts of his imprisonment, he is also figuratively castrated by his involuntary celibacy.

Now a number of writers have suggested that men in prison undergo a reduction of the sexual drive and that the sexual frustrations of prisoners are therefore less than they might appear to be at first glance. The reports of reduced sexual interest have, however, been largely confined to accounts of men imprisoned in concentration camps or similar extreme situations where starvation, torture, and physical exhaustion have reduced life to a simple struggle for survival or left the captive sunk in apathy. But in the American prison these factors are not at work to any significant extent and Lindner has noted that the prisoner's access to mass media, pornography circulated among inmates, and similar stimuli serve to keep alive the prisoner's sexual impulses.[9] The same thought is expressed more crudely by the inmates of the New Jersey State Prison in a variety of obscene expressions and it is clear that the lack of heterosexual intercourse is a frustrating experience for the imprisoned criminal and that it is a frustration which weights heavily and painfully on his mind during his prolonged confinement. There are, of course, some "habitual" homosexuals in the prison—men who were homosexuals before their arrival and who continue their particular form of deviant behavior within the all-male society of the custodial institution. For these inmates, perhaps, the deprivation of heterosexual intercourse cannot be counted as one of the pains of imprisonment. They are few in number, however, and are only too apt to be victimized or raped by aggressive prisoners who have turned to homosexuality as a temporary means of relieving their frustration.

Yet as important as frustration in the sexual sphere may be in physiological terms, the psychological problems created by the lack of heterosexual relationships can be even more serious. A society composed exclusively of men tends to generate anxieties in its members concerning their masculinity regardless of whether or not they are coerced, bribed, or seduced into an overt homosexual liaison. Latent homosexual tendencies may be activated in the individual without being translated into open behavior and yet still arouse strong guilt feelings at either the conscious or unconscious level. In the tense atmosphere of the prison with its known perversions, its importunities of admitted homosexuals, and its constant references to the problems of sexual frustration by guards and inmates alike, there are few prisoners who can escape the fact that an essential component of a man's self conception—his status of male—is called into question. And if an inmate has in fact engaged in homosexual behavior within the walls, not as a continuation of an habitual pattern but as a rare act of sexual deviance under the intolerable pressure of mounting physical desire, the psychological onslaughts on his ego image will be particularly acute.[10]

In addition to these problems stemming from sexual frustration per se, the deprivation of heterosexual relationships carries with it another threat to the prisoner's image of himself—more diffuse, perhaps, and more difficult to state precisely and yet no less disturbing. The inmate is shut off from the world of women which by its very polarity gives the male world much of its meaning. Like most men, the inmate must search for his identity not simply within himself but also in the picture of himself which he finds reflected in the eyes of others; and since a significant half of his audience is denied him, the inmate's self image is in danger of becoming half complete, fractured, a monochrome without the hues of reality. The prisoner's looking-glass self, in short—to use Cooley's fine phrase—is only that portion of the prisoner's personality which is recognized or appreciated by men and this partial identity is made hazy by the lack of contrast.

The Deprivation of Autonomy

We have noted before that the inmate suffers from what we have called a loss of autonomy in that he is subjected to a vast body of rules and commands which are designed to control his behavior in minute detail. To the casual observer, however, it might seem that the many areas of life in which self-determination is withheld, such as the language used in a letter, the hours of sleeping and eating, or the route to work, are relatively unimportant. Perhaps, it might be argued, as in the case of material deprivation, that the inmate in prison is not much worse off than the individual in the free community who is regulated in a great many aspects of his life by the iron fist of custom. It could even be argued, as some writers have done, that for a number of imprisoned criminals, the extensive control of the custodians provides a welcome escape from freedom and that the prison officials thus supply an external Super-Ego which serves to reduce the anxieties arising from an awareness of deviant impulses. But from the viewpoint of the inmate population, it is precisely the triviality of much of the officials' control which often proves to be most galling. Regulation by a bureaucratic staff is felt far differently than regulation by custom. And even though a few prisoners do welcome the strict regime of the custodians as a means of checking their own aberrant behavior which they would like to curb but cannot, most prisoners look on the matter in a different light. Most prisoners, in fact, express an intense hostility against their far-reaching dependence on the decisions of their captors and the restricted ability to make choices must be included among the pains of imprisonment along with restrictions of physical liberty, the possession of goods and services, and heterosexual relationships.

Now the loss of autonomy experienced by the inmates of the prison does not represent a grant of power freely given by the ruled to the rulers for a limited and specific end. Rather, it is total and it is imposed—and for these reasons it is less endurable. The nominal objectives of the custodians are not, in general, the objectives of the prisoners.[11] Yet regardless of whether or not the inmate population shares some aims with the custodial bureaucracy, the many regulations and orders of the New Jersey State Prison's official regime often arouse the prisoner's hostility because they don't "make sense" from the prisoner's point of view. Indeed, the incomprehensible order or rule is a basic feature of life in prison. Inmates, for example, are forbidden to take food from the messhall to their cells. Some prisoners see this as a move designed to promote cleanliness; others are convinced that the regulation is for the purpose of preventing inmates from obtaining anything that might be used in the *sub rosa* system of barter. Most, however, simply see the measure as another irritating, pointless gesture of authoritarianism. Similary, prisoners are denied parole but are left in ignorance of the reasons for the decision. Prisoners are informed that the delivery of mail will be delayed—but they are not told why.

Now some of the inmate population's ignorance might be described as "accidental"; it arises from what we can call the principle of bureaucratic indifference, i.e. events which seem important or vital to those at the bottom of the heap are viewed with an increasing lack of concern with each step upward. The rules, the commands, the decisions which flow down to those who are controlled are not accompanied by explanations on the grounds that it is "impractical" or "too much trouble." Some of the inmate population's ignorance, however, is deliberately fostered by the prison officials in that explanations are often withheld as a matter of calculated policy. Providing explanations carries an implication that those who are ruled have a right to know—and this in turn suggests that if the explanations are not satisfactory, the rule or order will be changed. But this is in direct contradiction to the theoretical power relationship of the inmates and the prison officials. Imprisoned criminals are individuals who are being punished by society and they must be brought to their knees. If the inmate population maintains the right to argue with its captors, it takes on the appearance of an enemy nation with its own sovereignty; and in so doing it raises disturbing questions about the nature of the offender's deviance. The criminal is no longer simply a man who has broken the law; he has become a part of a group with an alternative viewpoint and thus attacks the validity of the law itself. The custodians' refusal to give reasons for many aspects of their regime can be seen in part as an attempt to avoid such an intolerable situation.

The indignation aroused by the "bargaining inmate" or the necessity of justifying the custodial regime is particularly evident during a riot when prisoners have the "impudence" to present a list of demands. In discussing the disturbances at the New Jersey State Prison in the Spring of 1952, for example, a newspaper editorial angrily noted that "the storm, like a nightmarish April Fool's dream, has passed, leaving in its wake a partially wrecked State Prison as a debasing monument to the ignominious rage of desperate men."

The important point, however, is that the frustration of the prisoner's ability to make choices and the frequent refusals to provide an explanation for the regulations and commands descending from the bureaucratic staff involve a profound threat to the prisoner's self image because they reduce the prisoner to the weak, helpless, dependent status of childhood. As Bettelheim has tellingly noted in his comments on the concentration camp, men under guard stand in constant danger of losing their identification with the normal definition of an adult and the imprisoned criminal finds his picture of himself as a self-determining individual being destroyed by the regime of the custodians.[12] It is possible that this psychological attack is particularly painful in American culture because of the deep-lying insecurities produced by the delays, the conditionality and the uneven progress so often observed in the granting of adulthood. It is also possible that the criminal is frequently an individual who has experienced great difficulty in adjusting himself to figures of authority and who finds the many restraints of prison life particularly threatening in so far as earlier struggles over the establishment of self are reactivated in a more virulent form. But without asserting that Americans in general or criminals in particular are notably ill-equipped to deal with the problems posed by the deprivation of autonomy, the helpless or dependent status of the prisoner clearly represents a serious threat to the prisoner's self image as a fully accredited member of adult society. And of the many threats which may confront the individual, either in or out of prison, there are few better calculated to arouse acute anxieties than the attempt to reimpose the subservience of youth. Public humiliation, enforced respect and deference, the finality of authoritarian decisions, the demands for a specified course of conduct because, in the judgment of another, it is in the individual's best interest—all are features of childhood's helplessness in the face of a superior adult world. Such things may be both irksome and disturbing for a child, especially if the child envisions himself as having outgrown such servitude. But for the adult who has escaped such helplessness with the passage of years, to be thrust back into childhood's helplessness is even more painful, and the inmate of the prison must somehow find a means of coping with the issue.

The Deprivation of Security

However strange it may appear that society has chosen to reduce the criminality of the offender by forcing him to associate with more than a thousand other criminals for years on end, there is one meaning of this involuntary union which is obvious—the individual prisoner is thrown into prolonged intimacy with other men who in many cases have a long history of violent, aggressive behavior. It is a situation which can prove to be anxiety-provoking even for the hardened recidivist and it is in this light that we can understand the comment of an inmate of the New Jersey State Prison who said, "The worst thing about prison is you have to live with other prisoners."

The fact that the imprisoned criminal sometimes views his fellow prisoners as "vicious" or "dangerous" may seem a trifle unreasonable. Other inmates, after all, are men like himself, bearing the legal stigma of conviction. But even if the individual prisoner believes that he himself is not the sort of person who is likely to attack or exploit weaker and less resourceful fellow captives, he is apt to view others with more suspicion. And if he himself is prepared to commit crimes while in prison, he is likely to feel that many others will be at least equally ready.... Regardless of the patterns of mutual aid and support which may flourish in the inmate population, there are a sufficient number of outlaws within this group of outlaws to deprive the average prisoner of that sense of security which comes from living among men who can be reasonably expected to abide by the rules of society. While it is true that every prisoner does not live in constant fear of being robbed or beaten, the constant companionship of thieves, rapists, murderers, and aggressive homosexuals is far from reassuring.

An important aspect of this disturbingly problematical world is the fact that the inmate is acutely aware that sooner or later he will be "tested"— that someone will "push" him to see how far they can go and that he must be prepared to fight for the safety of his person and his possessions. If he should fail, he will thereafter be an object of contempt, constantly in danger of being attacked by other inmates who view him as an obvious victim, as a man who cannot or will not defend his rights. And yet if he succeeds, he may well become a target for the prisoner who wishes to prove himself, who seeks to enhance his own prestige by defeating the man with a reputation for toughness. Thus both success and failure in defending one's self against the aggressions of fellow captives may serve to provoke fresh attacks and no man stands assured of the future.[13]

The prisoner's loss of security arouses acute anxiety, in short, not just because violent acts of aggression and exploitation occur but also because behavior constantly calls into question the individual's ability to cope with it, in terms of his own inner resources, his courage, his "nerve." Can he stand up and take it? Will he prove to be tough enough? These uncertainties constitute an ego threat for the individual forced to live in prolonged intimacy with criminals, regardless of the nature or extent of his own criminality; and we can catch a glimpse of this tense and fearful existence in the comment of one prisoner who said, "It takes a pretty good man to be able to stand on an equal plane with a guy that's in for rape, with a guy that's in for murder, with a man who's well respected in the institution because he's a real tough cookie...." His expectations concerning the conforming behavior of others destroyed, unable and unwilling to rely on the officials for protection, uncertain of whether or not today's joke will be tomorrow's bitter insult, the prison inmate can never feel safe. And at a deeper level lies the anxiety about his reactions to this unstable world, for then his manhood will be evaluated in the public view.

Notes

[1]Cf. Edwin H. Sutherland, *The Professional Thief,* Chicago: The University of Chicago Press, 1937.

[2]Cf. William and Joan McCord, *Psychopathy and Delinquency*, New York: Grune and Stratton, 1956.

[3]For an excellent discussion of the symbolic overtones of imprisonment, see Walter C. Reckless, *The Crime Problem,* New York: Appleton-Century-Crofts, Inc., 1955, pp. 428-429.

[4]Western culture has long placed a peculiar emphasis on shaving the head as a symbol of degradation, ranging from the enraged treatment of collaborators in occupied Europe to the more measured barbering of recruits in the Armed Forces. In the latter case, as in the prison, the nominal purpose has been cleanliness and neatness, but for the person who is shaved the meaning is somewhat different. In the New Jersey State Prison, the prisoner is clipped to the skull on arrival but not thereafter.

[5]See T.H. Marshall. *Citizenship and Social Class,* Cambridge, England: The Cambridge University Press, 1950.

[6]Paul W. Tappan, "The Legal Rights of Prisoners," *The Annals of the American Academy of Political and Social Science,* Vol. 293, May 1954, pp. 99-111.

[7]See Lloyd W. McCorkle and Richard R. Korn, "Resocialization Within Walls." *Ibid.,* pp. 88-98.

[8]Komarovsky's discussion of the psychological implications of unemployment is particularly apposite here, despite the markedly different context, for she notes that economic failure

provokes acute anxiety as humiliation cuts away at the individual's conception of his manhood. He feels useless, undeserving of respect, disorganized, adrift in a society where economic status is a major anchoring point. Cf. Mirra Komarovsky's, *The Unemployed Man and His Family*, New York: The Dryden Press, 1940, pp. 74-77.

[9] See Robert M. Lindner, "Sex in Prison," *Complex*, Vol. 6, Fall 1951, pp. 5-20.

[10] Estimates of the proportion of inmates who engage in homosexuality during their confinement in the prison are apt to vary. In the New Jersey State Prison, however, Wing Guards and Shop Guards examined a random sample of inmates who were well known to them from prolonged observation and identified 35 per cent of the men as individuals believed to have engaged in homosexual acts. The judgments of these officials were substantially in agreement with the judgments of a prisoner who possessed an apparently well-founded reputation as an aggressive homosexual deeply involved in patterns of sexual deviance within the institution and who had been convicted of sodomy. But the validity of these judgments remains largely unknown and we present the following conclusions, based on a variety of sources, as provisional at best: First, a fairly large proportion of prisoners engage in homosexual behavior during their period of confinement. Second, for many of those prisoners who do engage in homosexual behavior, their sexual deviance is rare or sporadic rather than chronic. And third, as we have indicated before, much of the homosexuality which does occur in prison is not part of a life pattern existing before and after confinement; rather, it is a response to the peculiar rigors of imprisonment.

[11] The nominal objectives of the officials tend to be compromised as they are translated into the actual routines of day-to-day life. The modus vivendi reached by guards and their prisoners is oriented toward certain goals which are in fact shared by captors and captives. In this limited sense, the control of the prison officials is partly concurred in by the inmates as well as imposed on them from above. In discussing the pains of imprisonment our attention is focused on the frustrations or threats posed by confinement rather than the devices which meet these frustrations or threats and render them tolerable. Our interest here is in the vectors of the person's social system — if we may use an analogy from the physical sciences — rather than the resultant.

[12] Cf. Bruno Bettelheim, "Individual and Mass Behavior in Extreme Situations," in *Readings in Social Psychology*, edited by T.M. Newcomb and E.L. Hartley, New York: Henry Holt and Company, 1947.

[13] As the Warden of the New Jersey State Prison has pointed out, the arrival of an obviously tough professional hoodlum creates a serious problem for the recognized "bad man" in a cellblock who is expected to challenge the newcomer immediately.

14

Prison Rackets

Anthony L. Guenther

I'm just up from Atlanta. That was a hotel, I've been in a lot worse.
...But Atlanta was just fine. I ran two poker games...the guy who had
the games liked me,. so when he left he gave them to me. Now my partner has them. There's no money, it's all done in cigarettes. A guy may
owe you forty or fifty boxes.[1]

Recent interest in the prisoner's market system[2] has brought to light its
effect upon relationships among various sectors of the institution. From the
moment of commitment to a penitentiary a new man will be thrust into a
system of economic exchange in which his possessions, his commissary
account—indeed, his own body—are subjected to the wants, needs and
desires of others. Those who know how to do time quickly establish themselves as independent operators or find their niche in the exchange system.
Those who are new to the penitentiary go through a period of reconnais-
sance even as they find themselves scrutinized by the inmate population.
They discover that a Spartan existence is ahead for those who are not
affluent when they enter the prison, but that opportunities for getting ahead
financially are abundant. Almost no one in the institution needs to
experience poverty, assuming, of course, he is willing to incur some possible

Guenther, Anthony L. "Prison Rackets," from *The Social Dimensions of a Penitentiary*
an unpublished report to the National Institute of Law Enforcement and Criminal Justice,
1975, pp. 64-71, 78-92.

costs. This section examines at close range the major types of "hustles" in the prison community and the artifacts of their operation.

Currency, Loan Sharking and Storekeeping

Since currency and coins are contraband in the prison an illicit medium of exchange arises to take their place. This medium is cigarettes, which appear to be a universal form of currency in total institutions....

Williams and Fish[3] have pointed out that cigarettes come in three levels of buying power resembling denominations. Small purchases and minor favors can be repaid with individual cigarettes, moderately large purchases and slightly greater services can be secured with packs of twenty cigarettes, and large transactions can be made with a carton ("box") of ten packs.

Equally universal are the proclivities of inmates to borrow and loan cigarettes and to operate businesses of loaning "money" within the prison. A person who engages in these activities is referred to by Sykes and Messinger as a merchant or peddler who "exploits his fellow captives not by force but by manipulation and trickery, and who typically sells or trades goods that are in short supply."[4] Merchants, then, may operate a "store," usually from their cells, which supplies at inflated rates the goods ordinarily available from the commissary.[5] Credit is generally extended to prisoners who have drawn the full month's allotment from their commissary accounts. Although records of financial transactions pose a risk for the storekeeper, they are essential if the size of his operation is very large. A merchant may also engage in loan sharking, which works behind walls almost identically to its counterpart in the home world. The loan shark preys upon those who are unable to obtain credit elsewhere. In exchange for the risk he takes, the lender charges a widely known interest rate, often expressed as a "two for one," or a "three for two." The loan's duration is short, for example, a week or two at the end of which the borrower returns the principal and one hundred percent or fifty percent, respectively. To default on a loan in prison is not just economically inadvisable; it is often unhealthy as well. The inmate who cannot repay his loan at the end of the initial period is usually given an extension before he receives physical coercion. Men who owe others amounts they could not repay under the most relaxed conditions often request placement in segregation for protective custody. A storekeeper or loan shark in the penitentiary will hire enforcers to collect bad debts for him if his business is really professional. Experienced prison staff report that a sizeable proportion of the beatings quietly absorbed by inmates are caused by this system of usury. The following instance conveys the dangers attendant to purchasing beyond one's means. By providing information about a store, this inmate hopes his problem will be solved:

Dear Sir

I have borrow some cigarettes an other stuff from Clayton Edwards, he lives in B Cellhouse and runs a store. Cookies he charges four or five pack [of cigarettes]. An coffy six pack. I did get this stuff an am willing to pay him for it but he tell me that I oews him double because I waited to long, that rates have gone up. And also said get out [inmate's name] before i put my knife in you. he has three books under his bed that he has peoples names an how much they owe him in them. You can pick them up right now. they are three little tablets like they used at the mill [industries]. Brown books them are. an you can see I don't owe him that much Sir. And I dont want to get hurt. He keep stuff in his locker (No. 7) and Billy Davis his home boy (No. 3) locker. an why cant everyone run a store if he can? You all have bust[ed] him in the Basement for running a store. they call him (skip) Clayton Edwards

(thank you, sir, very very much sir).

I am a white male. I live in B Cellhouse.[6]

If an inmate cannot or elects not to borrow money, there are numerous ways to earn it. Cigarettes are paid for a wide variety of services and for the supply of certain goods.[7] It will be informative to look at some of these in detail.

Gambling

Bets on the outcome of an event made between two inmates occur so often and are sufficiently innocuous that custodial staff take little notice. The troublesome forms of gambling which can produce serious incidents are large-scale bookmaking and betting in games of chance. A bookmaker at Atlanta makes up "pool tickets," which are sheets of paper listing the expected scores of impending sports events, and collects bets from interested speculators. He then holds his assets in a "bank" from which runners distribute payoffs to winners at the event's conclusion. Certain potential problems facing a banker can lead him to employ two kinds of personnel: "jiggers," who for a fee ensure that the bookmaking operation will avoid official notice, and enforcers, who ensure that the "bank" is secure even if the "banker" is placed in segregation or is hospitalized.

Prisoners, of course, are permitted to have decks of playing cards and these, in conjunction with "poker chips" made of cardboard by a silkscreen process (forms of nuisance contraband) are used in such games as poker, tonk and acey-deucy. The prudent gambler will hire a jigger whether he runs a card game, a dice game, or some other competition involving chance. Comparatively few prisoners are charged with misconduct for gambling, and it is rare for a gambler to be intimidated. Those who are compulsive gamblers often default on their financial responsibilities and suffer the usual retributions.

Gambling plays an important role for prisoners related to its function as a removal activity. Intelligent betting on a sporting event requires knowledge about the participants and their competition which is obtained from the outside world. A football fan who is the Washington Redskins' most unflappable cellblock spectator may spend several hours each week reading or debating about his team. In this way he derives many of the home world satisfactions which are otherwise denied him. Prison employees are not opposed to wagering among inmates for moral reasons; they are accustomed to the trouble, however, which often signals failure to collect a bad debt.

Pornography

Prison officials find it increasingly difficult to enforce regulations concerning erotic material because definitions of eroticism and pornography are highly subjective. In the absence of guidelines established by judicial authority, officers find themselves confiscating materials which *they* think are pornographic. The rule of thumb followed by most draws a distinction between "normal" heterosexual art, photography and literature as opposed to characterizations of homosexuality, lesbianism, transvestism, flagellation, sodomy or autoeroticism. Nuisance contraband, then, would consist of items which pertain to these "perversions." Among the most frequently confiscated materials are three-ring notebooks which contain cut-out photographs of nude women pasted onto sheets, "pornographic" novels ("Blow the Man Down," "Campus Stud Lust"), and home-drawn cartoon books. The latter have two curiously consistent features. Although they usually depict heterosexual intercourse, some comment by one of the participants will often indicate that homosexual intercourse would have been better. For example, in one cartoon booklet about twenty pages are devoted to a male and female copulating while the former engages in a variety of weightlifts. On the last page, following an extended climax, he says to her, "not bad, for a *woman*." The second unusual feature of cartoon books is a gross enlargement of male genitalia. If it can be assumed that imprisoned men had active sex lives before incarceration, the emphasis placed upon virility and potency in original drawings would seem to affirm those needs.

Cartoons, novels and three-ring notebooks are referred to as "fuck books" and are available to inmates on a rental basis. For instance, a notebook may be kep in one's cell overnight for two packs. The likelihood of an assault over debts incurred through rental of these materials is exceedingly rare. What operates to define "pornography" in the prison as contraband is an attempt by staff to discourage licentiousness. They operate not as agents of any tribunal or legal authority but as moral entrepreneurs.[8] Observations made at the Atlanta penitentiary revealed important differences between supervisors with respect to their feelings about "obscene" materials. During one quarter, erotic literature was readily available, and few if any "fuck books" were confiscated. The next quarter when job rotations produced a different set of Lieutenants who oversee the housing units, decorations, literature and booklets were seized in frequent raids. One of the hypocrisies of this system is that "good pornography" confiscated by officers usually made its way to the Lieutenant's office for "inspection" and eventually was recirculated back to the cellblock.

Many prison staff feel ambivalent about pornography in the institution. While they recognize that ostentatious display of nudes may offend some persons, particularly visitors and tour groups, and therefore may be in "bad taste," they assert that sexual fantasy is preferable to sexual expression in a monosexual environment.

"Homebrew" Beer and Drug Trafficking

Although alcoholic beverages are technically central nervous system (CNS) depressants and, therefore, qualify as drugs, it is useful to discuss these two topics separately. Alcohol is legitimately consumed in the general society on such a wide scale that many drinking occasions have become institutionalized. Its use in the facilitation of social gatherings, in the reduction of anxiety and as a ritual (e.g., the "TGIF" party) is well known outside the prison. It would be reasonable to assume that alcohol consumption among imprisoned felons functions as a compensation for the deprivations they perceive.

Drinking in prison appears to take place on a small scale, principally for two reasons. First, commercial distilled spirits are almost unobtainable because someone would have to arrange for their passage through a security checkpoint. Even the smallest container, a half-pint, is bulky and requires destruction after it is consumed. Second, the availability of other drugs which are easily concealed and may have greater potency makes drinking less attractive. Nevertheless, the manufacture, distribution and consumption of "homebrew" beer is a thriving industry in many institutions, and it demands constant attention from correctional officers.

Homebrew is made by combining sugar, yeast, water and some kind of fruit, fruit peelings, or potato peelings and storing them in a warm place for a few days' fermentation ("working off"). Yeast is usually the critical component, since sugar can be "liberated" from the dining hall and the basic substance for fermentation is readily obtainable. Homebrew, often called "jack," "juice," "buck," "hootch," or just "brew," is made from milk, fruit cocktail, prunes ("pruno"), figs, raisins ("raisin-jack"), apples ("apple-jack"), potato peelings, or apricots. When working off, the solution emits a distinctive odor. The major problem confronted by a homebrew specialist, therefore, is to find a place which is preferably warm but also secure from discovery by officers. Large "stingers" (heating coils) which heat the mixture and thereby hasten fermentation are popular contraband. Specially-engineered stashes for homebrew,[9] as we saw earlier, are created by Atlanta inmates. Williams and Fish report similarly that Alabama state prisoners seal the mixture in plastic bags which they place between their legs in bed at night for warmth.[10] Drinking homebrew beer more often results in sickness than euphoria, but many prisoners feel that their efforts are worthwhile if they become mildly intoxicated.

Prison custodial staff confiscate homebrew stashes and collections of other drugs in large quantities just before weekends and prior to holidays. Note, for example, the frequency of shakedowns and disciplinary actions related to homebrew and drugs at Christmas and New Year's, 1968-1969:[11]

December 18   Ten pounds of sugar found in cell 5-9.

December 19   Mr. Curry found...a bottle of pills in A [cellhouse] basement. Mr. Disson took four capsules off Franklin 66091. Franklin was placed in segregation.

December 20   Approximately 4½ gallon of peach brandy (homemade) found in the storeroom of the kitchen. Stone 78275 placed in administrative segregation, drunk on pills. Three needles, two syringes, and one gallon brew found in B basement.

December 21   Twenty gallons of brew found in B cellhouse, cell 8-11. Approximately twenty gallon brew found in cell 9-11. Small amount of glue for "sniffing" found in cell 9-15.

December 22   Five gallon of brew found in cell 9-12. Thirty gallons of brew, a case of dried figs...found in shakedown of mattress factory.

December 24   Binns 49373 and Slatterly 74516 placed in administrative segregation for drinking. Approximately five gallons of "brew" found in cells 5-1 and 5-2.

December 25   Small amount of brew in 4-8. Real nice Xmas evening this watch. The inmates must have used up all their booze and pills.

December 26   A search of E cellhouse revealed two syringes and two hypo needles. A small portion of what might be marijuana was turned over to Mr. Follett for identification.

December 27   Some rumors that pills were received in the institution today. Unable to determine if they were received. Five pounds of sugar and one needle and syringe found in D-4 dormitory. McKinley 62219 and Robertson 81711 placed in administrative segregation (drunk). Trash baskets full of brew found in cells 5-6 and 6-8.

December 28 One gallon of brew found in cell 5-8.

December 29 Mr. Yeager found two inmates holding a five gallon bag of brew back of a ventilator in C cellhouse. Fifteen pounds of sugar and a hot water bottle full of brew found in B cellhouse. Six gallon jugs of brew found in vegetable room electric panel.

December 30 One gallon brew found in 8-4. Two large bags of brew picked up in A cellhouse made of raisins and raw bread dough.

January 1 Approximately nine gallons brew found in B cellhouse cut-off [utility corridor] in a special bag hanging with the utility pipes.

Correctional staff have a great deal of ambivalence toward homebrew. On the one hand, they may well appreciate the enjoyment which can be derived from a drinking occasion. This is reflected in comments made while dumping confiscated homebrew down the drain: "It's a shame we have to ruin this fellow's Christmas spirits"; "It don't smell like much, but if I was doing time I'd need a jolt every so often."[12] On the other hand, veteran officers recall the number of times they have had to confront an inmate who had been drinking, became progressively antagonistic, and finally assaulted someone in the vicinity. From a staff viewpoint, homebrew production and consumption are serious rule infractions because some inmates, not otherwise behavior problems, become assaultive when their inhibitions are reduced. Consider, for example, these episodes:

A 222 call from F-ward in the hospital brought ten officers on the run. An inmate there named Goodlett was wrestling with two hospital employees and had partially torn their clothes. Goodlett was finally subdued by eight officers at which point he became incontinent. Other inmates in his work area stated that he had been drinking homebrew most of the morning.[13]

Inmate Tyberson 27222 became inebreated and went beserk in B cellhouse on the evening shift. He was swinging at any inmate near him until restrained and held down by other prisoners. Then he was taken to the hospital and placed in restraints until he sobered up and calmed down.[14]

Since homebrew must be concocted in small quantities and is usually made for one's own enjoyment, it does not often exhibit the properties of a racket. An occasional "Homebrew King" will appear in Atlanta's population, but hustling "brew" for profit is not very rewarding.

Some Atlanta officers and their supervisors believe that the appearance of homebrew is a healthy sign, since there is presumably an inverse relationship between homebrew production and drug trafficking in the institution. If searches for "brew" are unproductive, suspicion mounts that drugs are available in its place.

The prisoner who is determined to get "high" may select a number of solutions or substances for this purpose. He may seek access to lemon extract or nutmeg for a special effect, or he may "sniff" gasoline, ditto fluid, carbon tetrachloride (now prohibited in many prisons), lacquer thinner, or glue. For the drug user who is not squeamish, a solution made of concentrated coffee ("instant" or "freeze-dried") boiled down to a sludge and injected intravenously ("mainlined") is reported to induce a substantial "flash."[15]

Drug trafficking is considered a major form of misconduct in the penitentiary; drugs and their paraphernalia are classified as serious contraband. The demand for drugs makes it a profitable enterprise which in itself would explain the degree of staff attention given to it. But the fact that most drug supply systems involve *collusion* between those inside the walls with persons outside adds a special dimension to the problem. Aside from drugs stolen from the hospital (a comparatively rare event at Atlanta), most trafficking occurs when prisoners smuggle drugs supplied by a confederate past the security check points, arrange to have them concealed in shipments or on transportation vehicles traveling through the wall, have them brought into the visiting room, or conspire with an employee to bring them in. Few acts by a staff member are thought to be more reprehensible than supplying drugs to the inmates.

Several means have been devised for surreptitiously getting drugs into the prison. A "drop" is often made consisting of a package small enough to be picked up by a minimum custody prisoner working on the reservation. He then throws it over the wall at a prearranged spot, inserts it in a package or vehicle passing through the east gate, or conceals it on his body, anticipating that the officer routinely shaking him down as he reenters the institution will not discover it.

Another plan calls for a visitor to bring drugs to the prison in a very small plastic bag or tube-shaped receptacle.[16] In the course of his visit, the inmate takes the bag and swallows it, or takes the cylinder and inserts it in his rectum. A strip-search at the end of his visit usually proceeds uneventfully and the prisoner can then recover the package in his quarters. The occasional prisoner who is suspected of concealing drugs in this fashion may be removed to the hospital where fluoroscopic examination is made or a "finger-wave" (rectal inspection) performed to verify its presence.

Yet a third technique involves concealment of a package smuggled into the visiting room where it will be picked up by a member of the inmate cleanup crew later. A typical case here is:

> On March 24 information was received of an attempt to introduce contraband pills into the institution through the visiting room. The pills (one hundred "black beauties") were found under the sandwich machine in the visiting room as we were informed. The package was placed back where it was found, minus the pills, in an unsuccessful effort to apprehend the pickup [man].[17]

One of the reasons why drug hustles have their appeal is the comparative ease of concealing and transporting them. Heroin, for example, can be brought into the institution in a small, flat packet and later be "cut" with a number of substances, placed in "papers" or "one-shots," and distributed to users. The advantage of packaging drugs in foil or paper packets, of course, is their ease of disposal, especially in the commode, if a shakedown is imminent. Most inmates, as this episode demonstrates, avoid carrying drugs on their persons:

> I received information from Lieutenant Willington this subject [Oliver 57893] had some form of narcotic in his possession. Officers Jones, Scranton, Phillips, Mumford and I went to D basement to search for this contraband. As Mr. Phillips and I approached Oliver's stall [cubicle], he stepped out. I stopped him and strip searched him there and found nothing on him. I went into his stall and searched a brown paper bag that was being used for a trash container. I found a Kent cigarette pack with an assortment of contraband pills and capsules and a white powder substance wrapped in gray cellophane. This package was found at approximately 2:50 p.m. this date. It was turned over to Lieutenants Willington and Burcham.[18]

An incredible array of drugs is found in prison settings. They range from those which induce mild intoxication or sedation to some which create psychological or physical dependency. A listing of some drugs [19] encountered at the Atlanta penitentiary in the last five years is found in Table I.

Drug trafficking in the prison receives about the same reaction by correctional staff as it is given in the outside community by law enforcement authorities. Correctional institutions experience violence from drug activity, e.g., homicides, overdose deaths, and drug-related suicides, which in the minds of staff is ample justification for its prohibition. The drug business and its profit potential are also likely to produce secondary problems, such as employed complicity, intimidation and favoritism. A closer look at drug distribution in the Atlanta penitentiary will show how this process operates.

Although no Atlanta inmates are likely to remain addicted to a drug after commitment by the court, it is theoretically possible to "score" intermittently over a relatively long period. For those who were intimately connected with the drug scene outside, the opiates are perhaps most sought after. "Drug busts" in the penitentiary reveal paraphernalia similar to that found outside, such as a spoon or bottle cap for cooking the solution, eyedroppers or disposable syringes and needles for injection, and material for a tourniquet. Paraphernalia associated with marijuana or hashish smoking are conventional pipes, water pipes, cigarette papers and "roach" (butt) holders. Heroin confiscated in Atlanta has been found to have twenty percent purity, but most "papers" contain three to five percent heroin.

Table I
Some Drugs Found at the Atlanta Penitentiary

Drug Type	Specimen Recovered	Pharmacology	Street and Prison Names
Opiates	Heroin "one-shots" or "papers"	Central Nervous System (CNS) Depressant	Smack, Shit, Dope, H, Junk
Cocaine	Cocaine "one-shots" or "papers"; vial of powder	Stimulant or Anesthetic	Coke, Snow
Marijuana/Hashish	Cigarettes; loose seeds, leaves, stems and flowering tops; foil packets of hashish in brown chunks	Intoxicant	Joints, Sticks, Reefers; Grass, Pot, Hash
Hallucinogens	LSD tablets, sugar cubes	Hallucinogen	Acid
	STP ("Serenity, Tranquility, Peace") liquid ampule	Hallucinogen	STP
Barbiturates	Sodium seconal capsules, Tuinal capsules, Pamine PB tablets, Nembudonna capsules, Nembutal capsules	CNS Depressant	Red Birds, Rainbows, Red Devils, Yellow Jackets, Blue Devils, Christmas Trees
Nonbarbiturate Sedative-Hypnotics and Minor Tranquilizers	Cortrax tablets, Darvon capsules	Tanquilizer without CNS depression	None
	Chloral hydrate liquid	Sedative for sleep	In combination with alcohol: "Mickey Finn" or knock-out drops
	Valium ampules	Anti-anxiety tranquilizer	None
Amphetamines	Methamphetamine powder, Dexedrine tablets, Obedrine LA (long-action) tablets, Dexamyl spansules, Biphetamine and Biphetamine-T (Tuazone) capsules	CNS Stimulant, mood elevator	Speed, Dexies, Hearts, Bennies, Black Beauties, Pep Pills, Footballs, L.A. Turnabouts, Co-Pilots, Uppers

Before the virtual disappearance of amphetamines from the pharma-
ceutical market, black beauties, footballs and L.A. turnarounds[20] were
among the most frequently confiscated drugs at Atlanta. In recent years,
these have been replaced by the barbiturates, while hallocinogenic and other
drugs of experimentation are rarely found.

Most drugs are quite expensive even by street standards, and the "going
price" varies with the supply. By way of illustration, at one time during the
field research for this project, a single black beauty was worth a carton and
a half of cigarettes. Heroin in large quantities is sometimes said to be worth
"several human lives" if it falls into the wrong hands. Even by the most
conservative estimates (authorities are prone to gross exaggeration when
calculating the "street" value of confiscated drugs), correctional staff in
Atlanta destroy thousands of dollars worth of drugs seized as contraband
each year, usually by flushing them down the commode.

The characteristics of drug hustling or racketeering are intricate and not
often clearly understood by staff. Sometimes all they know is that a
prisoner dies from a homicidal attack and that snitches allege he failed to
produce revenue for a shipment of drugs. Few cases of drug-related misconduct are prosecuted for lack of a suspect, witnesses, or even evidence. The
drug dealer usually covers himself with protective layers of other personnel
who maintain an outside source, arrange the means of importing supplies,
create a distribution system, divert official surveillance, and collect debts
indirectly. If drug trafficking in the institution flourishes, as it does sporad-
ically at Atlanta, it almost certainly indicates financing ("bank-rolling") by
sources beyond the walls. Arrangements for payments to outside
participants in this network can be handled by visitors, by unscrupulous
attorneys, or by a compromised employee.

Personalized Services

The final hustle found in the penitentiary delivers personalized services to
inmates. Many of these are innocuous and represent attempts to earn
cigarette money. At an established rate of two packs, for example, one's
clothes are given special attention in the laundry or one receives a custom
haircut in the barber shop. Many prisoners ("runners") offer to deliver
goods, ranging from weapons, escape equipment and drugs, to
pornography, outdated newspapers or magazines, and sandwiches. For the
risk he takes being caught en route with contraband (sometimes concealed
in books with cut-out interiors) or being out-of-bounds, the runner collects
a fee. In this same category are jiggers who maintain lookout for an officer
or divert his attention for a fee.

More sophisticated hustles delivering personalized services operate within walls. There are "jailhouse lawyers" who, for modest retainers (two "boxes" or more), will instruct a fellow prisoner in how to write a writ or will assist with his appeal. Inmate seers place their contraband advertisements in the cellblocks, offering to tell fortunes, remove curses, or confer a "hex" on enemies. Fortune-telling is popular because many things in a prisoner's life are problematic: whether he will make parole, when he will be released, whether his wife will await his return. Inmate prophets sometimes offer their services to staff, as in the case of a prisoner who devised his own "computerized" glimpse of the future. A "cop-out" bearing matrices of numbers and symbols (311 311 311 1-1-1 000) made this offer:

> Lt. Ramey—
>
> Please read [these symbols] computorially. And when you are alone.
>
> If you wish to take a course from me I'll make you better than the Banker who I've robbed. Thank you, Lt.
>
> E. Bledsoe 69871[21]

The "protection" racket is another means by which some inmates earn an income. Exploitation is most likely among new, "weak" prisoners, those who are disabled or afflicted, and those who are elderly. Most inmates who come to Atlanta know better than to divulge their financial holdings, but subtle means can be used to determine who can afford "services." Sometimes a prisoner will be told that he should "take out insurance" against "accidents" or for protection from "the psychopaths, killers, and perverts" in the population. Alternatively, he will be given to understand that a specific offender or a group of prisoners dislikes him and plans to take action. Extortion usually succeeds because most inmates will not seek assistance from the staff, but even if they do, protective cutody or transfer is the only alternative. As one officer explained: "We can't do much for a convict who gets all 'jammed up.' Every third one of them's got somebody after his ass and if we locked them all up for protection we'd need a segregation building big as this institution."[22]

Occasionally an ingenious hustle will surface, causing no small amount of conflict among staff. A good case in point is the following:

> Coming before the adjustment committee was a "shot" on Howery 72448. Several officers present were surprised that Howery had gotten picked up on a contraband "rap" since he reportedly dabbled in nothing less than narcotics.
>
> The contraband in question was examined at great length. It consisted of a cigar box overflowing with magnifying glasses, sandpaper, pliers, screwdrivers, watch crystals, a container of banana oil, containers of shellac, aluminum foil, three spoons, and several ballpoint pen replacement cartridges.

Howery's explanation to the committee was that he had been given permission to repair watches. He produced a certificate authorizing his service and bearing the signatures of a Captain and an Associate Warden (both since transferred to other institutions). He was told the case would be taken under advisement.

In later discussion it was revealed that the present Captain had Howery's cell shaken down and personally wrote the "shot." Two Lieutenants then tried to "lawyer" for Howery by arguing that he was going to hustle cigarettes one way or another and repairing watches was better than having him dealing drugs.

Howery was later given ninety days suspended segregation, his certificate was taken and his tool kit was destroyed."[23]

Notes

[1]M. Yanow, *Observations from the Treadmill,* New York: Viking, 1973, pp. 64-65.

[2]A very fine account of this marketplace is Heather Strange and Joseph McCrory, "Bulls and Bears in the Cellblock," *Society,* 11 (July/August, 1974), pp. 51-59. A more lengthy account is Vergil L. Williams and Mary Fish, *Convicts, Codes, and Contraband: The Prison Life of Men and Women*, Cambridge, Massachusetts: Ballinger, 1974.

[3]Williams and Fish, *op. cit.,* p. 55.

[4]Gresham M. Sykes and Sheldon Messinger, "The Inmate Social System," *Theoretical Studies in Social Organization of the Prison,* New York: Social Science Research Council, Pamphlet no. 15, 1960, p. 9.

[5]Predictably, "knocking lockers" is a gang activity which selects a locker used for a store and burglarizes it.

[6]Note dated December 30, 1969, U.S. Penitentiary, Atlanta.

[7]For an exhaustive description of these as they operate at the Rahway, New Jersey prison see Strange and McCrory, *op. cit.,* pp. 55-58.

[8]For a discussion of this role, see Howard S. Becker, *Outsiders: Studies in the Sociology of Deviance,* New York: The Free Press of Glencoe, 1963, pp. 147-163.

[9]Steel pans fabricated to exact dimensions are sometimes made to fit in the hollow space underneath cell lockers.

[10]Williams and Fish, *op cit.,* p. 72.

[11]Derived from the Lieutenant's Log, U.S. Penitentiary, Atlanta, December 18, 1968 through January 1, 1969.

[12]Field notes, U.S. Penitentiary, Atlanta, December 23, 1969.

[13]Field notes, U.S. Penitentiary, Atlanta, January 7, 1970.

[14]Field notes, U.S. Penitentiary, Atlanta, December 12, 1969.

[15]Darvon was manufactured for some years in a capsule containing buffer powder and a tiny bead. Referred to by inmates as a "time bomb," this particle was put in solution and injected for extraordinary intoxication.

[16]Favorite containers are a standard "Benzedrex" nasal inhaler filled with drugs or a "fingerstall" made by cutting the finger from a rubber glove, filling it with tablets or capsules and closing the end with a rubber band. Either of these coated with a lubricant such as Vaseline can then be inserted in the rectum.

[17]Memorandum, U.S. Penitentiary, Atlanta, March 25, 1972.

[18]Memorandum, U.S. Penitentiary, Atlanta, February 4, 1970.

[19]Excluded are alcohol and toxic vapors, which have already been discussed.

[20]These references are based in the first two cases upon physical appearance of the capsules. The third is a favorite of truck drivers who can hypothetically drive a tractor-trailer from the east coast to Los Angeles, turn around and drive back nonstop after ingesting one capsule.

[21]Inmate letter, U.S. Penitentiary, Atlanta, March 3, 1970.

[22]Field notes, U.S. Penitentiary, Atlanta, January 22, 1970.

[23]Memoranda, Adjustment Committee transcript, and field notes, U.S. Penitentiary, Atlanta, October 27, 1969.

15

Incarcerated Women

Arthur L. Paddock, III
Robert G. Culbertson

A significant body of knowledge about female criminality is emerging as we enter the 1980s. For the most part, female criminality and women's prisons have been ignored by writers in the field of criminal justice. The current flurry of research activity reflects fifty years of neglect and reveals a considerable amount of bias and myth in much of the earlier research on the female offender. Problems in regard to bias have been articulated by Smith (1965). Smith contends that issues in female criminality have been neglected or glossed over by sentiment and unreliable male intuition. Other writers link the absence of research on female criminality to the fact that women comprise less than five percent of the prison population in the United States. Historically, female criminality has not been viewed as "dangerous." Rather, the criminal behavior which brought women to court was considered socially offensive. As a result, intensive study of the behavior was not accomplished. There are other issues in this area. For example, male domination of graduate research programs has generated more research interest in large maximum security institutions for men than in institutions for women.

It is important to note that the traditional role of the criminologist has been to maintain a close relationship with corrections policy-making bodies and officials. As a result, research has focused primarily on those issues which officials distributing grants and consulting monies defined as problematic. Historically, major management problems have been centered in maximum security prisons for men. Policy issues tended to focus on these types of institutions. As a consequence, women's prisons were ignored. Significant changes began to occur in the late 1960s and the focus of research and study shifted dramatically in the direction of female criminality and women in prison. Some content the attention given to female criminality was the result of the emergence of women's rights movement which became an increasingly powerful force in American society in the late 1960s and 1970s. Others claim that increased involvement of women in serious crime produced the new attention to female criminality. Still others contend that the myth and bias which pervaded much of the earlier research on female criminality enhanced the potential for new efforts reflecting less biased and prejudiced research strategies.

Women are becoming an increasingly dominant force in American society. Refusing to play subordinate roles linked to traditional sex roles, women are aggressively pursuing Constitutional rights in a variety of settings. At the same time, as opportunities increase for women in the field of employment, opportunities have also increased in the area of crime. Because positions of financial trust were historically restricted to men, women were rarely charged with embezzlement or related offenses involving financial trust. However, as women overcome employment barriers and assume positions in the area of finance and banking, it is not longer uncommon to find women charged with the same offenses as men who hold these positions.

In the following discussion we have summarized a number of perspectives on female criminality and incarcerated women. Relying extensively on the work of Glick and Neto (1977) a profile of incarcerated women is presented. The data are demographic for the most part but contribute to an understanding of the problems of incarceration for the female offender. Attention is then given to programs for women in prison. Finally, the experience of incarceration is discussed with a focus on roles which women come to play in prison.

A Profile of Incarcerated Women

The demographic data provided by Glick and Neto indicate that women in prison are young; two-thirds of those incarcerated are under thirty years of age. The median age for unsentenced women and misdemeanants held in jails is twenty-four. While black women comprise approximately ten percent of the adult female population in the United States, studies indicate that about fifty percent of the incarcerated women are black. Based on demographic data, Indians and Hispanic women are also over-represented in prison populations. It is difficult to develop conclusions from these data. However, it should be noted that minorities also tend to be overrepresented in men's institutions when demographic comparisons are made. Research focusing on the interaction of race and crime rates has produced conflicting results depending on the sample and research strategy used by the investigator. It is important to note, however, that if opportunities for criminal behavior are opening for women, so are the opportunities for incarceration. This is especially true for minority women.

When compared to the national population of women, incarcerated women tend to be less educated. It is important to note that educational attainment levels are related to ethnic group status. That is, white and Indian women tend to be better educated, followed by black women. Hispanic women had significantly lower educational attainment levels when compared to other ethnic groups. The data on marital relationships reveal that at the time of incarceration, twenty-seven percent of the women indicated that they were single. Nineteen percent were reportedly not married but indicated that they were living with a man. Twenty percent reported that they were married. Twenty-eight percent of the incarcerated women indicated that they were separated or divorced. Finally, while sixty percent of the women in the Glick and Neto study had been married at least once, only ten percent of this population reported living with a husband immediately prior to incarceration.

1975 Census Bureau data indicate that incarcerated women tend to have more children when compared to non-incarcerated women. These data indicate that incarcerated women have an average of 2.4 children compared to an average of 2.0 children for all families reported on the Census Bureau data. Offense data, compiled by Glick and Neto for women incarcerated for felonies, indicate that forty-three percent of the women were incarcerated for violent crimes such as murder, manslaughter and armed robbery. The remainder were incarcerated for property offenses which tended to be drug related such as forgery, fraud and larceny. Data on offense histories show that nearly one-third of the incarcerated women had been arrested before their seventeenth birthday and that one-third of the women had been previously incarcerated in a juvenile institution. These data indicate that a substantial number of incarcerated women began their criminal careers at an early age.

In compiling this profile, Glick and Neto note that the search for good demographic data on women incarcerated in our prisons is hampered by a lack of information. The Bureau of Census, through its National Prisoner Statistics Program, has produced data on men and women in state and federal prisons. However, a prisoner census taken in 1972 was not designed to provide data on women. Data collection problems are even more serious when efforts are made to obtain information on women incarcerated in jails and city lockups.

What do these data tell us about incarcerated women? First, there is some evidence that the criminal justice system may be discriminatory in the processing of female racial minorities. Second, family histories of incarcerated women often indicate family instability. Third, the number of women involved in violent crimes seemingly destroys the myth that women are not involved in dangerous behavior. When we compare these data to data on men incarcerated in prison, there are a number of similarities which reflect unresolved issues in the criminal justice system.

Educational and Vocational Programs for the Incarcerated Woman

Educational and vocational programs for women in prison appear to have been introduced randomly over time with little consideration to planning and relevancy. The development, of programming in women's prisons, much like the development of programming in men's prisons, was initially designed to relieve boredom. Administrators often failed to develop educational and training programs which would prepare women for occupational roles after release from prison. Programs in women's prisons reinforced traditional sex roles. Vocational programs in the areas of cosmetology, horticulture, sewing, cake decorating and flower arrangement reflect this programming perspective. Non-incarcerated women, in increasing numbers, are entering industrial positions previously restricted to men. There is little evidence that incarcerated women are being prepared for these opportunities.

There are a number of problems in this area which reflect institutional constraints. Scpecifically, institutional size, location, budget and philosophical perspective of the administrator interact and ultimately affect programming for incarcerated women. In some women's prisons it is impossible to differentiate between programs designed for vocational training and prison industries designed to serve the institution and perhaps other institutions in the system. For example, programs in the area of sewing may consist of an assembly line operation where women participate in very specific tasks. As a result they do not learn the skills necessary to enhance employment potentials after release. Institutions which require a considerable amount of inmate labor in the area of maintenance tend to have the most limited range of program offerings. Prisons which require that women handle a major part of the cooking and maintenance tend to have few vocational or educational programs. Prison maintenance is the "program."

While no two women's prisons are identical, it is possible to identify a number of program/service units which are generally present in a women's prison. The most prevalent program/service units include: intake/classification, work assignment, education, recreation, health care, counseling/treatment, religious programs, food service and maintenance. The first contact between the woman and the institution occurs in the intake or admissions unit. At this point the woman is finger-printed, photographed, given a basic physical examination, and initial social history information is collected. Generally she is given a set of institutional regulations and is assigned to the classification housing unit. During the classification process comprehensive social history data are collected and attention is given to offense history. A major consideration in the classification process is the issue of security risk. If a woman's offense history and current offense indicate the need for strong custody measures, it is likely that she will be assigned to a maximum security unit within the prison. On the other hand, if the woman is considered a "good risk" it is likely that she will be assigned to a minimum or medium security unit.

It is important to note at this point that in most states a woman does not leave the prison to which she was initially incarcerated until her release date. In many states the classification process for a man results in his assignment to a particular institution depending on security status and he may be moved from institution to institution. The classification process is exceedingly important in that the security status will determine the extent to which each woman participates in institutional programs. Women incarcerated in maximum security units have fewer opportunities for program participation and the consequences of incarceration are more severe for this group.

Evaluation of programs in both men's and women's prisons tends to support the contention that women have fewer opportunities to become involved in vocational and education programs (Hendrix, 1972). We should not be surprised that recidivism rates for incarcerated women tend to be high. In addition to our failure to prepare women for new opportunities after release, we fail to understand the criminal subcultures of drugs and prostitution. These subcultures provide important financial incentives for the newly released offender. It is in these subcultures that a woman is accepted and rewarded for those skills which contributed to her incarceration.

The Prison Experience: A Sociological Perspective

Research on the role taking process in a women's prison seems to focus on two areas: the psychological needs of the women involved in the role taking process and the social roles women play in the institutional context. Some of the theory and research in the area of psychological needs has been labeled sexist. The emphasis has been on the differences between men and women as reflected in the division of labor in our society. Some theories in this area are based on the premise that men come to prison as husbands, fathers and wage earners while women come to prison as wives, mothers and homemakers. As a result of this perspective, it has been assumed that the man's position of leadership in the family setting differentiates men from women. Furthermore, it is assumed that this differentiation is reflected in the role structure in the prison setting. The self-concepts of men, then, reflect occupational roles which those men held before incarceration. Women, on the other hand, suffer primarily from separation from their families.

Research conducted by Cassel and VanVorst (1961) supports the notion that women bring to prison identities and self-concepts which are linked to family roles such as wife, mother or daughter. This classic study is supported by subsequent studies (Burkhart, 1973; Chandler, 1973; Lockwood, 1980) which place women in a prison kinship system reflecting traditional family roles. As a result, it has been assumed that women are more dependent on family relationships than are men. This perspective suggests that women subordinate themselves to the economic interests of the husband and thereby tend to accept a limited range of activity. Dependency is then continually reinforced thus contributing to further power differentials. As a result, women tend to utilize physical attractiveness and seductivity as techniques in meeting needs and in manipulating authority stuctures. The social behavior of women in prison reflects psychological deprivation. Cassel and VanVorst, and Heffernan (1972) found that psychological deprivation manifests itself in the taking of argot roles in the prison setting. Cassel and VanVorst have identified three types of personal needs which women bring to prison and which have a significant impact on their behavior during the incarceration process.

The first of these needs is "affectional starvation" which Cassel and VanVorst define as, "the need for ego status among a very small group of intimate peers and some degree of sympathetic understanding for their personal problems by such intimate friends." (1961:28) The second need reflects the exaggeration of certain symbolic needs. That is, incarcerated women may engage in behaviors which are mutually advantageous and provide symbolic satisfaction to both partners in the relationship. The need to suckle a baby, for example, may manifest itself in the form of an intimate relationship which provides symbolic satisfaction but would not be socially approved outside the prison walls. Finally, the need for psycho-sexual gratification is identified as a "need for continuous interaction with the male member of the species or some surrogate symbol." (1961:28)

Cassel and VanVorst identify a number of argot roles which exist in the institutional context and which are adopted to lessen the impact of psychological deprivation. "Argot" is a special language developed by a specific group to express the group's unique experiences. By using the special language of the prison, the inmate demonstrates allegiance to the inmate subculture which reflects the conflicts and tensions in prison. When this special language is applied to a pattern of behavior the result is what has come to be referred to as an "argot role." (Sykes, 1958) Argot roles in a women's prison include the "femme," the female role in the homosexual relationship and the "butch," the male role in the homosexual relationship. Role determination in these homosexual relationships is based on the degree of dependence the incarcerated woman experiences. The greater the degree of dependence, the greater the likelihood that the woman will play the role of "femme."

Heffernan has identified three argot role adaptations. Each argot role carries major goal orientations and characteristics. In characterizing the "square," Heffernan notes that adaptation to this role is largely concerned with the preservation of "squareness." This involves the maintenance of a conventional way of life while incarcerated. The "life" role is characterized by the conscious belief that prison has become a way of life. The prison is seen as a world separate and distinct from the "real" world with a unique set of social norms, values and interaction patterns. The "life" role then is the antithesis of the "square" role. Adaptation to the "life" role involves a conscious effort to break prison rules for personal gain without regard to the costs of rule violation. The third role identified by Heffernan is that of the "cool." Women playing the "cool" role stay out of trouble and at the same time acquire the amenities that make for a more pleasant prison life. These women are exceptionally manipulative in the prison setting, yet they maintain an orientation external to the institution. Confinement is considered a temporary experience in the life cycle.

The data collected through the research efforts cited earlier clearly support the development of a pseudo-family in the prison setting with relationships quite similar to those found in the traditional American nuclear family. Roles of "wife," "daddy," "husband," "brother," and "sister" are the most common. It is important to note that these roles and relationships emerge as a result of the need to adapt to the deprivation of incarceration. A single sex prison, where inmates are deprived of interaction with family members and men, facilitates the development of homosexual relationships where traditional roles can be played and where important psychological needs can be met.

The authors recently completed a study at the correctional facility for women in Illinois. In the data collection process, women were observed as they came to the dining areas from their respective living units. It was noted that "families" sat together and each "family" had a table that was considered its own. "Husbands" sat at the head of the table while other "family members" took their respective places. "Femmes," "grandmothers," and "children" showed respect to the "husband" by sharing their food. Newly incarcerated women were isolated and ignored because they had not yet become "family" members. It was clear that if an incarcerated woman was to enjoy the benefits of interpersonal communication, she could only participate in accord with the subculture norms identified in our earlier discussion.

Giallombardo (1966) utilizes a different perspective in her examination of the roles incarcerated women play in the institutional setting. Giallombardo finds that roles reflect reactions of peers and over time the labeling process creates a social system for inmates and staff. The roles define certain behaviors that are a part of the interaction process in the prison setting. For example, the role of "snitch" reflects disloyalty to other women and has serious implications for the role-player. Some "snitches" engage in the behavior routinely while others are more sporadic. Motivation for this behavior is often related to the need to settle an economic dispute or a homosexual conflict. One who systematically provides custody staff with information in the role of "snitch" is referred to as the "good girl" by staff who use the needed information to control behavior. Anonymous "snitching" is rare. While "snitching" occasionally results in violence, there are other negative sanctions. One sanction is "panning" or gossiping about the inmate when she is not present. Another sanction is "signifying," which is done in the inmate's presence and which takes the form of a degradation ceremony.

The role of "inmate cop" is played by an inmate who is in a position of authority over other inmates because of her work assignment. Inmates resent taking orders from another inmate, therefore the "inmate cop" is excluded from a number of important relationships. Giallombardo's argot role of "square" is not totally dissimilar from the role of "square" described by Heffernan. Giallombardo's "square" is oriented toward the prison administration. There are "cube squares" and "hip squares." The "cube square" tends to be quite loyal to prison officials while the "hip square" is somewhat sympathetic to the inmate culture. The "jive bitch" is a troublemaker whose deviance is a deliberate, calculated strategy to cause conflict in the prison setting. The "jive bitch" stands in contrast to the "rap buddy." The "rap buddy" is one with whom an inmate finds herself compatible in that personal communications can be considered confidential. A similar role is that of the "homey," a person who comes from the same community as another inmate and is considered as close as "blood" relation. There is a bond of reciprocity in this relationship which includes mutual aid but generally excludes homosexual demands.

Inmates in women's prisons can get things such as extra cigarettes, contraband, candy and clothing through the "connect." The "connect" is an inmate who has a "good job" and can deliver valued information or scarce goods. The "booster," on the other hand, is a thief whose behavior consists solely of stealing from institutional supplies. There are "petty boosters" who are small time thieves and are differentiated from "boosters" who steal regularly and take items of considerable value. The "pinner" is a lookout who is placed as a sentry in key locations to prevent other inmates and institutional staff from learning about illicit activities such as homosexuality. A "pinner" is an admired person who is trusted and can tolerate institutional pressure without disclosing information.

Giallombardo also identifies a number of homosexual roles. A "penitentiary turnout" turns to homosexuality in the prison context because heterosexual relationships are not available. The "lesbian" prefers homosexual relationships in the free community and has little difficulty adapting to the single sex society of the women's prison. The "femme" or "mommy," the female role in the homosexual relationship, is a role most women prefer to play. The "stud broad" or "daddy" is the male role in the homosexual relationship. The "stud broad" has considerable prestige in the prison setting because she provides a masculine image and plays the male role. The authors' research in Illinois revealed a number of "stud broad" role types. These role types were characterized by distinctly male-looking hair styles parted to one side and cropped in the back. A number of women playing the "stud broad" role smoked pipes and wore slacks and shirts. On closer observation one could see that these women had strapped their breasts back in such a way to negate any exposure of their busts. On a number of occasions women playing the role of "stud broad" were referred to as the "main man around here." The role is difficult to sustain over long periods of time because the stud is expected to internalize external symbols of sex differentiation and incorporate behaviors which are socially expected of males. It is interesting to note that some women identified as "stud broads" had made written requests for sex change operations.

When a "stud" and a "femme" establish a homosexual relationship, they are said to be "making it" or "being tight." In the inmate subculture they are recognized as "married." This is a "sincere" relationship based on romantic love. The relationship is in contrast to that which exists between the "commissary hustler" and the "trick." The "commissary hustler" may establish a "sincere" relationship in her cottage or living unit, but she also has a number of relationships with "tricks" for economic reasons. The "chippie" role is unique in that the "chippie" exploits each situation for its unique possibilities be they sexual or eonomic. She does not establish "sincere" relationships and she is often seen as a prison prostitute. Finally, the role of "cherry" is reserved for the uncommitted woman who has not been initiated into a homosexual relationship and is generally a young, first offender.

It is important that further research be developed to increase our understanding of female criminality, inmate subcultures and women's prisons. It is clear that family type roles found in women's prisons generally do not exist in men's prisons although there is considerable homosexuality in those institutions. Also, the level of violence in women's prisons is less than that in men's prisons. At the same time, we cannot assume that women's prisons constitute a static environment. As societal perspectives on women continue to change, we can anticipate that there will be changes in inmate subcultures. At the same time it is important to understand argot roles in women's prisons and the features of the inmate subculture. If a woman is to survive incarceration, both phsyically and psychologically, it is important that she develop interpersonal relationships in the prison setting. These relationships and the roles she plays are determined by the social norms and rules of the prison community. In this regard, the prison community is a unique and artificial environment. Women adjust to the demands of this environment in ways that may shock the unknowing observer. Adjustments made by these women reflect the realities of prison life.

Bibliography

Burkhart, Kathryn Watterson. *Women in Prison.* New York: Elsevier, 1980.

Cassel, Russel N. and VanVorst, Robert B. "Psychological Needs of Women in a Correctional Institution." *American Journal of Correction.* 1961, *23*, 22-24.

Chandler, Edna Walker. *Women in Prison.* Indianapolis: Bobbs-Merril, 1973.

Giallombardo, R. *Society of Women: A Study of Women's Prison.* New York: John Wiley and Sons, 1966.

Glick, Ruth M. and Neto, Virginia V. *National Study of Women's Correctional Programs.* Washington: U.S. Government Printing Office, 1977.

Heffernan, Esther. *Making it in Prison.* New York: John Wiley and Sons, Inc., 1972.

Hendrix, Omar. *A Study in Neglect: A Report on Women Prisoners.* New York: Women's Prison Association, 1972.

Lockwood, Daniel. *Prison Sexual Violence.* New York: Elsevier, 1980.

Smith, A.D. *Women in Prison*. London: Stevens, 1962.

Smith, A.D. "Penal Policy and the Woman Offender." *The Sociological Review*. Monograph 9. Sociological Studies in the British Penal Services, University of Keele Press, 1965.

Sykes, Gresham. *The Society of Captives: A Study of A Maximum Security Prison*. Princeton, N.J.: Princeton University Press, 1958.

16

The Parole Board Hearing

David T. Stanley

"We have this terrible power; we sit up here playing God," said the chairman of the U.S. Board of Parole after a day's hearings that were reported in detail in a magazine article.[1] The power may seem godlike, but the premises and proceedings are on a decidedly lower level. The typical parole hearing takes place in a small, plain room inside the prison. In a hall outside half a dozen prisoners wait their turn under the eye of a guard. Inside the room the panel of two or three board members or hearing examiners[2] sits behind a table holding a stack of files and a tape recorder. Sitting nearby is a prison caseworker who maintains the docket, calls prisoners in to be heard, and records the decisions.

The Dialogue

When the prisoner enters, often visibly tense or sullen, he is greeted by the member who will question him. It is customary to take turns interviewing and for one to talk to the prisoner while the others review files of prisoners scheduled next and pay partial attention to the hearing.

Normally the questioner gives the others a chance to ask a question when

David T. Stanley, *Prisons Among Us: The Problem of Parole* (Brookings Institution, 1976), pp. 34-46. Copyright © 1976 by the Brookings Institution.

he is finished. About half of the time they do, generally only a single question or piece of advice. Wisconsin board members, however, all of whom are educated as social workers, were more likely to participate in hearings they do not conduct themselves, and at much greater length, than members in the other governments studied.

The prisoner is greeted by name—usually his first name—and an effort is made to put him at ease. The tone adopted is normally friendly, but in a majority of hearings observed in the present study it became patronizing and sometimes demeaning: "Well, John, have you been behaving yourself lately?" "What can we do with you now, Bill?" (In fairness to parole board members it must be acknowledged that the stakes in this proceeding are very high, that the situation is tense, and that anything the member says can be objected to by a rubbed-raw prisoner or a critical observer.) The conversation usually centers on one or more of three subjects: the inmate's prison record, his parole plans, and the circumstances of his crime. Whatever the topic, the members are watching for indications of the inmate's willingness to face his problems, both past and future.

Prison Record

Referring to the inmate's file, the board member moves quickly to discussion of disciplinary infractions, assigned duties, and training. Talking about discipline is usually not productive. The prisoner caught fighting, talking back to a correctional officer, or possessing weapons, drugs, or excess food has already been dealt with by a prison disciplinary board. He may simply acknowledge his offense to the parole board and say he will do better in the future. Sometimes he will claim that he was unfairly treated or argue about the specifics ("I was just carrying those pills to Robinson; he had forgotten them," or "I didn't do it; they wrote up the wrong man"). Infrequently there is an outburst, as when one hearing examiner kept criticizing the prisoner for disciplinary failures recorded in the file and the inmate angrily said, "When I come to the Board you never talk to me. You talk to my jacket [file]. That's not me. You should tell me how much progress I must make."

Board members whom we observed usually did tell prisoners what they expected of them in terms of improved behavior or participation in therapy or training. There was occasional resistance: "If I learn a trade I won't use it." "That group therapy—man, all they do is hassle you." Normally, however, prisoners try to sound cooperative: "Yeah, I been going to AA [Alcoholics Anonymous]." "Expect to get my high school certificate." Humor may appear:

> *Parole Board Member:* "Why did you have that knife, Jim?"
>
> *Inmate* (in very impressive manner): "Why *did* I have that knife, Mr. J____? Well, you might say it was for social purposes."

Parole Plans

This is another natural topic. Even though the board member has studied a report showing what the inmate expects to do when he gets out, he asks the prisoner to tell him about his job prospects and living arrangements. In the governments studied here the prisoner was not pressed for a specific job with a specific employer if his prospects seemed reasonable considering his qualifications ("I'll work with graders and bulldozers in the Tampa area").

A recent survey of fifty parole boards showed that thirty-eight of them require that an offender have a job or "satisfactory other resources, which could include a place to stay where the person would be taken care of until he could find a job, a social security check, personal financial resources, a training slot, and the like" before he can be released on parole.[3]

The inmate is also questioned about whom he will live with, what his relationship with that person has been, and whether he will have problems with transportation to work. Parole boards naturally object to a prospective parolee's living with someone who seems to have led him or driven him to crime in the past (though autocratic parents seem to be an exception to this). If he plans to go to school he will be asked about his expected income and residence.

This sort of questioning can be constructive. The board gets an understanding of how realistically and sensibly the inmate is facing the future (if he is being candid). The inmate, in turen, may benefit from the board members' reactions. The discussion will also be useful in cases where the board has conflicting recommendations in the file. It is not unusual, for example, for the prison staff to endorse the prisoner's wish to be paroled to San Diego, but for a parole officer in that area to recommend against it. In some cases, the board may defer decision until a satisfactory parole plan is agreed upon. In others, they may grant parole anyway, feeling that the prisoner is "ready," even if he has no job lined up and is headed for an unwholesome neighborhood.

The constructive tone was shattered in some hearings when the member abruptly and harshly asked something like "How do we know you can stay out of trouble there?" "What makes you think you can stay on the wagon?" Such questions are hard on a scared inmate, who feels that anything he replies will seem wrong. The more confident, experienced convicts handled them easily: "I've learned my lesson, sir. Nothing like that will ever happen again, sir."

"Retrying the Case."

The board member has "played God" in both of the above types of questioning. He does so also when he questions the prisoner about his crime. He "plays prosecutor," too. The prisoner may be interrogated in some detail about the facts of the crime: "What got you started on this?" "Who drove the car? How did you break in?" "Why didn't you go home sooner?" If the prisoner's answers do not match the reports in the file he is cross-examined. Some prisoners respond openly and penitently, others become defensive or evasive. We heard numerous arguments about locations, times, actions. The manner of the board member may be firm and objective, or sternly prosecutorial, or even morbidly interested. Some board members keep after inmates about sex crimes, others on drug-related cases. Their interests differ, and their motives are not always apparent. What appears to be pointless harassment may be an effort to get the inmate to face up to his responsibility for the crime. The effort is not always successful, as in the case of one convicted rapist who just kept saying that he had been drunk and the victim was willing.

Many of the offenders who come before parole boards have been imprisoned after plea bargaining. In the cases we observed, the board's questioning clearly assumed guilt of the major crime: armed robbery instead of possession of a dangerous weapon, burglary instead of possession of burglar's tools, murder instead of neglect resulting in death of a child. Such a course of questioning is defended by parole board members on the grounds that they are trying to find out more about the inmate—how dangerous a person is he? The opposing argument is that it is unfair to the prisoner to grill him about a crime other than the one for which he is in prison. It would be interesting to know (if one could find out) how frequently prosecutors accept plea bargains knowing that the parole board will take into account the greater crime and may therefore decide to deny parole for a few more months, or even longer.

Such retrials in general are pointless. They may contribute something to the board's understanding of the inmate by testing his attitude toward his crime and his intentions for the future. But how much does it mean for an inmate to look the board in the eye and say something contrite? It is not hard for a prisoner to be sincere when he tells the board that he regrets the crime that brought him to prison.

Counseling Efforts

In all the jurisdictions we visited, particularly Colorado and Wisconsin, the hearings were used for counseling as well as inquisition. Inmates were advised to "get their heads together," that is, to make up their minds to stay out of trouble. More specifically they were told to quit fighting, to attend alcohol or drug therapy sessions, to work for their high school equivalency certificates, or to learn a trade. Inmates usually respond cooperatively but sometimes explain why it is difficult to take part: they can't leave their work; there are no vacancies in the class; even "the therapist turns me off."

Some counseling efforts are decidedly inexpert and unhelpful, like these observations from members of the board:

> "You are small in stature. Do you feel inadequate?"
> "You have a fear syndrome."
> "You have made a career of avoidance and underachieving."
> "Tony, when are you going to stop acting like a juvenile delinquent?"
> "It's just a matter of time before you are a rumdum again, walking down the street with a stolen eight-dollar radio under your arm."

To the convict the hearing is a big moment — which is about how long it seems. He has only a few minutes to present his case for a crucial decision. Jessica Mitford writes that the California Adult Authority averages a little less than seventeen minutes per prisoner, but she was told by one prisoner, "In my experience, five to seven minutes is more like it."[4] Both statements are probably right.

The average numbers-of hearings per day conducted by parole boards in fifty-one jurisdictions, according to the National Council on Crime and Delinquency survey, are as follows:[5]

Average number of cases per day	Number of jurisdictions
1-19	11
20-29	15
30-39	14
40 and over	11

The national median based on these figures is twenty-nine cases a day. Field observations for this study show a far lower number: board members and hearing examiners thought they were doing "well" if they got through more than fourteen or fifteen cases in a day.

First of all, a board panel probably spends only six hours a day in actual sessions, hearing and deciding cases. Why not eight hours? Because they use some time in the morning traveling to the institution, then conducting necessary business with the warden or members of his staff. An hour must be subtracted for lunch, coffee breaks, other discussions with prison staff, and rest periods. And they cannot run late in the afternoon because prisoners may have a 4:30 p.m. "count" in their cells or a 5:00 p.m. evening meal. Of the six hours left in the day our field observations suggest that two thirds is spent hearing cases and one-third deciding them and dictating or noting the decision. So four hours are available for hearing prisoners.

This means that at ten cases a day, each prisoner gets twenty-four minutes; at fifteen cases a day, fifteen minutes; at twenty cases, twelve minutes; at twenty-six cases, nine minutes; at thirty-five cases, seven minutes; at forty cases, six minutes. Fifteen cases a day was our own observation; twenty is the maximum recommended by the National Advisory Commission on Criminal Justice Standards and Goals;[6] and twenty-nine is the median of the boards surveyed by NCCD.[7] Six minutes was the average time per prisoner in New York State hearings, "including the time for reading the inmate's file and deliberation," according to the commission that investigated the Attica prison disaster.[8] A later New York study showed a range of four to twenty-five minutes, with the majority between six and twelve.[9]

Prisoners are plainly right when they say, in effect, that any of these periods is a short time to get acquainted with a man and size him up for a decision that will affect his liberty for months or years. Parole boards would reply that the hearing is only a part of what they base their decision on. They have test results, prison caseworkers' reports, recommendations of psychologists, comments on the parole plan, and other data to consider. They could add that prisoners are bitterly and understandably critical of any process that does not result in their prompt release.

Attorneys, Witnesses, Records

Brief as the hearings are, informal as they are, there must still be some procedural protections of the parolee's rights. Due process in the usual legal meaning of that term does not as yet apply to parole release hearings,[10] but some states have taken modest steps in that direction. The NCCD survey in 1972 showed that twenty-one out of fifty-one boards allowed inmates to have counsel present but that the prisoners rarely did so because they were unable to pay for attorneys[11]. Seventeen boards permitted the inmate to present witnesses, "but in no instance are witnesses permitted when counsel is not."[12]

The prisoner may need a lawyer in a parole hearing, but not in the same way that he needs one in a court trial. Parole is not an adversary proceeding, and courtroom rules of evidence are not applicable. Nevertheless the typical prisoner needs a better advocate than himself. Some inmates are indeed articulate, forceful "jailhouse lawyers," but most have limited analytical powers and verbal facility; they do not have the skill to "sell" their readiness for parole. Nor are the witnesses they call—wives, other relatives, former employers—likely to be better. Any reasonably competent attorney (or for that matter law student or even lay volunteer) could help them present themselves more effectively, by putting adverse material in perspective and by emphasizing the inmate's progress in gaining responsibility and skills. But the inmate rarely has an advocate of any kind to assist him.

Hearings were recorded verbatim in twenty of the ,fifty-one boards surveyed by the NCCD[13] and in four of the six covered in the present study. The normal practice is not to transcribe the proceedings but to save the tapes, disks, or belts for replay if there are later inquiries or challenges. In some cases this can be helpful to the prisoner (or the board) if the record shows that certain factors were or were not considered in the hearing.

The Prison Caseworker's Role

The prison caseworker (variously called social worker, counselor, classification and parole officer, or by some other title) present at the hearings does more than hand records to the board and make sure its decisions are recorded. He may be called upon to solve a problem about eligibility dates, clarify some discussion of a training assignment or a disciplinary problem, or supply other information needed by the board. He may even help an inarticulate prisoner make a point to the board.

Caseworkers sometimes feel they can offer their own judgments about inmates' readiness for release: "If there are grounds for parole, sir, there are community-based psychiatric program [sic] in his home state. He needs very intensive individual psychotherapy. He won't recover in a state institution. He *might* in a community-based program."[14] Another example comes from the present study. We heard one caseworker turn to the board member after the prisoner had left the room and say, "that son of a bitch will never make it on parole." Another one said after another hearing, "I think he can probably make it this time." Such comments may or may not be valid, but two points should be made about them. First, they amplify the influence that information from prison authorities already has on the presumably independent parole board. Second, as a matter of fairness in this important proceeding, adverse comments should be made in the presence of the inmate or his attorney. (One board we observed prohibited such "late shots" from prison personnel.)

Appraising the Hearings

Members of parole boards interviewed for this study do not question the need for hearings; they take it for granted that a prisoner must be heard before a decision is made. Board members differ in their confidence in their own ability to appraise prisoners, but most of them believe they can tell when the inmate is trying to con them, whether his attitude toward crime has changed, and whether he has violent propensities. Sometimes they predict well, sometimes poorly. Mainly, however, board members wanted to talk to us about the rigors of their hearing work — days away from home, hours spent in automobiles, excessive caseloads of inmates to see, and the tensions involved in making wise, safe decisions under the hostile scrutiny of inmates, prison officers, judges, and the press.

The Prisoner's View

The hearing is a highly traumatic experience for the inmate, according to board members, prison officials, and the prisoners themselves. A statement by a prisoner in one of the states we studied is particularly vivid. He describes on tape what it is like to anticipate and take part in a hearing.

> Sat down by myself and starting thinking really heavy on what the parole board was going to say to me and what I was going to say to them. God, I really caught a drag.
>
> I was sort of expecting the parole board to be loud and more or less belligerent and tell me where I messed up at and get on my case over bad things I had done and I spent all that night up thinking about what I was going to say and what I was going to do. I did sleep that night for about two hours but woke up when the doors opened and I was bright-eyed, I was ready to go and meet that parole board.
>
> I went to breakfast, came back and thought a little more about what I was going to say—their questions, my answers—and they called me that afternoon, it wasn't till afternoon and they called me down about 2:15, I think it was, and I sat down to wait for the parole board and I started thinking and thinking hard. I started pacing back and forth and then I walked back to my house [cell] and got sick, vomited. It as just something. All of a sudden my mind was a blur. I couldn't think, I couldn't talk or nothing. Then they came to the door and told me to come in and I walked to the door and sort of stood there for a second or so and looked the room over. The man in the middle was the guy that really struck me. I felt as though he knew what he was talking about just by looking at him. The other two I didn't think too highly of. They looked like second-rate people types. I walked over, I sat down and said my hellos more or less and I was still feeling upset over being sick and my mind wasn't working at all. The first question that guy asked me took me a long time to answer. The first big question. He asked me what I was trying to prove to the world and all the questions that ran through my mind the night before and all that day that wasn't one of them that I thought about. That question I just didn't have an answer for and I just couldn't rap to this guy and I couldn't tell him what it was. I couldn't speak right. I was nervous and shaky and my hands were twitching.
>
> I wanted to look around the room and see who else was there. You know, I just couldn't move my head. I couldn't take my eyes off this guy because I was afraid he was going to throw something under the table. You know a question under the table I wasn't ready for and I wanted to be ready for it. I waited for the other two guys to start firing you know saying you should have done this or you shouldn't have done that or why didn't you do that and they never said a word, not once. I got uptight because nobody yelled at me. No one yelled and no one said

you should have done this or you should have done that. Nobody got on my case. It upset me."[15]

This reaction is typical of prisoners' feelings about parole hearings, though milder perhaps than some in the literature.[16]

The Value of Hearings

Parole hearings need to be evaluated both in themselves and as part of the criminal justice decision-making process. To begin with the most important point, they are of little use in finding out whether the inmate is likely to succeed on parole. The authors of a large-scale research project on parole point out that "evidence that interviews are useful in parole prediction... has been preponderantly negative; repeatedly, comparisons have shown that statistical prediction devices are more valid.... Interviewer judgments disagree notoriously with one another and have little to do with parole outcome."[17]

A strong case can be made for abolishing hearings on commonsense grounds alone. In cases where the information in the file and the board's own precedents plainly show that parole must surely be granted or denied, the hearing is a charade. In cases where the outcome is not so obvious it is a proceeding in which the inmate is at a great disadvantage and in which he has reason to say anything that will help his chances for parole. The atmosphere at such a hearing is full of tension and latent hostility. Under these circumstances the hearing is an ineffective way to elicit information, evaluate character traits, and give advice, all of which parole boards try to do. Hearings entail expense for travel, recording equipment, and paperwork that would otherwise be unnecessary. Prison routine is disrupted; inmates must be excused from classes or tasks; guards and caseworkers must be diverted from other duties. Board members are fatigued and strained; prisoners are upset. So why have hearings at all?

Given the present parole system, hearings are necessary as an expression of our national tradition and culture. A man has his day in court before he is convicted and sentenced. In all sorts of situations we feel outraged if a person is not even confronted with the evidence before something adverse is done to him. In the hearing the prisoner is at least given a chance to state his case, correct erroneous statements, and impress the board with his determination (real or alleged) to reform. Board members feel that they have at least a chance to learn more about the prisoner. His

"employment history, relations with his family, feelings about authority, his disappointments and his expectations, all are frequent topics. The interview may reveal something of his abilities and interests, his sexual attitudes or defenses against anxiety, his values, and his plans....[It] may suggest a further treatment plan (on parole or in prison), particular

areas of weakness to be guarded against, and special potentials to favorable adjustment in certain situations."[18]

Nice work if the board members can get all this out of an overpowered and
resentful individual in nine, eleven, or even fifteen minutes!

Nevertheless, as a matter of apparent fairness and decency the prisoner
has to be interviewed, and the information gained is believed by the board
to be useful. The prisoners themselves believe they must be heard, although
they denounce any hearing with an adverse outcome. Board members feel
frustrated and guilty if they make decisions about a person who is only a
name, a number, and a collection of data in a file. Hearings are called for
by the standards recommended by the American Correctional Association[19]
and by the National Advisory Commission on Criminal Justice Standards
and Goals.[20] So as long as there are parole decisions there will be hearings.

Making the Decision and Notifying the Prisoner

As soon as the inmate leaves the hearing room the parole board or panel
makes its decision.[21] These are complex and difficult problems, but the
board usually decides quickly. The member who led the questioning of the
prisoner generally states his view, which may be phrased in figures, initials,
or abbreviations unintelligible to an uninitiated observer, or even conveyed
by a wink or a gesture. Examples of the most common decisions are:

> To grant parole effective in six months and recommend a work-
> release assignment (to prepare for parole) as soon as possible.

> To continue in prison and reconsider parole at a future time,
> such as in three, six, twelve, eighteen, or twenty-four months
> (some state laws require reconsideration every year).

> To continue imprisonment until expiration of the prisoner's
> maximum term.

The other one or two members present agreed with the decision in most
cases observed. In a few there was discussion of a condition of parole, such
as the need for drug therapy or an injuction to stay away from certain
people or places. Strong disagreement over whether or when to parole the
man was rare. In a three-person board or panel this is resolved by a vote.
When two are present one gives way, probably the member with the milder
personality.

There may be no decision, only a recommendation at this stage. A panel
may refer its recommendation for later decision by the full board, as in
some cases of famous or notorious persons, or a panel may have a disagreement that needs to be resolved by the full board. When hearings are held by

examiners or representatives without power to parole they also record their recommendations at this time. The usual practice in the hearings observed was for the member who led the discussion with the prisoner to dictate or write the decision, giving reasons for the decision in those systems that followed this practice (only eleven of the fifty-one boards in the NCCD survey recorded reasons).[22]

The prisoner, tense and anxious after his ordeal and, indeed, about his whole future, may get his answer right away or may have to wait weeks for it. The typical inmate can predict whether his parole will be granted or denied from the way the board has questioned him. The members do not conceal their reactions to the inmates progress, behavior, and attitude. They may state, or hint, their conclusions as to whether he has been punished enough or whether he can safely be returned to the community. In any event he wants to know, and know soon, what the decision is.

In twenty-two of the fifty-one governments where hearings are held, the prisoner gets the news at once in person from whoever conducted the hearing.[23] In the others, as in those that do not hold hearings, the inmate is notified by mail or by prison staff (usually his caseworker) after the prison receives the board's decision. Getting the word in writing varies from "immediately" (Maine) and "same day" (Kentucky) to "4-6 weeks" (South Carolina.)[24] For news of such importance a short time is a long time, and a long time unbearable. The intensity of a prisoner's feeling when parole is deferred, even when the wait for notification is brief, is suggested by more of the taped observations of the inmate quoted earlier.[25] (In this case he did not predict the board's decision correctly.)

> It was about 1:00. I just came back from lunch and they shut my door. I heard them call work lines out and I knew they weren't going to open my door because you know I was going to find out if I was going home or find out if I got a set-back. Everybody left and on the way they stopped and said what did you get. I told them I hadn't got it yet and about five minutes later it was really quiet. It was nice and easy, no disturbance, my radio was off and I heard the footsteps coming from the house. I knew who was coming down. I sat down on my bed. He sort of knocked on my door and gave me a big smile and he said "here you go," and he slipped it under the door. I just brooded. I sat there for a minute or so and I flashed back on the parole board before I picked it up. You know, I flashed on them not yelling at me. I flashed on them just talking about my home town, my wife and so on and how they had talked real good to me. I thought there was a good possibility I'll go home and I stood up and the paper was face down, the writing was down, and reached over and picked it up. I didn't look at it right away. I walked over to my desk and sat down. I flipped the paper up and started reading from the top. It had my name and the date and started running it down. I got to the bottom where it said I had been deferred

parole by a unanimous vote and that part really didn't bother me because I was really sort of expecting that but it said I would meet the board again in July. When I seen the July part I counted the months on my fingers and just said well fuck it. That's a fucking six and dropped the paper down and sort of leaned back and started thinking well let's see, let's make sure. That's February, March, April, May, June, July. God damn, that's a fucking six. They just gave it to me just like that. Well shit! I got up and paced around and walked back over to my desk and put the paper in my hand and looked at it and set it back down and made sure the name was mine on there. Walked over to my door and sort of knocked on it and asked them to let me out. I was getting upset and I didn't want to be in my house. I walked back and sat down on my bed. I was feeling like I was going to be sick for a minute so I took the cover off my shitter and was getting already in case I did get sick. Then I flashed back on the parole board again and thought what a bunch of bastards. Those guys are really fucking pricks. To slap a six on me the way they did and talk to me the way they did, as good as they did. It was a trip.

This prisoner was told the board's decision fairly soon, but the message was impersonal and gave no reasons.

Prompt personal notification by the board is obviously most desirable: the anxious period is shortened, and the inmate hears just what they have decided and why, in some of the states. Mail notification has the advantage of official clarity, but it is a chilling way to convey bad news. When the prisoner is notified by prison staff there is an opportunity for discussion and for ventilation of feelings. The caseworker or other staff member may be able to explain the board's policy or to make some constructive suggestions.

Notes

Reprinted with permission from *Prisoners Among Us: The Problem of Parole*. Washington: The Brookings Institutions, 1976. Pp. 34-46.

[1] Robert Wool, "The New Parole and the Case of Mr. Simms," *New York Times Magazine* (July 29. 1973), pp. 14-16, 18-20, 24-25, 30.

[2] Those who conduct the hearing will be called "members" whether they are actually board members or employees.

[3] William Parker, *Parole: Origins, Development, Current Practices and Statues,* American Correctional Association, Parole Corrections Project Resource Document no. 1 (College Park, Md., 1975), p. 217.

[4] Jessica Mitford, "Kind and Usual Punishment in California," *Atlantic Monthly,* vol. 227 (March 1971), p. 49.

[5] O'Leary and Nuffield, *Organization of Parole Systems in the United States* (Hackensack, N.J.: N.C.C.D., 1972), p. xxx. Data exclude Georgia, Hawaii, and Texas, where no hearings were conducted at the time.

[6]National Advisory Commission on Criminal Justice Standards and Goals, *Corrections* (GPO, 1973), p. 422.

[7]O'Leary and Nuffield, *Organization of Parole Systems,* p. xxx.

[8]New York State Special Commission on Attica, *Attica* (Bantam Books, 1972), p. 96.

[9]Citizens' Inquiry on Parole and Criminal Justice, *Prison without Walls: Report on New York Parole* (Praeger, 1975), p. 49.

[10]For a brief general discussion of due process in parole release decisions see David Gilman, "Developments in Correctional Law," *Crime and Delinquency,* vol. 21 (April 1975), pp. 163, 167-68.

[11]O'Leary and Nuffield, *Organization of Parole Systems,* p. xxxiv.

[12]*Ibid.,* pp. xxxiv, xxxvi.

[13]*Ibid.,* p. xxxiv.

[14]Wool, "The New Parole," pp. 15-16.

[15]Remarks of a state reformatory inmate taped by a parole officer; tape loaned to the author.

[16]See Robert J. Minton, Jr., ed., *Inside: Prison American Style* (Random House, 1971), pp. 176-93.

[17]Don M. Gottfredson, Leslie T. Wilkins, and Peter B. Hoffman, *Summarizing Experience for Parole Decision-Making,* National Council on Crime and Delinquency, Research Center, Report no. 5 (Davis, Calif.: 1972), p. 8.

[18]*Ibid.,* pp. 8-9.

[19]American Correctional Association, *Manual of Correctional Standards* (1956), p. 116.

[20]National Advisory Commission, *Corrections,* p. 422.

[21]Although this statement is a fair generalization it is oversimple. The boards that hold hearings differ widely in number of members, use of panels, delegation to nonmember examiners, and voting procedure. See O'Leary and Nuffield, *Organization of Parole Systems,* pp. xix-xxxi, xxxii-xxxiii, and, in much greater detail, 1-167.

[22]*Ibid.,* p. xxxiv.

[23]*Ibid.,* p. xxxi.

[24]*Igid.,* pp. 1-167 passim.

[25]See n. 15 above.

17

Residential Alternatives
to Incarceration

Paul Hahn

"It is difficult to train an aviator in a submarine. He can learn theory, one can discuss aeronautical and navigational problems with him,; if funds and space allow, he may even be provided with a simulated trainer; but sooner or later, if he is to fly, he must try and re-try his wings aloft, preferably guided and assisted. So it is with the prison and the reformatory as training grounds for responsible community life."[1]

This eloquent statement probably states the rationale for community-based programs as adequately as any other statement found anywhere in the voluminous literature of the field today.

New Mandate for Corrections

The need for translating such progressive correctional thinking into actual planning was given great impetus by the President's Crime Commission, Task Force on Corrections, in 1967: "The general underlying premise for the new direction in corrections is that crime and delinquency are symptoms of failure and disorganization of the community as well as of the individual offenders. In particular, these failures are seen as depriving

Hahn, Paul, "Residential Alternatives to Incarceration," in *Community Based Corrections and the Criminal Justice System.* Santa Cruz: Davis Publishing, 1976, pp. 153-70.

offenders of contact with the institutions (of society) that are basically responsible for assuring the developing of law-abiding conduct...

"The task of corrections, therefore, includes building or rebuilding solid ties between the offender and the community, integrating or reintegrating the offender into community life, restoring family ties, obtaining employment and education, securing in a larger sense a place for the offender in the routine functioning of society..."[2]

Objections to the Present Institutional System

At the same time that these positive arguments for community-based corrections were gaining a greater amount of serious consideration among correctional planners, the overwhelming weight of evidence of the bankruptcy of the existing mass-custody institutional system was rapidly accumulating. Over and over again, impartial observers were reporting that the existing institutional system, at both the adult and juvenile levels, was simply: (1) ineffective; (2) far too costly; (3) often inhuman.

While the subject matter of this present chapter does not allow for a detailed exposition of the many problems inherent in the mass-custody institutional system, the author would like briefly to summarize the results of the reported observation of almost countless numbers of commissions and study groups, the learned writings of many scholars in the field, and the criticisms advanced by many fine practitioners in the following points: (1) There is no empirical evidence which substantiates that prison does deter many of those whose acts we fear the most: crimes of passion, crimes of those who have no stake in conformity in our society, or of those who are seeking punishment or notoriety, or of the obviously severely deranged or retarded, etc. (2) Much of the deterrent value for others is quickly lost after incarceration because of the contamination, lowering of self concept, prison acculturation, "sick" dependency, sexual perversion, deprivation of family contacts, etc., which are much too often part of the mass-custody institutional experience. (3) The recidivism rate tends to indicate that the huge institutions do not provide the protection which society expects and genuinely wants. (And from a cost-effectiveness standpoint it is impossible to justify their existence on this score.) (4) The financial cost of the institutional operation is staggering in all too many cases because of: a) the per-diem rate of the inmate care. b) the cost of new construction of such facilities. c) the loss of tax revenue from the services of those incarcerated, from the use of land so allocated, etc. d) the cost of welfare assistance to the families of the incarcerated in many cases. (5) Realistic programming which could provide for a lowering of the crime rate by reducing recidivism, is very difficult, and in some cases impossible because of the structure of the institution. (6) By their very nature, the mass-custody institutions tend to force a ritualistic or "role-playing" response and thus encourage the cheapest forms of hypocrisy on the part of the inmates, and often on the part of the staff. (7) Such institutions tend to create the most deprived community in our entire society (which society tends to verbalize a commitment toward alleviating deprivation) by depriving those confined of: a) liberty; b) most family contacts; c) most social contacts (personal friends, neighbors, merchants, etc.); d) all heterosexual contacts of a personal nature; e) autonomy; f) freedom of expression (in many areas more than just in speech); g) many essential goods and services as judged by today's civilized standards; h) essential life roles (such as breadwinner, office-holder, club-member, etc.); i) in all too many cases, even of his personal safety, bodily integrity and security of person and belongings at the physical level.

Need for Smaller Residential Settings

The author again wishes to reiterate that the above comments concerning the deficiencies of the traditional mass-custody institutional system is **not** intended to imply that the American correctional system can dispense entirely with residential care for all offenders; however, it is intended to emphasize that through the use of enlightened diversionary programs and alternative facilities, a much smaller group which would ultimately require secure residential care, could receive it much more effectively in smaller settings, carefully designed to avoid many of the problems mentioned above. Small secure institutions, at the very end of the criminal-justice process, if properly designed and resourced, could much more easily avoid the horrible indictment leveled recently at our antiquated mass-custody system by one observer, who said that they contain "totalitarian social organizations" and "pathology-ridden, anti-therapeutic inmate subcultures."[3]

Stratified System Required

If, as was suggested in earlier chapters, every possible offender at the juvenile and adult level is diverted from entrance into the criminal justice system, and if those in the system, as far as possible, are served with a variety of individualized non-institutional programs, such as intensive probation services, family oriented programs for treating offenders from multi-problem families, demonstration projects utilizing indigenous workers and para-professionals, mutual-help efforts using ex-offenders, fellow alcoholics, etc., intensive vocational training and job-placement efforts, availability of individual and group therapy sessions when indicated, and a whole host of other services available outside of residential facilities in an enlightened community, there still remains a large group of offenders, both adult and juvenile, who require residential facilities, but not with the strict security and high degree of structure which would be provided in the small security institutions at the very end of the criminal justice cycle to the smaller group who would still require such facilities.

If the emphasis on a decision-making model to control needless incarceration is successful as stated above, then institutional caseloads would be reduced drastically (anywhere from 20% to 60% depending upon the localities involved) and substantial resources would eventually be made available in order to implement community-based, residential facilities containing viable treatment modalities which could be adapted to the particular needs of those offenders who then would enter such programs.

Types of Services Delivered in Alternative Facilities

There are all sorts of possible alternative facilities, but they can probably be reduced, for the sake of simplification, to those which provide any or all of the following services: (1) housing; (2) guidance and assistance with decision-making; (3) vocational training and or placement; (4) remedial or continuing education; (5) a stable environment; (6) cultural enrichment; (7) guided group-interaction, encounter groups, or other "self-awareness" kinds of experiences; (8) the entire complex of traditional psycho-social services.

The settings housing such services can themselves take on an almost infinite variety of shapes and forms, but some of the most frequently mentioned as being currently in operation, or planned for the immediate future in many jurisdictions, are: (1) halfway house; (2) reintegration center; (3) community corrections center; (4) alcohol detoxification unit; (5) drug-abuse center; (6) restitution house.

Eclectic Nature of Such Facilities

It is important, in this author's opinion, to note that whether a halfway house is "half-way in" or "half-way out," and whether the community corrections center is more highly structured or practically indistinguishable from a reintegration center, and whether some of the programs in the reintegration center should more appropriately technically be called efforts at resocialization or rehabilitation, all of these settings are capable of implementing a variety of program-elements and utilizing many therapeutic ingredients, and many of them are currently operating in a very eclectic fashion already.

The wide variety of programs already in existence, and the overlap in program-elements and methodologies, make it virtually impossible to totally delineate or to establish "ironclad" criteria as to what kind of characteristics, or how many of each, are required to establish what kind of a named facility.

Two Basic Errors

It is, however, of fundamental importance to the success of planning and operating any of the various types of alternative residential facilities, that two major "pitfalls" be avoided carefully: (1) the tendency to merely move institutional practice and programs into smaller community-based units in the community. Traditional penal methods and many of the established programs associated with them have not been successful historically in preparing offenders to make responsible decisions when the repressive and coercive atmosphere of the penal institution is removed. When these restraints are therefore removed, inmate involvement and participation in decision-making must be an actuality, not just a dream, if the open-type program is to be successful. (2) the mere placement of offenders in open, non-secure residences does not guarantee that they will be able to instantly handle such new-found responsibility without a large amount of assistance and support. There is no assurance that the residents, if program does not succeed in getting their involvement, will remain crime-free, or for that matter, even be good neighbors, in their new surroundings.

There is no empirical evidence to indicate that those recently released from a prison, or placed in an open-setting instead of the institution, will be "so grateful" that they will instantly change their life-habits or value-system. Effective program and offender-involvement are the elements which tend to prevent recidivism, not "wishful thinking" or popular myths about the nature of offender behavior.

Careful planning and programming can avoid the two disastrous errors of on the one-hand, feeling that any open program will be successful for any offender at any time (which is a very dangerous form of simple wishful thinking), or on the other, that we should simply move the repressive, restraint-oriented programs from the mass-custody institutions into our open-type facilities (which builds in a "failure factor" that no program can ever overcome). When these errors are avoided, much good can be accomplished from utilizing facilities designed to meet the real needs of the offenders placed within while still providing for the safety-needs of the surrounding community.

Advantages of Community-Based Settings

The advantages of such programs are many: (1) Community-based facilities by their very nature tend to place subtle pressure on the citizens of the community to recognize that they have a definite role to play in restoring offenders to useful citizenship. (2) Greater responsibility for adequate decision making is placed on the offender who is constantly confronted with real choices, since the regimented order of the institution is removed; and because he is exposed to a wide variety of situations calling for realistic decision-making each day while placed in the outside community. (3) Placement in open-type, community-oriented facilities eliminates the "ritualistic responses" and forced conformity which is so prevalent in the institutions. (4) Opportunity for individual decision-making and responsible choice removes the "excuse" that "I never had a chance," or "How can you learn to make good choices in a place like this?" which are heard each day in the institutional programs. (5) Open-type programs are invaluable as therapeutic agents in that they constantly present the opportunity to "hold up a mirror" in which the offender must recognize his real motives and actual values based on the conduct he exhibits in real-life situations. (6) Such placement also presents regular opportunities on a much more frequent basis for ego-supportive experiences, ranging from the more normal life-style itself through such special circumstances as the opportunity to do volunteer work in hospitals, to assist "an old lady to cross the street," etc. (7) Life in the community presents many more adequate "role-models" who can be observed regularly overcoming real-life difficulties and coping with real-life situations instead of such artificial kinds of images as institutional life presents. (8) Community-based correctional facilities, based upon a reintegration model, lend themselves much more effectively to a departure from the purely "medical model," and permit the offender to interact with, and to be acted upon by, a variety of helping figures. (The traditional notion that the offender is "sick" and that the therapist is "normal" or "well" has quite often been seen as totally "phony" from the offender's viewpoint and has numerous other inadequacies as an exclusive treatment model.) (9) Correctional workers, in such progressive settings, are able to develop new roles and begin to function as "brokers for services," "connectors," "advocate-mediator," members of a treatment team, and much more fully realize the need to "plug-in the offender" by utilization of an eclectic approach. (10) The individual rights of the offender are much more easily safeguarded in such settings. (The number of civil and criminal actions, class-action suits, grand jury investigations, etc., all indicate that this has been a major area of concern within the mass-custody institutions in the recent past.)

Importance of Selection Process

The secret of the success of such program operations lies in the area of offender and staff selection, combined with program and staff development. Community-based correctional facilities which are poorly conceived, poorly programmed, inadequately staffed and not extremely careful in the selection of "who fits into which program," can fail miserably, and with great cost to the community and to the cause of advanced correctional thinking. Unfortunately, there have been many examples of so-called "community-based programs" which in reality were totally without realism in their conception and operation. Such facilities notoriously have provided only the "human warehousing" that was part of the institutional arrangement, or they deteriorated into "delinquent sub-cultures" with little program and little control. In either case, the failure of such settings results in great harm to the community who does not receive the degree of safety which it longs for; great harm to the offender who has not received the realistic programming directed at a level to satisfy his real needs and presenting him with the opportunity to exercise adequate non-criminal options; and great harm to progressive corrections because the outraged citizens eventually scream that such facilities "do not work."

There is a "terrible responsibility" involved in the planning and operation of community-based facilities, and this should not be easily ignored. When someone selected for such a facility, does unfortunately exhibit severe criminal behavior, it graphically illustrates that we have simply "put the wrong person in the wrong place at the wrong time." This can either indicate faulty selection process, lack of effective programming, or some staff deficiency; but in any case it does not indicate that the concept of community-based programs is in error. It simply indicates that for this person at this time in this facility something was inadequate.

It is of fundamental importance to note that when such tragedies do occur, especially if the criminal act involves murder, rape, notorious act of grand theft, etc., programs should not be abandoned; and above all, we should not revert back to the rigid structure and tight security which turns a "group home" into just another prison. To do so is to admit that the highly-structured, regimented program of tight security is the only way to control human behavior and the great weight of evidence has long indicated that this is not a correct assumption. What should be done after such tragic incidents do occur, and their occurrence has been much less frequent than the critics of such programs would have us believe; is to re-evaluate the selection process, the staff development and all program ingredients, so that the program can continue to be productive and such unfortunate occurrences can be eliminated.

This common-sense consideration was brought graphically into focus in a statement contained in a detailed study of the 13 year old California community treatment project: "Dr. Palmer reports that, overall, the arrest rate during parole for youthful offenders in the CTP program was 63% lower than for a similar group that went through the California Youth Authority's normal institution parole cycle.

"The complex study shows, however, that not all types of offender did this well in the CTP. For some categories, the arrest rate was no better, and occasionally worse, when offenders were handled in CTP rather than in the traditional program.

"...since the study indicates that some types of offenders respond to community treatment better than others, he suggests that the criminal justice system focus on the proper placement of offenders on an individual basis."[4]

Need for Program-Flexibility

The residential community-based treatment programs as alternatives to incarceration in secure institutions should offer a wide range of flexible, eclectic programs capable of responding to ever changing needs within the offender population and the community served. It is especially important to note that the needs of each community vary widely in reference to planning residential community-based facilities. Therefore total transferrence of experience or concepts from other areas can often be fraught with danger. For example, a program which may serve well the needs of a sophisticated inner-city area with a high incidence of hard narcotic addiction would probably be eminently unsuitable for practical purposes in a small rural environment with no "hard-core" addiction problem and perhaps just a small amount of soft drug abuse.

The notion of flexibility must also be extended into a temporal context because many centers of various types have found that after 90 days or even an entire year of operation, experience readily dictates that the program must be changed, that basic ingredients must be added or subtracted. It is in this frame of reference, the need for flexibility, that those planning or operating such facilities must constantly be aware to avoid the trap of commitment to one treatment modality or "professional bag."

Overlap of Names and Functions of Facilities

Because of the high incidence of situations in which there is not only an overlap in the methodology employed inside, but in the very concept of the purpose and goals of the facility itself, it is practically impossible to "define" the various kinds of facilities in such a way that there are clear lines of distinction drawn and that overlap is eliminated. For example, the notion of "community correction center" often includes the concept of the halfway houses: "In addition, the bureau operates more than a dozen community treatment centers which function primarily as halfway houses for offenders on pre-release status but also accept short-sentence prisoners and female offenders."[5]

The wide-ranging, almost generic, usage of the term halfway house is illustrated in a description of that concept contained in one of the best available texts on the subject: "As the term is used throughout this book, halfway house refers to any relatively small facility, either residential or non-residential, usually located in or close by a city or town.... the halfway house stands, literally half-way between the community and the institution, and may serve persons who are released from an institution, as well as those received directly from a court."[6]

In the most recent Directory of the International Halfway House Association (1974), there are about 1,000 listings of facilities who at least have a sufficient common thread of function and goal that they asked to be listed in the Directory of "halfway houses." These range from "men's social service center" through "community correctional center," and with an almost infinite variety in between.

Beyond the generic nature of the halfway house, there is also much overlap in many of the other names of facilities used as alternatives to secure incarceration. For example, in some communities the notion of "reintegration center" implies simply a residential facility for "technical parole and furlough violators" while in other areas there are many other roles which others would ascribe to the "reintegration center." In like manner, the "community corrections center," as observed around the country, does not seem to be restricted to simply one function, but can be observed to be providing pre-release programming, housing for work and educational furlough grantees, probation shelter facilities, and alternative placement for those who violate probation, parole, or furlough and for others who might be seen as needing more intensive supervision than they previously received.

The wide variety in programming can be visualized very simply from an analysis of the enabling legislation permitting such programs to be established in various states. A very brief sampling by direct reading from the statutes involved, will very quickly demonstrate the high degree of differing community expectancies and program requirements in relation to each facility.[7]

Restitution Houses or Centers

One of the programs whose very name specifies a rather unique purpose for its existence, even though it incorporates many similar ingredients found in other settings, is the "restitution house" or "restitution center." In general, this term denotes a residential facility in which the occupants are "making restitution" or in some cases doing public work where actual restitution would not be possible.

While from the outside, such a setting would be probably indistinguishable from others, it would differ in that persons would be assigned primarily due to their inability to pay restitution because of unemployment or because of improper budget management or because a sentencing court felt that some sort of service exchange should be required in a particular case. Such settings usually offer relatively close supervision, and especially those supportive services related to economics, employment, etc. The State of Georgia has on the "drawing board," or already in operation, four such centers designed to service some 600 offenders. Several other states, and at least one local community are seriously considering the development of such facilities.

Alcohol and Drug-Abuse Units

Alcoholic detoxification and other drug-abuse treatment units offer a wide variety of services to a specialized offender-group as their individual names imply. The services rendered in each setting can range from complete diagnosis and treatment through formalized psycho-social services, and in many cases includes simply peer-operated "alternative communities" with voluntary or required encounter-groups, or simply such informal ingredients as "a positive life style" or "a chance to get your head together."

Again, except for those that are operated in or in conjunction with hospitals or other medical facilities, most of these settings are indistinguishable physically from other kinds of community-based residential centers.

Work-Release and Work Furlough

Throughout the existing legislation and the voluminous literature relating to residential facilities of an "open type" within the community, one of the most popular and best documented success stories, is in relation to the concept called "work release" and the kindred notion of educational or "school release." While differing in some features as implemented in different localities, basically the concept of work-release and work furlough (and educational or school release or furlough) involve some variety of a convicted and institutionalized offender being released into the community to pursue vocational or academic training or employment opportunities, and while so doing, he either returns to the institution, in some instances to sleep and perform other maintenance functions, or he stays in a separate facility designed simply as a residence for members of such a program, or in some rare cases, he receives permission to live in school dormitories or near his work site. The varieties of such programs currently in use by the separate states and numerous individual communities within the states, and in the federal system, is almost limitless. The one consistent strain which seems to be found in all studies of such programs, even though specific ingredients are ever so different, is that such programs have met with a high degree of success in most instances. This success-factor seems to be present whether the program simply consists of release in order to perform a menial job with tight security upon return and notable absence of supportive services, or whether in other programs the releasee receives a much better degree of freedom and is given intensive counseling and other supportive services along with the opportunity to work or study in the free community. In the city of Cincinnati, after 142 inmates were placed in a work release situation at the Cincinnati Correctional Institution, studies indicate that the recidivism rate dropped from an average institutional rate of 65% to less than 3% for those in the work release program.[8]

In Massachusetts, out of 3,000 such furloughs given during a five-month program, there were only 38 absconders thus the program there exhibited a 98.1 security factor.[9]

In South Carolina, it was recently reported that after six years of work release experience, 2,477 inmates had completed work release with only 27.1% committing any violation while involved in the program.[10]

And more significantly, during an experiment at Vacaville, California with a group of 18 inmates who were selected by the Corrections Department as "highly likely to recidivate within a year of release" it was found that with a combined program utilizing experimental techniques and dynamic motivational efforts combined with the opportunity to do meaning ful work in relation to social problems and projects, only two of the eighteen returned to prison, and several are reported to "now have high positions in government and private organizations."[11]

These random samplings of a widespread success experience led most observers to give additional credence to the notion that work in itself is ego-supportive, and that when combined with the opportunity to "support my family" or to pay bills, it tends to be an important problem-solving exercise as well. But more deeply than that, as was stated recently in a fine article on the subject in *Federal Probation,* "Deep in the ethos of the United States is the normative value of work, historically, at least. While the history of work for inmates is spotty and loaded with incredible inconsistencies, work-furlough supports the work ethic with its emphasis on frugality, industriousness and the determination to get ahead."[12]

The deep rooting of such motivations in our culture cannot be denied, and certainly lends its weight to the whole notion of work release and work furlough as therapeutic programs.

Educational Release and Educational Furlough

The same kind of reasoning can be applied to the favorable record which is currently being accumulated in relation to educational release. While statistics are currently being assembled in many places, the observation of a university faculty member recently says the whole thing very adequately:

"We have consistently been impressed by the positive attitude we have observed on the part of the incarcerated students. Several of them who have been released on furlough or parole during the school year have remained in school after their release to continue their efforts toward a University degree."[13]

"If You Can't Help — Don't Hurt

No matter what particular names might be placed on the community-based residential facility, and despite specific differences in treatment modalities, such settings have a distinctive advantage over the formal large prison settings because by their very nature, they follow the basic principle which should underlie all treatment approaches: "If you can't help, don't hurt; and if you must hurt, hurt as little as possible."

This injuction seems to be carried out excellently in the open type community-based settings because by its very structure and purpose it tends to remove the most severe consequences of mass-custody imprisonment. Among those eliminated or minimized open-type settings are deprivation of all liberty, of important goods and services, of heterosexual relationships, of most autonomy and choice, and even often of physical and emotional security. A properly developed and well-run open-type, community-based setting significantly reduces the impact of deprivation in all of these important areas.

For this reason, if for no other, such facilities represent a very definite contribution to "correctional reform" and not just to "prison reform." The author believes that these two terms need to be carefully distinguished because "prison reform" can be understood to mean merely the development of decent health and living conditions inside basically inadequate mass-custody institutions; while on the other hand, "correctional reform" implies an effort to reduce the rate of crime, the rate of imprisonment, and especially the rate of returns to prison by developing truly viable programs without the use of the unsuccessful mass-custody institutions.

To simply develop a system of peaceful, clean, "well run" institutions would seem, at this late date in the history of humanity, to be a totally unacceptable goal for any "reform movement." What we need is to work toward the development of a "system that works," and open-type residential facilities complemented by small secure institutional settings for the carefully selected few who cannot profit from the open type settings, seems to hold the best promise for truly protecting society and for delivering needed services to the offender population at this time.

Need for Immersion Into Community

The well-developed residential facility within the community should eventually blend totally into the community environment, in which case it would become practically invisible. All efforts should be made in this direction so that it is not seen as a setting "apart" from the regular community or identified simply as "another huge public building." Along with those efforts, the administration of such a setting should become so much a part of ordinary community life that neighbors would be able to relate to administrators personally, and even come to depend upon them for advice and other services. In such an atmosphere, the "house director" and others in authority could then make their important decisions based upon the real needs of the community and the real needs of the offender population in relation to that community. This kind of mutual involvement of all those involved in the decision-making process would remove the historically destructive practice of the authority figures being "remote" and making their decisions in important matters affecting both offenders and the community totally without input from either source.

Need for Staff Inter-Action and Decentralization of Treatment Authority

Finally, and of most fundamental importance, if such settings are to be successful, they depend upon a constant realistic interaction between staff and residents, and they demand that the old stereotyped concept of the "helpers and the helped" be abandoned. When such interaction exists, everyone knows everyone else very well and danger signs can often be detected far in advance and with sufficient time to resolve incipient problems. This constant interaction necessarily involves "staff exposure" of their own attitudes, values and capabilities, and this can become very threatening, especially to those committed to "old ideas," but the risk is well worth taking.

The decentralization of treatment authority and the interaction of staff with residents, rather than the "stand-offish" attitude encouraged by the "professional elite" so popular in the past, seems to be absolutely necessary to the successful implementation of programs in open-type residential, community-based facility because: (1) The rigid, hierarchical structure of "keepers and kept" or "helpers and helped" or "sick and well" or "them and us" are all primarily based on attitudes oriented to meeting the needs of the system and of the vested interests of professional groups rather than the needs of the residents or the community-at-large. (2) In traditional setttings, based on the above mentioned attitudes, inter-professional rivalries and friction were often constant and frequently were propagated by departmentalization and professional vested-interest approaches in which: a) each group competed for "favored son" status as most efficient, most professinal, etc.; b) each group claimed "superior therapeutic potential"; c) each claimed special efficacy at "relating" to inmates or patients or clients, etc.; d) each constantly seemed to be seeking for a higher professional standing and acceptance by the community; (3) In such a setting, the constant assumption was that each representative of a different professional discipline (or his department) was always planning "for the good of the patient or client," but this was almost always done without consulting the person being "planned for" and all too often was done without "considering his needs." Evidence of this can readily be seen by the fact that programs were often started or stopped for reasons totally without consideration of the "needs of the client" and based entirely upon administrative necessity or staff convenience. Many beneficial new ideas were rejected, or when attempted, were frowned upon and resisted, because they were "upsetting to the system" or especially to the existing organizational order. And many really therapeutic efforts became horribly fragmented and dissipated because there was a lack of unifying force and personnel often ended up acting for "cross-purposes" because of either departmental-vested interests or personal commitments to a particular "treatment modality" or organizational sub-goal. These difficulties must be recognized and dealt with.

Also, when an effective "treatment team" kind of approach is developed, and when the decision-making process is decentralized as far as possible, to even include involvement of the persons affected by the decisions, several great difficulties tend to arise which normally impede the successful implementation, or at least disrupt the smoothness and speed with which this administrative development can take place.

Difficulties in Implementing

These difficulties tend to be deeply rooted in such factors as tradition, cultural bias, politics, financial limitations, etc.; but they also tend to be based in the very important factor that staff, expecially those trained in older methodologies, can become extremely threatened by various elements in the new program: (1) The sweeping nature of the change itself. (2) The fact that positions and functions (job-roles) have become atrophied. (3) The rigidity of personalities. (4) A program of inter-action with residents and confrontation of behavior, as opposed to the older situation in which there was a carefully drawn line of distinction between the "treatment elite" and all others; and the fact that certain members of professional groups could engage in "intellectualizing about behavior" without ever having to confront it "in the raw" tends to expose professional incompetence and personal inadequacy because: a) everyone must work in much closer contact with each other, thus causing a greater visibility. b) the job role has now changed so that each one has to actually "handle" behavior, crisis, etc. c) each worker now has to relate at the "human level" and so his social and "human skills," or the obvious lack of them, become readily apparent (this is especially threatening to those professionals who have permitted their "professional veneer" to be used for many years to cover "personal callousness"). d) all personnel are literally "stripped naked" of their defenses, protections and barriers which had been erected by the traditional, rigid structure. (For example, at times of crisis or disruption, many professionals in the past have simply taken comfort in the position that "we have a staff meeting" or "this conference is too important to omit"; and thus they have avoided behavioral confrontation or relegated such tasks to "inferior members" of the organizational structure.) e) new situations, many for which no guidelines have ever been established due to the newness of the program, must be faced regularly. This is extremely threatening to those who are familiar with a "high degree of order" or especially with "doing things the way we always did."

The decentralization of the decision-making process certainly demands a high degree of flexibility and of "staff tolerance" for departure from the "familiar and comfortable ways of the past."

Tremendous Advantages of Decentralized Approach

While these difficulties in implementing such a program are formidable, the advantages far outweigh the difficulties when administration is capable and courageous enough to successfully implement such a program. Some of the most notable advantages are: 1) opportunity is presented for every staff-member, and for residents, to use all of their natural talents and initiative in a constructive way. (2) All suddenly are made to feel more responsible for their individual actions. (3) Sufficient time and "administrative tolerance" is more readily available for constructive program-change and innovative idea-testing. (In the old system, "administrative patience" at times of innovation was notoriously lacking in many settings.) (4) A continuity of therapeutic efforts is more easily maintained because there is not always a "new therapist" coming into the picture, because even when one staff-member leaves, the team remains virtually intact under the new arrangement. (5) A much greater consistency of therapeutic efforts is present because of the constant group communication and the removal of "fear of mistakes" and "administrative reprisals" because all shared in the decision-making at the onset. (6) Individual whims and "blind spots" are minimized because the group makes the most important decisions as a group. (7) Feedback is much more reliable because of "built in" evaluation of each person's efforts due to the high degree of visibility regarding each ongoing part of the program. (8) Resentment towards decisions is minimized because all members of the group are part of making them in the first place. (9) Much greater flexibility and room for original thought and effort is easily provided. (10) A totally much healthier environment for residents tends to develop because they cease to be "tools" in staff jealousies, there is less confusion as to rules, there is an elimination of the feeling of alienation from important decisions, etc. (11) Such a setting tends very readily to eliminate the idea of the professional in his "ivory tower" doing the ordering, prescribing, directing, while the "lower level staff" actually has to remain on the "field of combat" doing all of the cleaning, shouting and comforting; and especially it tends to eliminate the idea of the residents being "caught in-between" or finding themselves in situations where they can use professionals against professionals, staff against staff, or in turn where they are used by professionals of staff in "inter-departmental warfare." This is especially important to notice, because in many of the traditional settings, the atmosphere was such that because of inter-departmental of inter-personal jealousies, and the inmates' ability to manipulate such situations, the atmosphere became horribly anti-therapeutic.[14]

Summary

Thus it seems to be extremely important that we develop well-functioning community-based residential facilities of a variety of types, suited to a variety of needs, and arranged in such a way that there is real resident involvement, de-centralization of decision-making and treatment authority, and a tearing down of the barriers that have separated staff and residents and especially the barriers which have separated residents and community. Such facilities, when properly planned and programmed, and especially when staffed by a dedicated "crew," working with residents who have really been given the opportunity to become involved in the program, have a high degree of success expectancy and hold great promise for the future of corrections.

While such settings certainly are founded in sound correctional principles and utilize the knowledge-base drawn from the very best in the behavioral sciences, their greatest advantage seems to be that they tend to give the opportunity to the residents, to the staff and to the community-at-large to fulfill the age-old admonition: "It's great to be great, but it is greater to be human."

Notes

[1]Morris, Norval, "Foreword," *Half-way Houses,* by Keller, O.J. and Alper, Benedict S., Heath Lexington Books, Lexington, Massachusetts (1970), page X.

[2]Report of the Task Force on Corrections, President's Crime Commission (1967).

[3]Martin, John M., "Toward a Political Definition of Juvenile Delinquency," Department of Health, Education, and Welfare, Washington, D.C. (1970), page 3.

[4]"California Releases 13 Year Juvenile Project Evaluation," Juvenile Justice Digest, Volume 2, No. 9, September 1974, (page 4.).

[5]"Community Alternatives to Prison," Nora Klapmuts, Assistant Director, Information Center, NCCD, (Reprinted from Crime and Delinquency, June 1973.).

[6]Keller, O.J., and Alper, Benedict S., op. cit., page 10.

[7](1) Ohio Revised Code Section 2968.26. (2) General and Special Laws of Texas, C-493.3. (3) New York Criminal Law, Article 26. (4) City of New York, Criminal Law, Article 6A. (5) Illinois Code, Chapter 13, S123-127. (6) Pennsylvania Statutes C-19, S1052. (7) Oregon Revised Statutes C421.170.

[8]"Continuance of Work Release Program Urged," Cincinnati Enquirer, August 3, 1973.

[9]"Penal Chief, Hope of Prisoners, Fired," Cincinnati Enquirer, Sunday, July 8, 1973.

[10]Corrections Digest, Volume 4, No. 21, October 3, 1973, page 3.

[11]"Criminal Rehabilitation Should Be Our Top Priority," Honorable Lee H. Hamilton, Criminal Law Bulletin, Volume 7, No. 3, page 233.

[12]"Evaluating Work Furlough: A Follow-up," Alvin Rudolff and T.C. Esselstyn, Federal Probation, June 1973, page 48.

[13]The Communicator, August-September, 1973, page 15.

[14]The author wishes to acknowledge that the above analysis of the concepts of "decentralization of treatment authority," etc., is based heavily upon the fine work in this area done by Dr. Roger S. Kiger of Provo, Utah, and Dr. Garcia Bruniel of Boulder, Colorado — both published and reported at conferences.